BREAKING SILENCE

A Novel of
the SERRAted Edge

BREAKING SILENCE

A Novel of
the SERRAted Edge

MERCEDES LACKEY
CODY MARTIN

BREAKING SILENCE

Copyright © 2020 by Mercedes Lackey and Cody Martin

A Baen Book

Baen Publishing Enterprises
P.O. Box 1403
Riverdale, NY 10471
www.baen.com

ISBN: 978-1-9821-2434-2
Cover art by Larry Dixon

First Baen printing, February 2020

Distributed by Simon & Schuster
1230 Avenue of the Americas
New York, NY 10020

Library of Congress Cataloging-in-Publication Data

Names: Lackey, Mercedes, author. | Martin, Cody, 1987- author.
Title: Breaking silence / Mercedes Lackey and Cody Martin.
Description: Riverdale, NY : Baen Publishing Enterprises, [2020] | Series:
   Serrated edge
Identifiers: LCCN 2019050949 | ISBN 9781982124342 (hardcover)
Subjects: LCSH: Domestic fiction. | GSAFD: Fantasy fiction.
Classification: LCC PS3562.A246 B74 2020 | DDC 813/.54--dc23
LC record available at https://lccn.loc.gov/2019050949

Printed in the United States of America

10 9 8 7 6 5 4 3 2 1

BREAKING SILENCE

A Novel of
the SERRAted Edge

CHAPTER ONE

The worst thing about bugbears wasn't so much how horrifying they looked. It was how bad they *smelled*. Take equal parts hot garbage, wet dog, and rotting fish, marinate it in sewage, and let it simmer for a day on high heat, and you have roughly what a bugbear smells like. It was Staci's first clue that she wasn't alone in the woods surrounding the ruined Blackthorne Manor. She had known that there would be guards of some sort, though she wasn't expecting them this soon; she was still a half mile from the mansion's walls, and had been proceeding slowly on foot so as to maintain some semblance of stealth. Bugbears weren't terribly smart, but they were tough and vicious. If she kept her wits about her (and didn't throw up from the stink), she should be able to sneak past the sentries.

It took her another hundred feet of walking in quick little rushes, pausing to listen intermittently, before she finally saw what she had been smelling. There were two of them; from a distance, they looked like mangy black bears standing on their hind legs. Once she got closer, the differences were very clear. Both had shoulders that were hunched forward in such a way that they didn't look like they were really meant to walk upright. Heavyset and barrel-chested, their skin was covered with coarse and filthy dark fur; leaves, mud, and worse were matted into it. She realized that if either of the creatures were to lie down, they would probably blend into the ground almost perfectly. The hands were as big as dinner plates and ended in cruelly curved black claws. The absolute worst part of the bugbears were their faces, however. All similarity to bears ended there. Instead of a snout and close together, ursine eyes, their faces were flat and vaguely human. The jaw was broad and square, with broken and yellowed tusks protruding from the top and bottom lips. The nose consisted of two slits, constantly sniffing the air and dripping with mucus. Then there were the eyes; wide set and disproportionately large, they gaped wide open and had blood red irises.

The bugbears hadn't noticed her. As much as Staci wanted to be invisible, that was out of her power. She had done as well as she could, though, with the next best thing. Her clothing was all close-fitting without anything that could snag on branches, and was colored in earth-tones that fit the season and the area that she was in. Most of her skin was covered: a brown and green long-sleeved cotton turtleneck shirt that she had gotten off a website that specialized in "natural" and "forest camouflage" clothing, ending with a pair of thin leather gloves. The rest of her gear was cotton cargo pants and a leather belt covered with various pouches, along with a pair of dark brown, all-leather hiking boots. Maybe it was her imagination, but wearing stuff made of all natural materials seemed to work better with magic. For her, anyway.

She hadn't used any face-paint to cover up with, or any natural foliage to break up her outline; the shape of a person is one of the most recognizable things in the world, especially when contrasted against a natural backdrop. Instead . . . she had used magic. It was a spell that Tim, her mentor in all things supernatural, had taught her. Invisibility was far outside anything that she could do. There were some creatures that could do it, and rumors and legends of certain people achieving it, but nothing beyond that was known to Tim. What her spell did was good enough, though. It basically made it so that people (and other things with eyes) didn't want to look at you. It was an entrancement spell wrapped with a minor illusion; it suggested to someone that there were other places that they wanted to look. If they did happen to look at you, they would either see you as someone utterly forgettable, someone or something they expected to see there, or something fuzzy and hard to pin down if they really tried to search for you. It didn't work on everyone, and she couldn't do it indefinitely; the spell was constantly draining energy from her. If she let it go on for too long, she wouldn't have enough "juice" to power any other spells, and would be almost magically defenseless.

The two bugbears weren't making a circuit or patrol of any sort, or if they were they had come up short for some reason. Staci couldn't afford to wait all day to get to the mansion; she had to *move*, and going around the sentries would cost her time. She was standing tight against a tree, barely peeking around the edge of it to observe her quarries.

Just need a little bit of a distraction. Nothing too flashy.

She reached into one of the pouches on her belt, producing a small tuft of rabbit fur bundled with a bit of twine string. Clasping her hands around it, she concentrated for a moment. Her mind's eye swam with formulae, incantations, and the shining power of her own will. She sent all of it into the fur between her gloved hands. The fur and twine collapsed into dust, sifting through her fingers. A moment later, there was the sound of a rabbit's distress cries in the distance; the opposite direction she was in. The bugbears both immediately perked up, then seemed to confer with each other for a moment before setting off at a stumpy jog towards the noise. Again, bugbears were not very smart, and tended to think with their stomachs. They were probably thinking that not only could they make a meal of that "rabbit," but if they were quick enough, they could feast on whatever had attacked it, too.

Yeah, that's right; Staci could do *magic*. Not sleight of hand—though that was a skill that often helped with magework—or party tricks, not stage magic. Real deal, turn-reality-inside-out magic. She hadn't always been able to. Not even a year ago, she was just another normal, utterly average teen. Plucked from her home of New York City and essentially dumped by her father in the town of Silence, Maine, she had been torn free from everything and everyone that she had ever known. Silence was a quiet fishing town, and devoid of nearly everything that made modern life bearable for a young teen; no internet, spotty and unreliable cell phone service, and no shopping worth mentioning. Stuck with an alcoholic and not entirely stable mother, she had thought she would die of boredom in Silence.

Until she got caught up with elves. Not the kind that come on the packages of cookies, and not nearly as nice as the ones in Tolkien's books. Fantastic beings that lived for millennia and wielded magic as easily as a teenager used cell phone apps. Staci had discovered that, somewhere in her family line, someone had intermarried with an elf.

So, she had some elven blood in her, giving her inborn magic potential. Learning that fact, and that magic, elves, and even darker and more dangerous creatures existed had brought her here; an apprentice mage to the town's local bookshop owner and mage-in-hiding, Tim.

It was funny how life could take you to the strangest of places, especially when you least expected it.

Not wanting to be around when two disappointed bugbears returned, Staci waited until they were out of sight before she continued on. It didn't take her long before she caught sight of the Blackthornes' mansion, or what was left of it. In only six months, since she and her friends had last been at the estate, it had fallen into ruin. The grounds were unkempt and wild, with waist-high grass over the lawns and grass and weeds sprouting in every crack and crevice, and all of the stonework and masonry was half-buried under vines and behind bushes that seemed to have grown at an unnatural rate.

She could *feel* the magical pulse of the object she was looking for. It was like a warm heartbeat, rhythmically thumping against her skin. Whatever it was, it was deeper in the manor, somewhere near the center. Staci licked her lips, working her way through the trees until she was nearly to the outer wall. Memories flooded back to her; clearing the wall with Dylan, being attacked by dark elves and worse creatures, the Gate . . .

Give your head a shake, girl, she heard Tim saying in her mind. She couldn't get lost in the past; she had a job to do.

Effortlessly, she gripped the edge of the wall and pulled herself up high enough so that she could see over the top of it. *I've gotten stronger in the last few months, that's for sure.* If she had thought the exterior looked bad, the interior was worse. What had once been well-groomed and maintained yards and gardens was now gone completely to pot; wild flowers, weeds, and what had been carefully confined and well-tended plants had sprouted everywhere, the grass now grown to well over waist height, with the hedges and bushes that had made up the maze or dotted the yard now unrecognizably overgrown. There were hints of broken furniture here and there, covered by the weeds. The swimming pool was full of stagnant water, scummy and so thick with algae it looked like pea soup, and there were invisible *things* in it, making ripples on the surface. *Probably bugs and frogs, but you couldn't tell with all the algae and duckweed.*

The important thing that stuck out to Staci was that she didn't see any guards. That was . . . odd.

There should be something, someone here protecting the manor. Other than those bugbears, I haven't seen anyone.

She felt goosebumps rising on her neck and arms. Something wasn't right. But she was so close! With a quiet grunt, she heaved herself up, settling on top of the wall in a low crouch. She couldn't stay up there for long; even with her cloaking spell, she would eventually stand out enough for someone to get suspicious. Reaching into her pouch again, she pulled out a bit of glass about the size of a silver dollar. It had a hole in its center, which she held up to her eye while breathing incantations. *Just because I'm cloaked, doesn't mean that someone else isn't using the same sort of trick. With any luck, this will reveal them.* It didn't take her long to complete her survey of the immediate area; there wasn't anyone cloaked by magic, as far as she could tell.

Staci dropped down off the wall on the inner side, and immediately knew that she had screwed up. She had felt ambient magic in the air, and just assumed that it was emanating from what she was after. As soon as her feet touched the ground, she felt a surge of magic and saw it racing lines through the tall grass and weeds. *Alarm spell!* Immediately she rolled to her right from the crouch she was in; a trio of spikes appeared out of nowhere, embedding themselves in the wall behind her. She dropped most of the enchantment spell, leaving only the part that would help her in combat; she was still blurry to the unaided eye, and would be harder to pin down. She started running, a hard sprint for the object. She drew on her magic, making her strides a little bit longer, her speed that much faster. She dodged and weaved randomly; arrows and spears fell from everywhere and nowhere, trying to find her. It took her a moment to realize that the projectiles were driving her somewhere, intentionally pushing her in a certain direction. *Away from the mansion.*

Staci faked to her left, her right, and then her left again. *There!* She found a gap to her right side between a pair of spears and slipped through them, turning her body sideways at the last second.

Now the arrows and spears were falling in earnest; she had to duck several times in quick succession to keep from having some new and lethal headgear. She was getting closer; she could feel the pulses of magic coming from the unknown object much stronger now. They were waves crashing and breaking against her, guiding her. She only had a half-dozen strides left until she was inside the house, safe from the arrows, safe from the spears. If only she could get her hands around it—

Her sight had been attuned for magic when she hit the tripwire. A simple physical tangle trap wrapped itself around her ankle, bringing Staci down to the ground hard. She almost landed on her face, throwing her arms up just in time to prevent breaking her nose. The cord around her ankle tightened the more she struggled; she had to get it off if she wanted any chance to make it through this. She flipped over, reaching for a knife on her belt. Before the blade even touched the cord it was struck by an arrow, knocking the grip from her hand. She reached for it—another arrow, pinning it to the ground. She tried to roll out of the way, but three more arrows planted themselves in the ground, expertly placed to catch a bit of her pants with their points. Now she was pinned, as well. Before she could start working the arrows free, a large shadow loomed above her, and she felt a sharp pain in the center of her chest as she was knocked to the ground.

When Staci opened her eyes again, she saw that she was still in the forest. The traces of the illusion spell that she had been inside were still fading away, wisps of magic disintegrating into the air. Above her and to her sides were Wanda and Seth; Wanda was removing the string from her longbow with a self-satisfied smirk, while Seth was shaking his head and coiling a length of cord. At least he had the decency to look like he felt a little bit sorry for Staci. In the middle was Tim, with a long stave that had its tip resting against her breastbone.

"You get distracted, you lose, apprentice," he said, calmly. "You are focusing on the wrong things at the wrong time. Magic is addictive; you can get lost in it if you're not careful. You were so busy looking for magic that you forgot the mundane, even though I've told you over and over again, that magic is the *least* efficient and *least* practical way of getting most things done. It's better to conserve your energy and do things with your hands than to do it with magic, unless you absolutely have to. That's part of why the Unseleighe have so many minions."

"Plus, you're still clumsy as ever, girl." Wanda was wearing an off-the-shelf hunter's camo netting; the loops of burlap and nylon had been stuffed with tufts of grass, sticks, and other bits of local foliage. Next to her right shoulder, however, was a large and yellow "happy face" button.

"Smart ass," Staci muttered under her breath. She had already plucked the arrows up, freeing herself. Seth offered her a hand up, but she stood up on her own. She thrust her chin at him. "You're getting better with those snares. I should have seen that one, though."

"Yes, you should have." Tim looked at Wanda and Seth. "Wanda, you're turning into quite the marksman with that thing; there's not much more I can offer you in that regard. We'll have to find you a dedicated trainer, soon. And Seth, keep up on your studies. You're improving steadily, which is good." Without another word, Tim started walking back in the direction of town. When he was out of earshot, Wanda and Seth turned back to Staci.

"So, he's a little bit pissed." Wanda punched Staci lightly in the shoulder.

"No, he's right. I had my head full of magic. I need to keep my feet on the ground better, practice mundane skills more. It was dumb on my part." She worried the three holes in the side of her pants with her pinky finger. "You're totally stitching this up for me, by the way."

"It'll be all right. Let's get some food and coffee; Tim is probably going to just go straight to the bookstore, so we'll catch up with him later," Seth said.

With that, the trio set off back towards town. The diner was calling to them.

This had been the third training exercise that the group had done this week. Tim tried to give them three days of training and studying, with a day rest in between and weekends off . . . usually. They would set up in the forest, Tim would cast an illusion spell and outline a scenario, and they would work through it. Sometimes it was all three of them working together, or only one of them, or they would be paired off. After the exercise was over, there was an evaluation; depending on how the gang did, it would either be long and tortuous, or short and to the point. Today's had been unexpectedly brief. Staci didn't mind; she had had enough tear down sessions from Tim, and she was too tired to deal with it now. She knew what she had done wrong; her mistakes were obvious in retrospect and it wouldn't happen again. For his faults, Tim was still a good mentor; Staci never forgot an object lesson once it had sunk in.

"I wish Riley and Jake were still here," she said, as they began the long walk back to town. "They'd have had a lot of fun with this." Riley and Jake had been in the group of friends that Staci had become a part of when she first arrived in Silence. They had been through everything with her, from discovering magic to battling dark elves.

"They'd have handed our asses to us," Seth replied, with a grin. "They were the best LARP fighters we had. But..." He shrugged. "How the hell were a couple of high school seniors supposed to justify staying here when their families moved?"

"Better question, how they hell were they supposed to eat and get a roof over their heads?" Wanda pointed out. "It's not like any of our families would have been willing to bring in another mouth to feed. At least not mine." Staci noticed that Wanda quickly looked to her feet for a moment, and then her mask was back up. Wanda never talked much about her family, and everyone had learned not to pry.

"Maybe Tim?" Seth shrugged his shoulders. "They could work at the bookstore, maybe..."

"Tim tolerates us just barely, as it is. Besides, just because he's a mage doesn't mean he's made of money. Even in a town like Silence, it'd cost him to hire on two people."

"Yeah, I really don't think he's sitting behind the counter twelve hours a day all by his lonesome because he loves being there." Staci had had enough experience in juggling her mom's bills to have a firm handle on Life in the Real World by now. In fact, if it hadn't been for her dad's guilty generosity, they'd have been living on TANF and food stamps at this point. Mom had been getting better, though; she didn't bring home skuzzy types anymore, and she had been drinking a lot less. Still loopy as all get out, though. But harmless.

It didn't take them long to reach the edge of the woods; they were on a gentle hill that overlooked most of the town. To the west were the docks, where all of the fishing boats and their attendant canneries were located. Moving to the east was the town proper; most of the buildings were brick, the most recent dating back to the 1950s and most of them much earlier, and many of them looked their age. Things had been getting better, however. The Blackthornes, dark elves, had been secretly keeping the town locked in a sort of perpetual recession. Dark elves fed on misery, and Silence had been a miserable town if there ever was one. Now, it seemed like the town was coming back and even getting into *this* century, slowly. New stores were opening, the fishing industry was starting to recover, and people didn't seem to look at their feet all the time, shuffling from one place to the next. It was as if someone had opened a window in a stuffy room, letting fresh and clean air in. There were even rumors of a new company opening up a factory near town, which would mean jobs and a much needed boost to the economy.

"Maybe we could get some fast food chains in town." Seth often lamented the lack of variety in Silence cuisine, something that Staci agreed with him on.

"It wouldn't be like NYC, but I would kill for some decent Chinese food."

"Until then," Wanda said, "it's the diner for us. Greasy burgers on greasy buns, washed down with—somehow—greasy soda. Let's see whether or not Beth is working."

Beth had been one of the first people that Staci had met in Silence. She was one of the few waitresses at the diner, near the docks. She had stood out to Staci as someone who wasn't as beaten down by the dreary nature of the town as almost everyone else had been. On Staci's second day in town, she had visited the diner, and Beth had immediately been kind to her, even going so far as to draw her a map and give her the lowdown on Silence.

"Hey," Staci objected, mildly. "The food's been improving. It's way better than the drive-in."

"Or the pizzeria, though that's not saying much," added Seth, earning him a light elbow to his ribs from Staci.

"Let's get there, already. I'm starving after turning Staci into a pincushion." Wanda made as if she were pulling back a bowstring, eliciting chuckles from Staci and Seth.

When they finally arrived at the diner, Staci noticed that it was actually somewhat busy. A year ago, it would've been dead quiet at this time in the afternoon; the only relatively crowded times would be when people were getting off of shifts at the nearby canneries. The busiest times were late afternoon when the fishing boats came in, and Oh-Dark-Thirty just before they went out, and the fishermen were fortifying themselves with bacon and eggs and lots and lots of coffee.

Beth immediately spotted the trio as they entered, waving her order-pad and pen at them. "Hey, guys! Be with you in just a minute; find a space wherever you can."

The three friends found a corner booth that wasn't occupied and sat down. They mostly talked about the training exercise, or the tabletop campaign that Seth was running. Despite Staci's mistakes earlier, she was happy. Things were finally making sense for her; she had found a place in the world where she was doing something that she was good at, and was actually useful. Her friends seemed to share in her happiness, too. They had all been through hell, but they were stronger for it.

Eventually Beth extricated herself from her other customers and the demands of Ray, the diner's new cook, long enough to see her friends. They chatted for a moment and she took their orders, and before long the gang was hungrily chowing down. Using magic burned energy—and calories—whenever Staci did it; after a lot of magework she was usually famished. While they were eating, Staci's attention occasionally drifted to the new dishwasher and busser that Ray had hired. He was a new boy in town, just a year older than Staci and the others, and he was named David Parish. It wasn't much of a secret to the rest of the group that Staci had eyes for him, and they all encouraged her to try to get to know him better, in between bouts of teasing her about her crush.

After they had finished their meal, Staci caught sight of David getting a slight push to his back by Beth, sending him in the direction of the trio's table. She immediately felt her cheeks flush. David looked a little bit apprehensive, bringing over a bin for dirty dishes. "Uh, hi. Everyone enjoy the meal?"

Seth and Wanda traded a look, then nodded. "Oh, totally." Wanda faced Staci. "Hey, we'll get the check and catch up with you at the bookstore. Bye!" Before Staci could object, both of her friends had dropped a few bills for the check and were up and out of the booth, heading for the door. She watched them whisper to each other and felt her cheeks go even redder than they already were.

"Thanks. David, right?" Staci had fought dark elves, Red Caps, and all sorts of other nasty beasts. But the prospect of talking to a boy that she liked terrified her. *Staci, you're absolutely hopeless sometimes.* "You're new in town. I only moved here a few months ago myself."

"That's right. Beth told me," he said, chuckling lightly. *Of course she did. Love that girl, even when she's trying to play matchmaker.*

Part of Staci's problem wasn't just that she was nervous around the new boy because he was cute. It was that she was still dealing with what had happened months ago. She thought she had been in love back then. Dylan . . . he had first shown her how to use magic, how to fight back. And he had been an elf, full-blooded. Ridiculously handsome as most elves were, though in a slightly rougher way. She thought that he had cared about her. That was until, of course, he had left her alone, to live or die on her own. It had left a wound in her heart, and she wasn't sure that it was fully healed yet.

"Um, cool. How are you liking Silence?" Every word that came out of her mouth felt clumsy and forced. She hated small talk like this, anymore, and it didn't come easily to her. Then again, it wasn't like she could just blurt out her innermost feelings and secrets. How would that conversation go? *"Hi, my name is Staci and I'm a half-elven-blooded mage. I fell in love with an elf and saved the town from a magical plague. How are you?"*

"It's all right. Seems nice enough, and it didn't take me long to get a job after my folks moved here. Still trying to learn what the town has to offer." He seemed to have the same trouble finding things to say as she did. "They're here for the motorcycle works. We moved here from Georgia."

"Oh, is that what's getting built? The new factory or whatever?"

David nodded with more enthusiasm. "Yeah. They worked for a race-engine builder down in Georgia, and got the chance to transfer up here. Custom racing bikes. I—"

"Dave!" Ray barked. "I don't pay you to entertain girls!"

"Yessir!" Dave replied, and favored Staci with a rueful grin. "See you around later."

"See you!" Staci called after him.

CHAPTER TWO

Staci woke up the next day feeling sore all over. It wasn't nearly as bad as it had been when she first started training with Tim; she was getting stronger, getting tougher each day, but she still groaned a little as she moved. Now, mind, getting stronger didn't mean that it didn't still *hurt*. But, it was hurting less and less. Before, she would have been dreading the rays of sunlight coming through the blinds of her room's window, rolling over and covering her face with a pillow to squeeze in a few extra minutes of sleep. These days, she felt awake and actually eager to get up and get ready for the day.

But the bottom line was that she couldn't afford to be lazy anymore. Not given the things she knew, and the things she could do. Ignorance had been a sort of shield, in a way. Now it was gone, and she had a whole new set of priorities.

Rolling out of bed, she made her way to the bathroom to get showered and attend to the rest of her morning hygiene ritual; brushing her teeth, using moisturizer, getting her hair and makeup done right (she wore much less makeup now, as well), and practicing her protection charms forwards and backwards, in three languages. She was still having a bear of a time with Latin. Magic, especially older magic, "liked" to be done in certain ways. Sometimes that involved speaking in the language a certain incantation or ritual was first created in. Luckily, she hadn't had to work with goat entrails or anything gross like that. Yet, at least; Tim, when he felt like teasing Staci, would threaten to teach her some shamanistic magic from "the deepest, darkest primeval forests, where the word 'sanitation' has never been uttered."

Once she was done getting ready, Staci made her way downstairs. Her mother was already awake, sitting at the kitchen table and smoking a cigarette while she read a newspaper.

She gave her mother the death-glare. "Mom! You know the rules! Not in the house."

"Morning, pumpkin! I know, I know. Just needed a little something to wake up," her mother said as she stubbed the butt out in an ashtray. "Have fun yesterday?"

"Yep. Just hanging with Seth and Wanda, trying out some more LARP stuff." She whisked the ashtray off the table and dumped the ashes and butt in the trash, so her mother wouldn't use it as an excuse to light up again. "You really ought to try patches. Or vape."

"Oh, it just seems like such a bother. Anyway, I only made some coffee and some hash browns; I didn't know if you were going to meet your friends for breakfast, so I kept things light."

Staci moved over to the stove, peering down at the contents of the pan that was resting on it. "And you didn't burn them this time!"

"Your mother isn't *completely* useless, kiddo. Just . . . don't look at the coffee maker."

A quick bite and a farewell later, and Staci was off on her bike, heading to town. She had plans to meet up with the rest of the gang at Tim's book store, and she didn't want to be late. Glancing back over her shoulder at her house as her bike turned onto the road to town, Staci reflected how far her mother had come the last few months. The drinking had mostly stopped. No more blackouts. No more wandering around the house in an alcoholic daze. And Staci wasn't having to do more than what she considered to be a fair share of the chores, either. Her mother didn't bring home skuzzy losers anymore; in fact, Mom seemed to be right off boyfriends altogether, at least for now. Which, given that she worked in one of the town's several low-rent bars, and didn't really go anywhere other than to work and back home and didn't get any chances to meet anyone that wasn't a skuzzy loser, was probably just as well. Staci hadn't seen her mother this way since before the divorce.

Things had gone downhill for her mother after her father had left. She'd gone from being a bit flaky and given to slightly manic bouts, to a full-on crazy person, who could only seem to hold jobs in cheap bars, and then, not for long. She'd moved from one town to the next as she'd run out of people willing to keep paying her. Silence, and the influence of the Blackthornes, had taken what had been depression and turned it into substance abuse and borderline bipolar disorder. Well, that would be what a social worker would have said. Staci wasn't too sure about that. Tim was fairly certain that the elven-blood in her came from her mother's side of the family . . . and Mom had *always* been . . . interesting. All those fairy stories she'd told Staci when Staci was little, well, now that Staci could see the things that other people couldn't for herself, those stories sounded less made-up altogether, and more like something Mom had made up out of fragments of things *she* had seen. So some of those mental issues could very well have come from the conflict in Mom's mind of the two sorts of reality she could see: the reality everyone else knew, and the *other things*.

Tim had been helping to get her back to something close to her old self. "Magical therapy from afar," he had called it. "She'll never be 'normal' again, whatever that is. But she won't be driven insane. Best that I can do for her." It seemed to be working, slowly but surely. Having Staci around was a big part of it; the first bit of stability that her mother had had that didn't come in a brown bottle. Now Mom was a bit forgetful, and a little air-headed, but she dealt with that by having reminders on her own laptop (which in itself was a major step!) and her new cell phone (Hoorah for cell service *at last*) and the bills got paid, the groceries got bought, and no one was living on pizza anymore. That said, Staci hardly felt the urge to check her own cell phone unless it was to read a message from Tim or the gang. Mostly it was a convenience to not have to look for a pay phone if she was the one doing the shopping and wanted to know if her mom wanted something.

The Staci who had lived on her cell phone, Twitter feed and Facebook page was someone she didn't recognize anymore.

Okay, that wasn't entirely true. She *was* guilty of posting sad Facebook posts when the household needed something that wasn't going to fit into the budget, then texting Dad about it a couple days later. Dad knew very well that his clients were the kinds of people who checked the Facebook feeds of everyone in the family, and the last thing he wanted to do was make it look like he was a Deadbeat Dad. He still felt guilty about dumping her here, at the behest of his new wife, and she had every intention of feeding that guilt to keep her and her mom afloat. That was how she'd wrangled a new washing machine when the one that had come with the rental house tried to walk across the basement floor then threw up water, clothes and soap all over the place.

It's not like I picked the model he ordered, anyway. It didn't have to be the one that does steam-cleaning and has a freaking "sanitation cycle" for heaven's sake!

The bike ride into town was typical: warm but not too hot, with a nice breeze blowing in from the coast as she went down the hill. She stayed on the main drag into town; there were people out, doing their shopping or making their way to work. More cars were on the streets nowadays, and fewer of them were beat to hell and ready to die. Where before Silence had seemed deserted, now it actually had *life* and a pulse. Staci wondered if any of the other people living in Silence—those that didn't know about magic, or what had happened with the Blackthornes—noticed the changes, or if it had been gradual and unobtrusive. Like someone opening a window and letting air into a room; just enough of a difference so that the place aired out, the stale, nasty smell was gone, and you could actually *breathe*.

She pulled up in front of Tim's book shop, parking her bike and chaining it to the light post near the curb; just because Silence was getting to be less of a hole didn't mean she had gone completely naive. As soon as she opened the door, she was greeted with familiar smells; cinnamon, coffee, old paper and leather. The lighting was always a little bit dimmed in Tim's shop, but the banker-style lamps and wall sconces shed warm, golden light. Tim was in his accustomed spot; leaning on the cash register counter right next to the door, his head buried in a large tome, with two more, and an e-reader, open next to him.

"Morning, Staci," he said without even looking up to see who she was. No doubt he had felt her presence through magic long before she even opened the door; she was still having a little trouble masking her magical signature if she didn't pay strict attention to it. "The others are in the usual spot. Stomping goblins or kicking kobolds, I think."

"Thanks, Tim," she said over her shoulder without breaking her stride. Her first stop would be at the coffee machine, which was conveniently right across from her friends' usual spot; close enough to be really easy to reach for caffeine-refueling, without being right in the path of any other customers that were going for a cup. Thank goodness there wasn't enough elf in her to make caffeine a poison. As promised, all three of her friends were sitting in a circle of large, comfortable leather chairs and loveseats, centered on a low wooden table. One chair was left open for Staci, which she happily plopped down into after she finished getting a large cup of coffee. "Morning, goons. What's the adventure today?"

"Same as every other day . . . taking over the world!" Seth threw his arms wide, causing both Wanda and Beth to duck. "Or, y'know, dungeon crawling and dying horribly to one of my devious DM traps."

"Devious is one word for it. Obvious would be more appropriate," Wanda said, pushing Seth's arm out of the way. She wasn't dressed in her training clothes, of course; it was back to her Goth uniform of boots, tight long sleeve shirt, and baggy pants. All black, naturally. "Hey, Staci. I've got your pants sewn back up . . . and that sounded wrong."

"What happened to her pants?" Beth, out of her waitress uniform, and into the clothing she considered "comfortable," which was far too fussy for Staci and had caused Wanda to abduct the waitress for sewing lessons. Courtesy of those lessons, Beth wore soft, faded jeans with dainty applique patches and lace up the outer seams, and a frilly silk peasant blouse with a lace-trimmed "poet" collar, huge lace-trimmed sleeves, and a corset-belt of pale beige moleskin, also trimmed in lace. "Not my style," Wanda had observed, and then chuckled gleefully. "But *no one* in this town does Lolita, and *everyone* dumped Gramma and Great-gramma's old clothes at the thrift store. We're going to have a blast for a couple bucks."

"LARPing," Staci said succinctly. "We go full-contact and it's kind of hard on clothing. I had a serious wardrobe malfunction." The lie came very easily to Staci; that's another thing that had changed. She usually felt better about it when she remembered that, if she told anyone the truth about what she and the gang really did in the woods, they would either think she was insane . . . or worse, they would believe her. *It's safer to lie* had become a running mantra whenever she had to deal with people outside the circle of Tim and her friends. Most of the time it worked.

Beth made a face. "No thanks. Ticks. Mosquitoes. Giant beetles. Dirt. Grass stains. And now you add ripping up your wardrobe? I like my adventures with the Mocha Java within reach." Somewhat to Wanda's surprise, and Seth's complete astonishment, when she had been tentatively invited to the RPG group, Beth had accepted enthusiastically and turned out to be a good player. She tended to favor clerics and other healers, which was good, because Wanda and Staci . . . didn't.

"On that note, shall we get to it? Everyone got their dice, character sheets, and coffee? Oh, Beth, here's a pencil. All right, let's go!" Seth cleared his throat, unfolding his Dungeon Master screen and cracking his knuckles. "Where we last left off, you had just come upon a ruined caravan in the middle of the Queen's Road . . . "

It was mid-afternoon when the gang finished up their session; Staci and Beth's characters had both done relatively well, which was a nice change for Staci. Usually the dice fell the wrong way for her. Wanda's character had been knocked out several times, twice by the traps that Seth had been bragging about. Staci noticed that Wanda was fudging her rolls intentionally a few times, and she had a notion as to why; Wanda was crushing on Seth. It had been building for some time, and naturally Seth was oblivious. The entire situation pleased Staci immensely; it was so very normal, proof that life wasn't just magic and monsters and danger. She had felt a momentary pang of regret, however. Seeing Wanda mooning over Seth reminded her of her own love life . . . and Dylan. She had tamped that feeling down, and hard; she was hanging out with friends, and it wouldn't do for her to get all emotional. That would invite questions, and she didn't feel like lying to her friends any more than she had to.

The quartet were all stretching and cleaning up the table, some gathering the character sheets and dice while the rest took up the cups and saucers to a small sink near the coffee machine. It was Wanda's turn to wash up, which she did, complaining as usual about how much she hated washing dishes, and how one day she would have her own place with a dishwasher. Not that Staci blamed her. There wasn't a dishwasher at the house, and there wasn't a hookup for one even if they'd had one, and she hated washing dishes. *I wonder if I could guilt Dad into buying one of those portable ones you hook up to the sink?* The fact that she and Mom were cooking meals meant there were always dishes to wash . . . the downside of no longer getting most of her meals at the diner, the drive-in, or the pizza joint.

Once the cleanup was done, the gang finished getting their things together before filing out of the store, saying goodbye to Tim on their way out. Staci waited until the others were out the door before she stopped, turning to face him.

"Are we still on for training tomorrow?"

"Of course," Tim said, this time actually looking up to meet her eyes. "Have you been keeping up with your reading? I've got more books for you to study. There will *always* be more."

She nodded; those books were slow-going. Sometimes she wondered if advanced physics wouldn't be easier. "I have been; your notes help out bundles, on most of them. Anyways, I have to catch up with the others. See you tomorrow, Tim!"

"Always with the threats, apprentice?" He grinned, a rare display for Staci. "See you later, kiddo."

The others were waiting for her outside, chatting and laughing. "What's the hold up, slow poke? Forget which one was the exit?" Wanda crossed her eyes at Staci, sticking her tongue out.

"You're hilarious. No, I had to—had to special order a book from Tim." Staci caught herself at the last moment; sometimes she forgot that Beth wasn't privy to all of their secrets. The girl was likeable, and fit in so well with the rest of them; all of the in-jokes and mannerisms had quickly become comfortably familiar to her, as if Beth had been a part of their group from the beginning.

"Hey, you know that David is getting off of work soon, right?" Beth leaned against the light pole, her arms crossed in front of her chest as she watched Staci.

"No, in fact, I did not know that." A complete lie; she had become fairly knowledgeable about David's schedule at the diner, as of late. Totally not a stalker. "You know what guys, I think I'll catch up with you later. I need to . . . "

"Go suck face with the cute dishwasher? Please, don't let us keep you," Wanda finished for her. She had an infuriating habit of doing that, and usually with a remark that made Staci blush; with her fair skin, it was very, very obvious when that happened. Wanda smiled in satisfaction upon seeing that she had succeeded to do just that.

"Shut up, nerd. Anyways, I'll catch you guys later!" She unchained her bike and quickly began peddling towards the diner, eager to hide her embarrassment . . . and to see David. This was totally *not* a rebound crush. This was just . . . well David was cute and nice and *normal* and didn't have any Tragic Past Issues or Immortality Issues or, well . . . it would be nice to have one thing in her life that actually was normal. She deserved at least one thing, right?

She slowed down as she got nearer to the diner. She didn't want to be red-faced and sweaty when she saw David. As luck would have it, she caught him just as he was coming through the front door. He saw her and waved, stepping up to the curb and putting his hands into his pockets.

"Fancy seeing you here. Where's everyone else?"

Staci stopped her bike in front of him before leaning it against the curb after she stepped off. "Everyone? Oh, the gang. Uh, they had, stuff to do. Somewhere else." *Stuff to do?* She mentally kicked herself and continued on. "Just thought I would swing by, see if I could walk with you for a bit?" Now she really was freaking out. Where had that come from?

"Sure, that'd be nice. I'm a little ways away, but it shouldn't be too far." He laughed a bit. "Then again, isn't that true of everything in this town?"

"Hazards of living life at the end of the universe," she replied.

They walked quietly together for a couple of minutes before both of them started talking at the same time, then both of them laughed nervously. *At least he's as bad at this as I am.*

"You go first, then I'll go," he said, nodding towards her.

"Okay. Well, we didn't get a chance to really talk the other day, when you were at work. And it's probably not a good idea for me to get you in trouble that way. So, yeah." She paused for a second, thinking. "Tell me more about your family?"

"Not much to tell. Pa's a hotshot mechanic, but he's self-trained— old-school. It's hard to get the franchise-shops to give him a chance without certification. When he lucked into the job he's got now, we pretty much thanked our lucky stars, and figured when they said 'frog' we'd jump, you know?" He shrugged. "So Fairgrove said 'Move to Silence' and we said 'sure thing, boss,' and here we are."

Staci felt herself stiffen at the mention of Fairgrove. *Fairgrove . . . that's the name Dylan and Morrigan Blackthorne mentioned, the elves in Georgia, big shots. And they were into motorcycles . . . I need to tell Tim.*

" . . . and that's when the horn grew out of my forehead. Made for a nice hatrack." David looked at her expectantly, smiling.

"I'm sorry, what?" she said, then realized he'd been talking, but she hadn't been listening. Not at all. *Damn you, Dylan. You're even messing up my attention-span now.* "Oh, hell. Sorry, I got lost in my thoughts there, David. As you get to know me, you'll find out that I'm just a huge ditz, and not the wonderfully awesome specimen that I appear to be."

"It's okay." He gave her a cute, sideways look and a half-smile. "I get a bit fried after a long day of working, so I'm probably no better right now. Anyways, what about your family? Tell me some about them."

She made a face. "Ugh. Got a couch for me to lie on and a prescription pad? That's what it'd take to get all of the details about my family. Short version, Mom is a little crazy, but I guess a little crazy is pretty normal anymore. We live over on Waide Street. Dad's a lawyer, and a few months ago he dumped me here to keep his new wife happy, though I guess he feels bad about it. Mom and Dad separated about eight years ago, and I was living in NYC with Dad until he got remarried." She thought about telling David more about the situation. About Brenda. Would that make her look too . . . bitchy? "She was nice to me right up until the ring was on her finger, then it was *new wife, new life,* I guess."

"That sucks. I'm sorry, Staci. It couldn't have been easy getting uprooted like that; I know I have some friends that I miss back home, but that's rough." They walked along quietly for a few more moments before he began again. "Still, this town isn't all that bad."

"Lately, you'd be right. It was the pits before. No cell service, almost no internet." She shook her head. "Would you believe the best you could get was twenty-four baud with an old-fashioned modem over copper telephone wires? Even the school! Everyone was in a constant funk, and the economy was in the crapper. You had to go the next town over to see movies or do any shopping. But I guess that kind of forced me to make friends." She mock-shrugged. "Beth, and a few other kids; you met Seth and Wanda. Two of them moved, 'cause their families got jobs up the coast, but the rest are still here."

"Yeah, I heard that things started picking up a lot, which I guess is one reason why Fairgrove decided to start a new branch here. Get in while the real estate is still cheap, yeah?" His look invited an answer and she laughed a little. "Wasn't there also some sort of big tragedy a few months back? A fire or something?"

"It wasn't a fire." *It was a whole bunch of dark elves and monsters trying to kill me and my friends with magic.* "I was up there for a party, and I actually don't remember much. Cops said it was a gas explosion. It took out most of a big-time family here in Silence."

"That's right! The Blackthornes, or something. Crazy stuff." He looked at her, his brows knitting together. "You got hurt in that?"

"Yeah . . . Tim and the others came rushing up after the explosion, found me and helped me out. I'm fine now, I was mostly just in shock and shaken up." That was mostly true; she had also been left to die by someone that she thought she loved, but that was a detail that David didn't need to know about just this moment. Or ever.

"I'm glad that you're okay, Staci." He reached out and touched her shoulder for a moment. She felt as if she could kiss him right then; it had been a long while since she had received any of that kind of affection, and she had missed it. "This is me," he said, removing his hand—couldn't he keep it there just a few seconds longer?—and gesturing towards the house they were standing in front of. "Would it be okay for me to ask if you'd like to get a bite sometime? Not at the diner; maybe the drive-in?"

"More than okay. I'd really like that, David." She positively beamed. "I'm busy tomorrow, but . . . maybe the day after?" She knew that he was only working a half-shift that day; she only had practice tomorrow, with the next day being one of her days off.

"Cool. Can I have your number? I'll call you when I get off and pick you up." He chuckled a little. "Sad and pathetic, I don't have a car of my own, that's what I'm saving for, but I can probably borrow Ma's if you don't mind being seen in a relic of the last century. It's a Subaru Outback Sport."

Going to the drive-in in an actual car? That'll be a change! "Sure, that'll work great. Here's my number. And I like Subarus." Actually she didn't have the slightest idea what a Subaru looked like, but she wouldn't have cared if it was a barge at this point. *Well . . . maybe not a crapped-out pickup. I probably wouldn't want to go to the drive-in in*

a crapped-out pickup . . . which is what most of the boys in this town
seem to drive.

"The advantage of having a pa that's a mechanic is you can keep cars running forever. The *disadvantage* of having a pa that's a mechanic is that you can keep cars running forever." He laughed again. "Still it means I only have a couple hundred bucks to go before I'll have my own wheels, since Pa can run a resurrection spell on just about anything."

"As long as it isn't a zombie-car," she replied lightly. "Or Christine." And before she could think of anything else to say, a voice called from the green clapboard saltbox house above them.

"Dave! Can you come take out the garbage?"

"Well, I am summoned," he said, heading up the driveway to the house. "Later, Staci! Day after tomorrow!"

"I'll see you then, I guess!" She stayed there, watching David until he was back in the house, smiling the entire time. *Damn if he isn't cute. And nice.*

She checked her phone and was surprised to see that half an hour had gone by since they had started walking. It had seemed much shorter than that to her. Staci felt as if she was on a cloud the entire bike ride back to her house.

Maybe I'll have the guts to ask him to come to the bookstore sometime, have some coffee. Maybe.

CHAPTER THREE

Staci awoke the next morning to the smell of cooked bacon and coffee. All things considered, she had had much ruder awakenings. She felt well rested, despite having had a very odd dream during the night. She could only remember bits and pieces of it; her rolling a large stone up a hill, or trying to keep it from rolling down? There was a lot of thunder and lightning, and she had heard what sounded like a lot of scratching noises rising up all around her. Weird.

After a quick shower and a change of clothing she ran downstairs to find her mom had actually made a full breakfast for both of them without ruining anything. Pancakes, bacon (a little more on the burnt side of crisp, but still edible!), and coffee, and orange sections on the side. "Hey sweetie!" Mom greeted her, handing her a plate with the butter melting on top of the pancakes. "Remember when I used to make you mouse-head-pancakes?" she added wistfully. "You used to eat them until I thought you were going to pop."

"Yeah, I loved those. You started making them after our first trip to Disney when I was little." Staci looked at the pile of food before her. "You really did great on this, Mom. I just hope I can finish it all." Her mother beamed at the compliment. Staci had been trying to encourage her mother at every opportunity that she could; there were a lot of missteps on both of their parts, and sometimes her mother would break down and cry from frustration. But it had been a long time since that had happened, and it looked like her mother had learned to cope with the little setbacks much better. Before, the burnt bacon would have been enough to set off a crying jag, and

27

statements about not being good enough, a horrible mother, and a general failure. Staci had recently had her own bout of not feeling good enough for anyone; it was the one good thing to come from that experience, that she could help her mother with her own feelings.

"At least my tips are getting a lot better." Mom nodded at the jar, which was noticeably fuller than it used to be. How much of that was due to Mom not drinking her tips away? *Some, but not all of it. There's a good pile of money in there.*

Staci eyed the jar with a nod of approval. "Things getting better at the bar?"

"More guys coming in from the lumber mill." Mom filled her own plate and took it to the table and sat down. "You know, when they started talking about the mill going all *sustainable products* everyone thought that was the start of layoffs. But it isn't. The guys were all talking about it last night. They said that the bay is full of old sunk logs that are all old-growth wood. There's work for divers bringing them up. And they're milling out every single scrap, because that wood is so valuable, so instead of being less work, because they have to be so precise, there's more."

Staci blinked. Not at the idea of there being more work because of what the new owners were doing at the mill (and wouldn't that new owner be Morrigan? Wasn't she the only Blackthorne left alive on this side of the Portal?) but because her mother had actually *listened* to what the guys at the bar were saying and *remembered* it. "Wow," she said. "That sounds like something everybody can get behind."

"Mhmm. So, what adventures do you have planned? Another day at the bookstore?" her mother asked as she was clearing away the plates; Staci had demolished the breakfast, even having seconds. She would need her energy for today.

"Nope, heading out to play in the forest again with Seth and Wanda; more LARPing and hiking," Staci responded, as she slipped her jacket on and secured her leather knapsack. "I probably won't be back until late; we'll probably stop and get some lunch or dinner in town."

"Well, I can't complain that you're a couch-potato, that's for sure. You're in better shape than I am! Maybe you ought to make a fitness video or something." Her mother giggled at that. "Move over, Buns of Steel, right? You're so cute, you'd make a million dollars!"

Staci rolled her eyes a little. "Too many people doing those for free on YouTube, no way I could compete." She checked to make sure that she had everything: phone with its attached charm, backpack, and all of the books that she needed to return to Tim. "All right, I've got to get going. I'll see you later!" She pecked her mother on the cheek before starting for the door.

"Okay, sweetie. I'll be working tonight, so I'll see you in the morning. Be safe!"

Staci took a leisurely route through town on her way to the spot in the woods where she would meet the others. She had the time; Wanda hated getting up early, and Tim had to attend to things at the bookstore before he would be free to come out and help train them. Even getting there early, Staci would be able to keep herself occupied: first setting up a few wards to alert her if anyone was getting close, and then working on magic. Practicing magic produced a thrill in her that she hadn't even thought was possible, when she first moved to Silence. It was primordial: something that was old and impossibly powerful, but able to be manipulated. Used for purpose. Immediately after the attack on the Blackthorne mansion, Staci had thought that she wouldn't want anything to do with magic ever again. But, instead, she had thrown herself completely into studying it, and it had helped her cope. She loved using magic; that was part of why she had messed up during their last training day. She understood the need to practice mundane skills, even rely on them, since her magical energy stores could be drained, leaving her unable to cast even a simple cantrip, but magic was just more fascinating.

Deep inside of herself, she felt a burning urge to use magic more and more. Who wouldn't? To shape the world with your thoughts? To control the very elements and fibers of existence? It was addicting, and helped to mask the ache she experienced whenever she thought about Dylan.

It's always coming back to him, isn't it? Ugh. She shook her head as she pedaled along, trying to will the image of her erstwhile, elven pseudo-boyfriend away. Then she shook her head again that that was even a *thing*.

Staci decided to take a detour down towards the cannery and lumber mill to see for herself what her mother had mentioned. Plus . . . the route would take her past David's house. The thought of him made her smile. He would be at work right about now, without a doubt; serving all of the fishermen that had already brought in a good haul, or people from the industrial area getting off of swing shifts.

There were a lot of guys going into the cannery; the alley that had been mostly deserted at this hour before had activity in it. Mom was right; there had been all these rumors about the cannery going bust, that the fishermen would never be able to follow the new "zero bycatch rule" and still make enough to keep food on the table and fuel in the boat. That was why Jake and Riley's parents had both bailed. They'd been sure that their cannery and mill jobs would be done, so they'd headed up to Vermont where relatives were living. Even sold the houses that had been in their families for generations.

And yet . . . whoever the owner was, he'd (or she! It could be Morrigan!) managed to make it work, almost as if there was magic propelling everything. It turned out there were lots of fancy East Coast markets who'd pay top dollar for "certified zero-bycatch" sardines, and sardines were getting trendy instead of being a bar snack or a poor-man's lunch. So the cannery was doing well! Smaller cans than before, new brand, meant more work. *Jake and Riley could still be here, if only their folks had had faith. . . .*

But faith had been in very short supply in Silence, the town that was dying by inches . . . and anyway, Staci had gotten the very strong feeling that neither of the two had been even remotely comfortable with magic that was real, magic that could kill people, magic that wasn't safely contained in a book or on a screen. Their brush with it had been more than enough for the pair of them. Still, she missed them loads, and still kept up with them via texts and Facebook when she could. Sometimes Seth would do a special campaign and have them do telepresence through a laptop; it wasn't exactly the same, but it was still better than nothing.

You would think that the simple fact we can even do that now would prove to them that everything is better now.

"Maybe they'll come back one day, if they see how things are changing," she wondered aloud to herself. She'd have to remember to take some pictures of the town, especially the cannery; show that things were bouncing back. Something they could show their parents. She wouldn't mention the magic stuff; that would just be for her, Seth, Wanda, and Tim from now on.

Just as she had thought, Staci was the first person to arrive at their spot on the cliff, or rather, below it. Staci had stopped using Makeout Hill to practice magic, for a number of reasons. One, it reminded her of too much; the Blackthornes, Dylan, Sean even. Two, now that there was actual cell reception in the town, people didn't just use the spot to rarely get a signal, but for its actual namesake. Watching couples getting it on there would have been bad enough; having some unlucky couple drive up at the wrong time and catch a real display of magic would have been *far* worse.

Instead, they had decided on a spot that didn't give Staci any memories to speak of, and had the advantage of being very secluded—the Blackthornes' private beach. There was road access only to the top of the cliff over the beach. But because you had to climb down a cliff—even if there was a staircase cut into the side of it—no one around here bothered to use it. At least not for swimming. Probably it had been used during Prohibition to land booze, but there were easier ways to traffic drugs in and out of this area.

The Blackthornes had used the beach for parties, but the Blackthornes had had a million servants to schlep stuff around, and magic to make it, if they didn't even want to bother schlepping it. Whereas, if you were schlepping the stuff yourself, and were a normal teenager, or even a jock, you'd be too tired by the time you got to the beach to pop a beer. *So* much easier to swim off the docks, now that the weather was normal and Silence was actually warm and sunny during the day. Mostly. This *was* still Maine. It got in the 50s even in the summer, especially at night.

This, of course, meant that Staci and Company were toting their own practice gear down to the beach, and she really didn't want to think about how awful this stretch of sand would be once it turned cold . . . but that was for the future, and right now, this was a pretty good spot.

She left her bike chained to a tree at the top of the cliff, picked up her pack, and started down the stairs. Down below there wasn't a sign that anyone used the beach for anything. Not even litter. Well, that was because part of their warm-up was to police the place for anything that washed in on the tide. So that no one had to lug tons of practice weapons up and down the stairs, Tim would use a borrowed boat to bring that stuff in when he got here.

Her first chore was to set up a couple of alarm spells; just enough to let her know if anyone was getting too close, to where they could see what was going on. The last thing any of them wanted was for someone to roll up on them right in the middle of a spell, or a cop asking questions about why they had bows and arrows, knives, and other implements. Or, frankly, why the local bookstore owner was in a secluded spot with three teens.

She touched her phone charm and went to work. Staci knew that it was a stupid habit, and knew that she was being sentimental about it; it was something Dylan had given her. But, it had also helped to save her life, and to discover magic. Even Tim said that things that meant a lot to people could be powerful for them; like totems that could store magical energy. That's how she justified keeping the charm. Her fingers took a moment to warm up as she started weaving complex designs in the air; it was a little cool with the breeze, and her hands felt slightly stiff. As magic started to trickle into her limbs, all feelings of being tired or her hands being not quite warm enough vanished.

The great thing about this being a secluded beach was that nothing ever really changed here. So instead of needing to create some kind of illusion or put up something like a barrier, all she needed to do was to set up a kind of "magical screen" across the front of the cove that replayed a moment in time. And that time was an hour before she got here. She didn't even need to allow for anything but about a five second loop of waves washing up on the shore. Simple, easy to do, and required the minimum of magical "juice." She could keep the screen going even if she wasn't concentrating on it; there was a small piece of quartz in her jacket pocket that would turn to ash when the spell ran out, consumed as part of the spell. It was very handy, to say the least.

Now that her set-up was done, it was time for her to get to work. *It was a good thing I ate a large breakfast; this is going to burn up a lot of energy. Never mind what Tim will have me practice.* Staci started with a basic shield incantation; it would set up a barrier that would stop basic spells and small objects that were thrown at her, diverting them around her. It couldn't take much abuse; only one or two shots, and it was gone. But it wasn't supposed to be her only line of defense; it was the base that she needed in order to build the rest. *Now something a little fancier.* The next layer was a reflection spell; any spell launched at it would rebound along the same path, hopefully back to whoever had cast it. But Staci had been experimenting with a twist on the spell. It now had a minor illusion spell attached to it; whatever spell that was launched at her, if it had a visual component, would simply disappear. The idea was that if something got reflected, her opponent wouldn't be able to see their own spell coming back to smack them in the face. The illusion spell made the shield a little more unstable, but Staci figured that it was worth it if it took someone off-guard. She could see the trickle of magical energy flowing from herself to the shield, and willed it to be dampened until it was almost not even there. She could strengthen the connection—and thus the spell—at will, but this way it wouldn't be so obvious as to what she was doing if another caster was watching.

So much for set-up. She sighed, letting out a breath she had been holding. "Time for the offense."

There was an old piece of busted concrete pillar that had somehow found its way onto the beach; it made a good target. Since it was man made, it would stand up a little bit better to some of the stuff that she could throw at it than say a rock or a tree stump would; magic had an affinity for natural substances, which is why she wore a lot of leather and non-synthetic fabrics when she was practicing magic. She willed energy to collect in her hands, building up and coming from what felt like the center of her chest. She imagined what she wanted to happen, started mouthing the words . . . and then *looked* at the pillar. Her right hand shot forward while her fingers did an odd, twisting sort of contortion. There was a very audible *thwack* and a puff of dust that came from the pillar. It was a simple kinetic spell; like punching someone, without being right next to them and actually touching them. It was good for interrupting someone while they were casting, or to make someone sit down *hard* if you put a lot of energy into it. She repeated the spell a dozen times, varying it a little each time; once with a visual component so that it looked like a bolt of energy, once with a spell rider that would make the place that it struck itch like crazy if it landed on a person. Her head swam with calculations, chants, incantations, glyphs and symbols; underneath it all, however, was raw *power*. Willing what she wanted to have happen was just as important as knowing all of the mechanics of how to do it. Sometimes when she dreamed it was in the permutations for a spell; occasionally she would wake up half afraid that she had somehow cast it in her sleep and blown the house up.

Next came something a little flashier. "Seth's favorite: *fireball.*" This spell took substantially more power, and the result was equally impressive. A literal ball of flame shot towards the pillar, erupting into a cloud of flame and smoke like a small gas explosion when it impacted. Nothing fancy for that spell. Something you want to be on fire? Congratulations, it is now probably on fire and hopefully not bothering you anymore. A lot of the elemental attacks were variations on the same theme; create a big hunk of something with magic, then use magic to basically throw it at whatever you wanted. She still hadn't gotten used to electricity; the magic got very "slippery" for her, and part of the magic would get away from her. The very first time she had tried ball lightning, she had shocked herself bad enough that when she came to, she could smell ozone and burnt hair.

Tim had told her to study up on spells that were both offensive and defensive, and the first one that had come up had been something to create a "tempest"—basically a dust-devil sort of thing, but a lot more powerful. She decided to go ahead and try it. This one you had to "anchor" to the place or thing you wanted to attack. The idea was, at the worst, your opponent would get a lot of dust and sand and debris in his face. And at best, he'd be knocked around and too busy trying to stay on his feet, *and* get scoured or cut up by the debris in the wind.

Staci poured magic into her arms, tracing a complex circular glyph in the air; her fingers and arms left after-image trails of magic as she moved, the trails sparking and disappearing as quickly as they had appeared. Finally, she offloaded the magic into her target; a patch of sand at the base of the pillar. *Damnit! Not again!* The spell started off just as she had wanted; a small cyclone, no more than a couple of inches high, swirling in the beach sand. Then the spell unraveled; the energy that she had put into the spell tore it apart, and the cyclone dug into the ground for a half-second before exploding, showering Staci and the immediate area in sand. And since she had her eyes open at the time, the sand flew into her eyes.

"Ow! Ow! Ow! Shit ow!" She dashed for the water and waded out knee-deep, opening her scalded-feeling eyes wide and splashing water in them to try to get the sand out. The salt water hurt, but it was better than the sand. That was the fifth time that had happened, and the worst. She still hadn't figured out what she was doing wrong; she would have to ask Tim when he got here. Finally, she got all of the grit out of her eyes. Then she realized what the scene would have looked like to an outsider; first the sound of the sand exploding, followed by a teenage girl cursing and *appearing* seemingly out of thin air in the middle of the surf. Her magical screen was still up, and she had run straight through it.

Good job, bonehead. It was a lucky thing that there wasn't anyone out on the water just then. Staci slogged through the knee-high water to get back to the shore; she felt the electric tingle on her skin that told her that she had passed through the magical screen again. Her boots were waterproof, but the salt water had splashed up high enough to soak into her pants. Clicking her tongue, she started to brush off the last remaining bits of sand from her clothing. *I probably have time to get a spell going to help dry off, at least a little bit.*

Staci had just begun to trace the lines for the spell when she came up short. Something was wrong; not with her magic, or with her. But she felt it all the same. It took her a moment to pinpoint it; then she recognized the feeling, remembered it. *This feels like that first time on Makeout Hill, when I had the Red Caps following me.*

Someone—or some*thing*—was watching her.

She didn't immediately move to cast a spell, or even look around suddenly. Tim had taught her that letting on that you knew you were being watched or followed wasn't the wisest strategy, most times. Instead, she went back brushing off the sand, pretending to get it out of her hair as she scanned with her eyes. *Whoever it is, they have to be in the forest. I would've seen them, otherwise, and there's still my alarm spells—*

What sounded like a fire alarm from the New York City apartment building she used to live in went off inside of Staci's head. Tim had taught her that spells were highly personal; you put something of yourself into them every time you cast. If you were creating your own spells, it was the same thing. Nothing in the world sounded like those fire alarms from her childhood; they had been old, '70s era fire alarms, outmoded and endlessly repaired instead of replaced. She would recognize the sound anywhere. Hearing them now meant only one thing; her alarm spells had been triggered. She started readying new defensive spells, and already had in mind a particularly nasty attack spell that would suspend someone in mid-air; if she did it right, it basically killed gravity in a small sphere. *And will probably make whoever is caught in it blow chunks.*

At the same time a familiar voice hailed her from the top of the cliff. *"Hey!"* She swiveled her head to look up, and there were Seth and Wanda, backpacks on their backs, standing at the edge of the staircase down. *"Already starting without us?"*

Wanda was snickering. *"You're supposed to take your pants* off *when you go swimming, Stace!"*

She dropped her hands to her sides, then glanced quickly to the forest behind them. Whatever had been there was surely gone now. But there had been *something*...hadn't there been? She had felt so sure, and Tim told her to trust her gut, but now she was having doubts. *All alone at the beach, and you're freaking yourself out. Some great warrior mage badass you are, Staci.*

The sound of an outboard motor puttering at low speed made her look towards the ocean, and there was Tim, in the borrowed green dinghy, heading in. It was the sort of old metal boat you could run right up onto the beach, and that was what he did, pulling the motor up after he killed it, on its swivel out of the water and letting momentum and waves carry him in. Staci trotted over to help him pull it all the way up past the waterline. It hardly mattered now, with her pant legs soaked.

As Tim was gathering up the equipment in the front of the boat, he noticed that something was off with Staci. "Are you okay?"

"My cyclone spell had a catastrophic system failure, and my alarm spells went off." She knew better than to lie to Tim at this point. "I don't know if the alarms went off because there was something in the woods, watching, if it was because the cyclone interacted with them somehow, or because I FUBARed and Wanda and Seth set them off."

Tim paused for a moment, as if weighing her words, and then

nodded. "We'll work on that spell. There are a couple of mnemonic tricks I can help you with that might fix it. As much as I like to drill that this is a certain kind of science that we're doing, there's still a lot of individual interpretation. Doesn't hurt to have the hard and fast stuff down pat, though." Staci mentally breathed a sigh of relief. She wasn't sure that she really *had* seen something or not; being too gung ho about it might make her come off as easily spooked or just nervy. She had moved past that; Tim trusted her, now, more than he ever had before. She wasn't just the little elven-blood girl who had ruined his town. She was his apprentice. He had done a lot in those early days to discourage her from training under him, hoping that, if he was hard enough on her, she'd give up, quit, and forget all about this magic business. But she had persevered . . . and earned his respect.

She treasured that, and wasn't about to throw it away because she got a little spooked on a beach. But she also didn't want to screw things up because she "didn't bother to tell him something," either. It was a balancing act. But then, everything in magic seemed to be a balancing act.

"All right," Tim said. "Stay alert and focused, because there might have been someone up there watching. Probably a kid, possibly a low-level Fae creature, but you never know. Now let's get training."

CHAPTER FOUR

By the time the gang had started up with practice in earnest, Staci had almost completely shaken off her unease. She simply didn't have time to worry about it; when the four of them practiced, they practiced *hard*. By now she knew this wasn't "normal." Tim had given her access to books that described the normal "path of the apprentice." Staci's training, had she been the average apprentice, would have been much more structured, slow-paced. Making sure she had time to chew on the very precepts of magic, to know it in her bones before she even got near a dangerous spell. As it was, due to the circumstances, Tim—and Dylan before him—had given Staci a crash course on how to be effective, even deadly, with magic. They'd taught her to shoot from the hip before she'd ever seen target practice. It was all born of necessity; due to her elven-blood, and her involvement with the Fae, she was already marked. No matter what happened from now on, she would always have magic and fantastical beings in her life. She needed to be able to defend herself.

What really surprised her was how quickly Wanda and Seth had accepted the situation. Granted, they had seen elves and magic up close. But the fact they had stuck around, had *wanted* to keep helping, even though they couldn't do magic themselves... it was insane. She loved them all the more for it, but she also worried about them. About how deep they would get into this, and if they could get back out again if they didn't like how things were going. Staci was stuck, she knew that. What was more, she didn't mind it; she had fallen in love with magic, and accepted that the danger was a part of

39

the price for that gift. Wanda and Seth were still just . . . *normal*. Regular people, in over their heads.

"Staci, focus. Get back on task," Tim said. Staci shook her head; she really must have been shaken up before, to let her mind wander like that. *You're here to work, so work.*

The three of them were all doing exercises that played to their talents, today. Staci was working magic; Tim's mnemonic trick was helping, but she still hadn't quite pinned down what was causing her cyclone spell to come undone at the seams. She was determined that she would figure it out before they broke for the day. Seth was building traps; perfecting them and hiding them was his game. There were a lot of ugly and nasty things out in the world that were far too dangerous to go after head on; trapping them wasn't just safer, it was smart. Wanda was the one that shone the most out of all of them, however; when it came to archery and knives, she had a true talent. She was perfecting her technique for firing on the move; if she did well enough today, she'd soon be graduating to moving targets.

Over all of them was Tim; surveying, appraising, critiquing. Staci felt like a god when she did magic; watching Tim, she felt like a mouse in the shadow of an elephant. She had only seen him at his full strength once, magically. It had been when he had rescued the entire gang from Blackthorne Manor. He had taken out several elves, with magic alone; the energy coming off him had been like a corona from the sun, and he had made it seem effortless. Only now, having seriously studied magic herself, did she realize how much self-discipline and concentration her mentor must possess. *To get as good as Tim, I'm going to have to work a lot harder.*

He tended to give them periodic breaks when it looked as if they were flagging, reminding them as he did so that "if we're fighting for our lives, nobody's going to give you a chance to rest, so get used to not having one."

Today, however, he stopped and looked all three of them over carefully. "Wanda, Seth, I have the feeling that you consider yourselves to be the also-rans," he said. "Or maybe the cannon fodder. That you think I'm indulging you by *letting you help*. I'm not. You two could end up being the front line the next time we face something."

When that penetrated, both Wanda and Seth's faces showed . . . shock. Then disbelief.

"I'm going to start handing you homework as well as Staci," he continued. "*History* homework. Mages are rare. Always have been. Good ones are rarer. Great ones are unicorns. When humans have fought Fae and Dark creatures in the past, it's been plain old *ordinary* people that did most of the work, and if they were lucky, there was *one* mage around, who might or might not have been any use, who backed them up. Half the time, the mage was just a healer, no combat abilities beyond the use of sword or bow. The people who protected their own homes and families and villages weren't special. Sometimes they couldn't even see what they were fighting against. But fought they did, and won they did, and Staci and I are damn lucky you've come along on this ride. We might as well have big fat targets pasted on us. Whatever comes next will come first after us. We need you far more than you need us."

Staci could see that they were both filled with more than a little pride at that. Tim seemed to have a knack for knowing when to boost people up, and when to be hard on them. Most of the time, he was hard on all of them. Staci especially. She had gotten over being jealous or being hurt by it; she saw that it was for her own good, as it was for the others. They all needed to be strong in their own ways if they were going to be any good to each other in a fight.

"Finish up with what you're working on. Let's give it fifteen minutes. Then we're going to try something fun . . . with a prize at the end." The three teens grinned at each other when Tim finished talking, redoubling their efforts with their current tasks. Tim's prizes tended to be books—wonderful, amazing books that were *not* part of their homework, things he had discovered over a lifetime of reading. Leather-bound, first editions, limited printings; always the sort of stuff you wouldn't be able to find at the local big box store. Somehow he was always able to pick out something that turned out to be the filet mignon of books. It wasn't a great surprise, his knack for finding choice volumes; he was a bookstore owner, and a magician to boot. But it still pleased the trio every time he came up with something new. They would all, of course, share whatever the prize was. The real treat was being the *first* to read whatever the book was that they received. Staci had always been a reader, but since coming to Silence—and especially since becoming an apprentice mage—she had become voracious in her reading habits. Possibly that had something to do with being cut off from the internet for so long. Fighting off boredom wasn't a matter of following crappy clickbait anymore.

Well, she *still* wasn't able to get the cyclone spell to work, but at least it wasn't blowing up in her face, it was just starting to spin up, then spinning down again before it got anywhere. Seth and Wanda were obviously having a lot more success than she was today. She closed everything down and erased all traces of having done any magical work, less with a feeling of defeat than of... well, it wasn't resignation, and it wasn't exactly determination. More like a combination of the two. Like *this is going to be harder than I thought,* combined with *but I'll get this like I've gotten everything else Tim has thrown at me.* She noticed that the others were already on their way to see Tim, and hurried to join them.

Tim waited until the three of them had assembled in front of him. "We'll do a breakdown on the afternoon after we get back to the bookstore. Before that, however, I have something new for all of you. We're going to be doing a scavenger hunt... of sorts." Tim held up a piece of paper; it was folded into a triangle. "This is your list. Not everything on here is going to be obvious. It's all going to be in the forest... and you're going to need to work together to find it all. You have one hour to get all of the items on the list. I'll be watching you as you work... so try not to embarrass yourselves." He sat down on the log he had been standing on, then placed the tip of the folded piece of paper on his knee. With a flick of his finger, he sent the list spinning at the group; Wanda was the one who caught it out of the air, sticking her tongue out at the others. When the three of them looked back, Tim was gone.

"Now... go!" Staci had been half-expecting it, but she still jumped when Tim's disembodied voice called out to them. She was the first one to regain her composure and start running, after elbowing Wanda and Seth simultaneously, of course. It had been a couple of weeks since they had done a learning game like this. They definitely needed the break, and Tim had no doubt sensed it.

"Where are you off to, you dingus! I've got the list!" Wanda and Seth chased after Staci anyways; the desire to run and blow off a little bit of steam was too great for any of them to stop. They finally regrouped at the edge of the treeline, breathing hard and smiling.

Wanda elbowed Staci back. "Going to be hard to find anything without this." She waved the paper football in front of Staci's nose, prompting Staci to swipe at it.

"Open it up! Let's get cracking on this."

Wanda unfolded the paper, then began reading the note. "We need to find a pin oak leaf, a lone mistletoe berry, a seashell where it shouldn't belong, and a movie ticket stub. At the bottom, it says, 'WORK TOGETHER.' Gee, you think we ought to help each other out?"

"Well, first of all, obviously it isn't going to be just any leaf or mistletoe berry or shell, or ticket stub. So . . . " Staci thought. "There's going to be something special about where these things are. Which means we have to look for clues that say 'this is different,' and since Tim just gave us that big talk about how magic isn't all-that, some or even all of those clues probably aren't going to be magic. What else does it say?"

"Um . . . *get jogging*. I wonder . . . *Oh!* They'll probably all be along the running trail we use," Wanda deduced.

Seth pointed. "There's the trailhead. Let's get moving. I want to be claiming our prize over burgers by dinner time."

They kept jogging along the path for about five minutes before Seth called out for them to stop.

"Getting tired already? Must be from the way you overeat—"

"No, look!" He pointed up; nestled in where two branches met in an old oak tree was a mistletoe plant.

Staci closed her eyes a moment and concentrated on the spell that allowed her to see magic. When she opened them again, the entire plant was glowing. "That's the one," she confirmed.

"The note says *one* berry. I bet we have to get a particular one down without getting the whole plant down."

"They're *all* lighting up," said Staci. "I guess the deal might be that we are going to have to be really careful. Maybe if we bring down too much of the plant, the magic dies on the berries."

Seth eyed the trunk. "We're not getting up that without some help."

"Well, in the South they hunt mistletoe with a shotgun," Wanda observed. "And I spy a cluster with only one berry on it." She pointed. They all looked. Sure enough there was what had been a cluster of berries that was now bare, with one single berry on the end. "I can take that," she said.

The others nodded. "Go for it," said Staci. Wanda considered her bow a moment, then took out a throwing knife.

"I think I've got the range. If I don't, I can try the arrow," she said, and threw. Staci held her breath as the knife flew end over end towards the mistletoe. The knife passed close to the plant, but it looked like it had missed. "Ha!" Wanda ran forward, catching something out of the air. When Staci and Seth caught up to her, Wanda opened her hand while smiling triumphantly; in her palm was a single mistletoe berry.

"That was incredible; I didn't even see it fall. You must have clipped it right at the stem." Seth's eyes were wide in amazement.

"What can I say? I'm just naturally amazing. Here," she said, tossing the berry to Seth. "Don't eat it."

"Har har. Let's keep moving. I'm getting hungry enough that I might actually eat it." He stuck a hand in his backpack and came up with an empty plastic container for breath mints. They all saved those, because they were so handy for storing small things. He popped the berry into it for safekeeping.

"Well, you wouldn't be hungry any more," Staci added. "They're poisonous."

The trio continued on; it didn't take them long to find the second item. A gigantic spider web was spread across the running trail. At least a couple dozen leaves were stuck in the web, all of them different.

"Now what?" Wanda put her fists on her hips out of frustration, huffing. "I hate spider webs; they always show up on black clothing."

"Which one is it? We can't take them all, can we?" Seth had walked up to the web, examining the individual leaves.

"That one," Staci said, pointing to a leaf that was near the top of the web, far out of reach for any of them. "I've been studying a lot of local plants and things like that; you never know when you'll need to find spell components on the fly. That's a pin oak leaf. The rest are all red oak. *One of these things is not like the other,*" she added in a sing-song voice.

Wanda and Seth both took several steps back, craning their necks to see the leaf. "No way I can get that with a knife or an arrow; it'll take the whole thing out. Plus, it looks really dried out, like it might crumble."

"I've got a couple of spells that might work... but I'm not really practiced at them. It'd be just as bad as throwing a rock at it and hoping." Flying was not something that Staci could do; she didn't even know if it was possible with magic, though she had secretly hoped it was ever since she became an apprentice.

"Step back, ladies. I can handle this." Seth gently brushed passed Wanda and Staci as he walked back up to the web.

"Whatever you say, Peter Parker. Just don't cry to me when a spider jumps on your face." Wanda repressed a shiver, rubbing her arms.

Seth reached into his jacket, producing what looked like a silver loop. He untwisted something on it, and suddenly the loop unfurled. "It's a car aerial I got off of a junker at the scrap yard. I use it for a trap probe; plus it hurts like hell if you whap someone with it." Carefully, he positioned the end of the thin metal wire near the leaf; it gave him just enough reach. He took his time, using the tip to gather up bits of web on both sides of the leaf, sort of wrapping it in the sticky threads. After a few minutes of effort, the leaf fell free from the web, which now had a gaping hole. It landed on the ground, but remained intact due to the bits of web holding it together. "Here; get out some notebook paper; we'll sandwich it in that and then put it in one of my books, make sure that it doesn't get crushed."

Once they had safely tucked the leaf away where it wouldn't get damaged, they started off again. They were halfway done; the sooner they finished, the sooner they would be able to get some grub... and their prize, whatever it was. Further on down, the trail they were on had a bend that came close to a man-made firebreak; just a simple dirt road with contoured sides. The road itself was just below eye level for the gang due to the sloped sides. Staci, jogging along with the others, almost missed their next clue; out of the corner of her eye as they rounded the bend she saw the glint of magic.

"Hey! Something back over by the road." The gang came to a stop, then followed Staci as she led them up the bank of the road. The road itself was meant to be a gap in the vegetation in case a fire happened, and as a way for wilderness management crews to get around. In reality, it was often used by locals for hunting, ATVs, mudding, and finding places for underage drinking where they were less likely to get busted. As a result, the road had a fair bit of trash on it and around it. The twinkle of magic that Staci had seen was coming from one of the trash piles. As they got closer, the magic became stronger and brighter; it was focused on a movie ticket stub. "It's the ticket," she said, pointing at it. "Looks like it's for that dumb teen vampire movie that came out last year."

They all made a face at that. Wanda, for all the Goth that she was, hated that movie especially; she had had enough catcalls and the like directed her way by folks that took exception to her style.

"Well, that was easy," Seth said, bending to pick it up. Staci's hand shot out, grabbing him by the wrist. "Hey, what gives?"

"You said it; 'easy.' Since when does Tim do 'easy'? There's something more to this." Staci concentrated, letting her eyes unfocus a little bit, blurring everything at the edges. She saw that the magic, while concentrated on the ticket stub, also had tendrils that extended down into the trash pile, rooting themselves in the ground. She held out her hand, drawing a few strands of the magic towards her to "taste" them. The ticket stub wasn't the true source of the magic; it was a beacon, meant to attract attention. The magic was coming from somewhere else . . . and it was fueling a trap spell.

"Trap?"

"Trap. I think . . . " She paused as she studied the patterns of the magical energy, cross-referencing it with what she knew. " . . . I think it's a fire spell of some kind. Something small. If we trigger it, it'll burn everything up; the trash and the ticket. Snatching the ticket won't work; it's the shiny that is supposed to catch our attention, but it's also the spring for the trap, I think."

"Well what can you do?" Seth asked. "How complicated is it?"

"Fiendishly," Staci replied and chewed on her lower lip, thinking. "The thing is, Tim always says to go with Occam's Razor in magic."

Wanda made a face, but Seth got it immediately. "The simplest answer is usually the right one," he replied. "So . . . um . . . this is about fire. The Fire Triangle is Fuel, Air and Heat. Take one away and you don't have a fire. So?"

"Can't take the fuel without setting the trap off. Can't take the heat away because that's the fiendishly complicated trap. I suppose I could try counter Fire with Cold, but the ticket's about the most flammable thing in the pile and might go up first. That leaves air." She chewed on her lip a little more. "Okay, let me give this a try."

She flexed her fingers a little and created a sort of force-dome, a shield that was, in fact, in some ways the very opposite of the shields she was used to setting up. This one would let anything in or out. Except air. Then with a snap of her fingers, she removed the air.

The other two couldn't see anything at all of course. Only someone who could see magic in action could see the little dome over the mound of trash. She reached in, snatched the ticket, and felt the trap go off—but nothing happened, and she handed Seth the ticket. "Back up," she said, and all three of them moved away from the trash pile. Then she dispelled the dome.

As soon as the dome was gone, the entire trash pile lit up; for a half-second, it looked like a regular fire. Then it sprang into a conflagration as tall as the teens were, the fire so intense that all of them could feel it on their skin even from a distance. Just as suddenly, the fire collapsed back in on itself . . . and the moldering pile of trash exploded, sending bits of gunk, mud, and ash in all direction. The three teens were just far enough away not to be completely covered with the mess, though they did get pelted with a few small rocks.

"Yeah . . . thanks for stopping me from picking it up. I kind of want my eyebrows to stay on my face."

Wanda laughed. "Aw . . . I could have painted some new ones on you. You'd be just *dawlin'*, Seth." Seth lightly shoved her shoulder with his, and Wanda smiled at his touch. *Those two are so cute I could vomit, sometimes,* Staci thought.

"Flirt later; we're almost done." Wanda and Seth both blushed at that, and the trio started down the trail. There wasn't much of it left; they would be back at the beach soon enough. "Do you think we missed the last thing?"

"It's a seashell that's out of place. I haven't seen anything that would've fit that. I mean, we could take the other trail, the one that leads farther in." Wanda thrust her chin towards a cairn that marked where they were. They had reached the one fork in the trail; the path they always took led back to the beach, where they had started. The other would take them deeper into the forest in another big loop; they generally didn't use that trail, since it took so long to actually follow. They were on a time limit, anyways; it wouldn't have made sense for Tim to put the last item too far away for them to actually reach, would it?

"Anyone notice anything different about the trail?" Both Staci and Wanda started looking around, trying to find something out of place; Staci was the first to pick up on it.

"The cairn. It's in a new spot, isn't it?"

"Wait, you're right," Wanda said. "It used to be at the foot of that tree, but now it's off to the left by a few feet." There wasn't a blank spot missing vegetation where the cairn had been; Tim must have used a spell to cover up the area, make it look natural. Or else he was so good at camouflaging things that he simply blended in the spot where the cairn had been with trash and leaves and things.

They all got closer to it, looking at it from multiple angles after Seth had checked the area to make sure there weren't any physical traps. "It's dead on magic, too," noted Staci. She wasn't even getting a flash of magical energy from it, just ambient stuff.

"I have the feeling we are going to have to do this the hard and tedious way," Wanda said, with a heavy sigh. "This is another of Tim's little lessons on *why we don't rush through things,* I bet."

Staci groaned; the pile of rocks was about shoulder height, and some of those stones looked *heavy.* "Might as well get started, if we want to make it back in time. Remember, we're looking for a seashell; let's try not to turn it to powder with one of the rocks." The trio started to dismantle the cairn; Wanda and Staci took the stones off, one at a time, while Seth organized them according to size, shape, even color. It took them about fifteen minutes to completely dismantle the cairn, and all of them were sweating and covered with dirt and smudges of moss.

"Okay. It's a shell, and since we aren't in the tropics it can't be all that big and it's probably a clam," said Seth. "So . . . " He indicated a place in the line of stones with his hand. "From here back, we can eliminate. I'll take this third—" he drew a line in the dirt. "Staci, you take this third, and Wanda, you take the last third."

Picking up the rocks one a time and examining them closely was tedious, but not all that hard, since none of them were bigger than her hand. But the moment Staci got the right one in her hand, it was obvious it was a shell and not a rock when she turned it over. The underside was concave, and you could see the smooth shell and some tinges of purple that told her it was a quahog clam.

"You were right, Seth. I think this is it!"

"Great! Do we put the cairn back together?" The pile of stones had taken a good chunk of time to unstack; it'd take even longer to get them sitting on top of each other properly.

"We don't have the time. I imagine Tim will have us come back and put it back together, maybe tomorrow." Wanda turned her right wrist up to reveal her watch; wearing it on her left got in the way of using her bow. "Right now, we've gotta go."

They ran all the way back to the beach. Tim was waiting, a backpack beside him that looked promisingly full. They carefully displayed their finds to him, waiting with anticipation while he looked them over carefully. When he got to Staci's clam-shell he finally nodded.

"I have good news and bad news. The good news is you found all the objects in the time limit. The bad news is that I am pretty sure that you left that cairn scattered all over the trail, so I want you to rebuild it in the original spot."

They all groaned, but nodded. Tim didn't tell them *why* he needed it rebuilt; they didn't ask. That had been another lesson—*sometimes you don't get all the information; just do what you are asked and you'll be told later.* It might be something as simple as the fact that the cairn was something historical. Or maybe some people were using it in a navigation game; there were a couple of those out there, and why spoil people's fun? Staci had looked into them, and thought she might like to try . . . someday . . . when she wasn't running around having to learn so much.

"And the good news again. You've won four books." He pulled them out of his backpack, four hardbacks with dust-covers that looked like heavy-metal albums. A series. *The Secret World Chronicle.* Wanda grabbed the last one and leafed through it. "Hey!" she said indignantly. "It's a five book series, and there are only four here!"

"The fifth one isn't out yet," said Tim with a smirk. "When it is I will let you know so you can buy it from me. While some places may be able to run on dreams and well-wishes, my shop is still a business. Got to make money to help support my free-loader students." He took the books back, replacing them in the backpack. "I'll have these for you at the bookstore, once you're done. I'll go ahead and clean up the area here and start heading back. Stick together, and I'll see you in town. Now, get!"

"I have the feeling I'll have to get copies of my own," Seth mourned. "Oh well. More of Tim's free coffee, fewer sodas I guess."

"You shouldn't be drinking any soda," Wanda scolded. "All that—"

Seth held up a hand. "No lectures. I've heard them all before. If I don't get my neon-green fix once in a while I'll have to turn in my geek card. And don't get started on cheesy puffs."

"No more talk of food. I'm about ready to start gnawing on one of you. Let's finish up, then *fooood.*" Since they weren't in a rush, the trio took their time to get back to the location of the cairn, talking about school, the new books and who would get to read them first, and what movies were coming out. It had been a good day so far for Staci, despite the weirdness on the beach and not quite getting the hang of her cyclone spell. That could wait for another day. They kept talking as they restacked the stones; it took them a couple of tries, as the stones fell over twice when they weren't paying attention to the order they were placing them. Seth finally got everything in order, with Wanda and Staci playing helpers and lugging the stones into their spots. Once they were done, it looked much as it had before; Staci liked it better, now, because the three of them had worked on it. It had a little of them in it, and would until someone else restacked it, if ever.

"Done as it's going to be," Wanda said. She turned to the cairn, then held her hands up placatingly. "Now . . . stay."

"Where are we going to eat?" As if on cue, Seth's stomach growled, eliciting laughter from all three of them.

Something caught Staci's eye as Wanda and Seth debated the various food options in town. Down the path that branched off deeper into the forest was a tree trunk. It must have been there before, but something stood out about it this time. She started walking down the path almost unbidden, drawn by the downed tree. It was only part of a much larger tree, she saw immediately. The upper part of it was still green, so it wasn't a deadfall tree. About fifteen feet from the top branches it looked . . . odd. The bark of the tree twisted in a spiral pattern, like a corkscrew. At the base of the trunk the twisting became much more violent; it looked like the bark had split and exploded, leaving jagged peaks and valleys in the living wood.

"Hey!" Staci started as a hand came down on her shoulder; she had been engrossed in the sight of the ruined tree trunk. She realized that Seth and Wanda had been talking to her; she hadn't even heard them. "What's going on, space cadet?"

"Get a look at this. Have you ever seen a tree that looked like that?" The others finally noticed the tree trunk, and stood by Staci while they examined it.

"That's freaky. Maybe a bear or something? Or a storm?" Wanda nudged some of the chunks of broken tree with her boot's toe.

"If it was a storm, it wouldn't be the only one. And I've seen plenty of trees used like scratching posts by bears. This is something else entirely... it isn't rotted. It's like..." Seth stopped short. "It's like something grabbed this tree in the middle, and twisted it off like a bottle cap."

Staci's eyes followed what looked like a trail of some kind; something had moved through the woods, and wasn't particularly stealthy about it. "Let's follow that. See where this came from."

"You're mental, right? The last thing we need is to run into a bear."

"I'm telling you, it wasn't a bear—"

"Whatever. Besides, we're all starving. Poor Seth is going to expire if we don't get some food into him soon."

"It'll just take a minute," Staci said, already starting to walk. "Come on; Tim told us to stick together, right?"

"Argh!" Wanda threw up her hands, then followed Staci. "Let's go, Seth; someone needs to be the brains to Staci's... whatever."

The trail was easy to follow. There weren't any footprints, but there were enough busted plants and branches that Staci could have tracked it in her sleep. When they found the origin of the trail, there was a collective intake of breath as they all came up short.

"Holy. Shit."

There was a small clearing. It clearly didn't used to be one. It looked like a small tornado had set down right in the middle of the trees, and ripped about a dozen of them to pieces. That was how many tree stumps Staci counted, though she couldn't be sure. Many of them looked like they could have been the other half of the trunk she had seen on the trail; others looked like their top halves had been busted off by a wrecking ball.

"Seth," Wanda said slowly, almost in a whisper. "Tell me that there's some natural phenomena that explains this. Like a beaver's union that was on strike, or something."

"I got nothing," Seth replied. "This is spooky as hell."

"Staci, this is your idea. What are we doing here?" There was an edge of nervousness in Wanda's voice. That sealed it for Staci.

"Getting the hell out of here and back to town. I'm too hungry, too tired and too sweaty to deal with this right now. This is a mystery we can leave for another day." She surveyed the entire area; there wasn't another trail leading away from the violent clearing. *Whatever did this didn't leave a trace as to where it went. Seth was right; spooky as hell.* "If ever," she added under her breath.

"I knew there was something I liked about you; you're not as dumb as you look, sometimes."

"Har har. Did you and Seth figure out where we're eating, or do I have to pick again?" Staci was already following the trail back out to the main path, heading towards the beach. She would have to tell Tim about this; maybe it was another trick of his? Something they were supposed to find and mess around with? He had told them to go and restack the cairn; it would make sense that he'd have something extra to mess with their heads, get them thinking around another problem. Even if that were the case, she figured it would hold; they had bigger problems. Like starvation.

CHAPTER FIVE

Amazingly, even the food at the diner had improved in the last few weeks. There was a new cook who'd introduced "'50s comfort food," but like Grandma made it, not like you'd get from the fast-food version. The fried chicken dinners were amazing, and that was what they had all opted for.

"You coming to the bookstore, Beth?" Seth asked, as the waitress flew by with refills for their tea and water.

"Not tonight, I'm on late shift," she said. "We're twenty-four hours now—"

"*Beth!*" her boss yelled from behind the counter, where he was working like he had six hands.

"Right, coming!" she called back, and ran to get a tray full of the "new" milkshakes, made with real ice cream and real milk.

"Phooey." Staci sighed. "That means David is probably on late shift too. I mean it's great they're making more money now but . . . "

"I'd say we should pick up late-shift jobs for ourselves for the extra cash, but school starts in a few weeks and that's a no-can-do," Wanda pointed out. "Plus our . . . extracurricular activities. I'm pretty sure that employers aren't ready to give sick days for magic-related injuries. Let's get our faces stuffed and get down to the bookstore and get our prizes."

When they got there, it turned out that the prizes were better than they'd thought. The hardback of the first book had come with a free CD with a bunch of the publisher's other books on it. Wanda gleefully claimed that, after Staci remembered she had just gotten a package that day that probably had a bunch of books she'd put on her "wish list" in it. She could survive until Wanda was finished. Dad was pretty reliable about sending her books whenever he felt guilty about dumping her here. *I guess books makes him think he's "participating in my education." Whatever.* The longer she was away from Dad . . . the less being dumped in favor of "new wife, new life" hurt. Besides, what could New York offer her *now?* Nothing but a bunch of phony friends who got in touch with her less and less and some shopping opportunities. Almost dying a bunch of times, discovering elves, magic, and worse were real, and getting her heart broken had radically shifted her priorities since she had moved to Silence.

None of them really wanted to game without Beth. For one, it didn't seem fair, and for another, the facts that she had a *great* imagination and really no concept of how RPGing was "supposed" to work meant she sprang stuff on the group that had livened up the games no end. Seth was always the Game Master, so he rarely got to play his own characters; Wanda would min-max hers, much to the chagrin of Seth. Beth's playstyle was more innocent and whimsical; she was a lot of fun to game with as a result. And things involving her characters tended to get really hilarious. Like the time that she'd parked her character in the inn, and said, when Seth told them all, "You are meeting for the first time," replied "And I'm talking to a bunch of dangerous looking strangers *why*, now?" forcing Seth to kick off a totally unplanned bar fight that had turned into a food fight and gotten the three of them united against the rest of the bar. . . . Or the time when she'd decided that sheep at a copper apiece were really good trap-detectors, had bought a herd of them and drove them into the dungeon in front of the party.

So instead, Staci was surprised by a huge stack of magazines that Tim had ordered for her, including some on Goth fashion that she and Wanda oo'd and ah'd over, while Seth dove straight into the first book so that Staci would get it faster—or so he said—and the coffee-fueled hours flew by. A lot of people had come into the store, probably because now that things were better, people actually had money to spend on stuff like books and magazines and stuff that Tim would special-order for them. Internet shopping was new and somewhat suspicious to a lot of the residents of Silence, given that for most of them, the new high-speed had exposed them to so many warnings about credit card fraud that Staci suspected some of them thought that if they even brought their card into proximity of the computer, a hacker would steal it. So they'd look up what they wanted when it came to books, magazines, or even DVDs, and come to Tim to have him order it for them.

That meant the store was busier than it ever had been, and didn't give them a chance to talk about their training tonight. Which was fine by Staci; they had all been going at it pretty hard lately, today especially, and a chance to relax a little was more than welcome. The hours passed, the three of them talking, reading, and drinking a likely unhealthy amount of coffee. Staci lost track of the time; all of them had, save for Tim. One moment she was absorbed in conversation over a new videogame that was coming out soon when Tim walked up to the seated trio.

"All right, night owls. Time to call it; you scared all of the respectable types out." Indeed, the bookstore was now empty, save for the four of them. Staci checked her phone for the time; ten minutes past when Tim normally closed. "We'll discuss our training schedule for next week tomorrow, whenever you all stop in. You did well today; enjoy the weekend. Get some rest tonight."

Staci was just about to tell Tim about the path of strange destruction they had found in the woods, when the bell over the door jingled again, and three strangers walked in.

She would have known they weren't natives to Silence just by their clothing alone; a sort of compromise between modern business attire and something out of Game of Thrones. The men both wore collarless wrapped jackets over collarless shirts and trousers tucked into leather boots that appeared handmade; the woman wore a tunic-top that looked as if it had been made by cutting a medieval gown short, over the same sort of boots and trousers. Staci couldn't identify the fabrics, but they looked rich and sleek, in blue and gray for the older of the two men, and green and brown for the younger man and the woman. There was a presence to all of them; powerful but relaxed. The three of them clearly were used to being looked at, and not caring who did so, in the way that beautiful people normally did. They weren't butterflies; they were living statues, perfectly carved. There was a hardness there.

Tim was the first to speak. "Sorry, folks. We're closed up. You'll have to come back—" and then he stopped dead, mid-sentence. A slight smile played on the lips of the oldest man, and Staci was probably the only one that noticed Tim tense up.

But of course, their clothing wasn't all that was different about them. All three of them had *intense* magical auras. And when Staci looked at them with mage-sight, she saw they all had . . . pointed ears and strange, green eyes.

She nearly gasped; she wasn't as controlled as Tim, so Seth and Wanda noticed that something was off almost immediately.

"Staci, what's wrong?" Wanda put a hand on Staci's wrist, shocking her back to reality a little bit.

"Elves," she whispered, keeping her eyes on the three newcomers. Elves had just walked into Tim's bookstore. Extremely powerful elves. The last time an elf had visited Tim's store . . . everything had changed for Staci. Her world had been shattered and only now was starting to make sense again. Both Seth and Wanda straightened in their seats, the gravity of the situation dawning on them.

Tim straightened, and then . . . took on an aura of authority and power, himself. Normally, he didn't display his own magical energy; he ran in a sort of "stealth mode" unless he was actually doing magic. He didn't like having a high profile, after all. He had been teaching Staci, and she was getting fairly good at it. Still, when he "showed" himself, it was like someone had turned on the lights in a dark room. "And what brings you here?" he asked, in a cold, yet neutral tone. Staci understood exactly why he phrased it that way. When you dealt with elves, you had to be very careful about what you said and how you said it. If he had asked "What can I do for you?" that would have been an opening for them to *compel* him to do what they asked, without repercussions. She still didn't know all of the rules concerning elven etiquette and their culture; even Tim didn't, but he still taught her as much as he could.

The older elf was the first to speak. *His* tone was dead-neutral; not cold, not warm, but there was a certain air of . . . haughtiness about it. "Before we get to that, I think introductions are in order. I am Ian Ironoak of Elfhame Silversun, allied with Elfhame Fairgrove. These are my companions, Caradoc ap Daffyd ap Gwalchmai, and his sister Branwen. You of course, need no introduction, Timothy

Carter, warrior-mage, onetime ally of Elfhame Myrddhin, conqueror of the Unseleighe Melisande and her progeny, decimator of—"

"That's enough." There was steel in Tim's voice, now. She had seen him angry, rarely, before. When he had last spoken with Dylan, or of elves in general. It startled her for a moment. "I'll ask again; what brings you here, into *my* store, and *my* town?"

"*Your* town, is it? I seem to recall that it belonged to the Blackthornes, not too long ago." That was the elf called Caradoc; he was clearly amused, but not *too* patronizing in his tone. He had a carefree air about himself, as if this exchange was a neat game. "And who are your friends?" His eyes played over the teens, tarrying for a moment longer than was polite when he came to Staci.

"That would be none of your business. For the third time I ask, what brings you here into *my* store, and *my* town, and *my* territory. Answer, or leave." Tim crossed his arms over his chest. Staci wondered just how he thought he was going to make three powerful, adult elves leave. . . .

Ian held up a hand lightly in front of Caradoc; the younger elf smiled at this, and nodded. Ian's demeanor softened a trifle. "We're not here to fight or be rude, Master Timothy. We're here to pay a species of . . . courtesy call, I suppose you could call it. To announce our plans for Silence and discuss them with you before we bring them before the town. Morrigan of Elfhame Blackthorne, the last of their kind on this side of Underhill, and as such the heir to the Blackthorne properties Overhill, has given over administration of those properties to Elfhame Fairgrove. I am here as Keighvin Silverhair's appointed representative. So . . . you will see, Master Timothy, that this is *shared* territory, outside these walls."

Staci remained silent, taking in the information and trying to process it. Morrigan was the only surviving Blackthorne in Silence, that was true enough. During the battle at the Manor, she had begged for sanctuary from Dylan, invoking the name of Keighvin Silverhair. He had been honor-bound to grant it and spare her her life, though clearly he wasn't happy about it. After learning about what the Blackthornes really were, Morrigan had seemed the most . . . *human*? She had befriended Wanda prior to that horrible night, and didn't seem to gel with the rest of her dark family. Since she was the last one left, she had inherited everything: the money, the lands, the businesses. Had she turned that over as a condition of her "sanctuary"?

Tim was quiet for a moment, digesting the information. "Lock the door and flip the sign over to 'closed,'" he said, thrusting his chin out at Caradoc. "We'll talk." Caradoc complied with the request, while Tim gestured for the three elves to come further into the store. "Have a seat. Would you like to have something to drink? We have an excellent selection of coffee and some espresso."

"No, thank you for the kind offer," Ian said, his eyes crinkling as he smiled. Staci remembered that elves were allergic to caffeine; it was a potent drug for them, acting like a heavy duty opiate that also made them hallucinate. The gang had used water guns filled with a mixture of energy drinks and caffeine powder to help give them an edge when they were fighting the Blackthornes; one good blast of the stuff in their faces pretty much turned them catatonic. Tim surely knew this of course . . . with one hand he "extended hospitality" as she supposed he had to do, but it was a poison pill.

"So, you said that you—and by extension, Keighvin—have plans for Silence," Tim said, as he sat down in a high backed leather chair. He didn't relax or lean back, however; he was still coiled and ready, though he kept his face much more neutral now. Whatever anger had flared up inside of him, he seemed to have under control. *If you want to find something out from someone, just let them talk . . . and talk, and talk. People will tell you whatever you want to know if you give them enough time to get it all out. I guess that applies to elves, too.*

"Keighvin's plans," Ian corrected. "We are merely here to implement them. Morrigan is no businesswoman; she knows that, and this is why she put the properties in Keighvin's hands rather than allow the town to die. The Blackthornes, as you are well aware, propped up the local economy just enough to permit Silence to exist to sate their need for misery-fueled power. Without that aid, in five years, if that, this town would be nothing but a shell, home to the few people in it who have incomes from outside. There would be no one here but the old, the dying, and those few who could continue to eke their living out of the old and the dying. As you yourself must know; you are no fool, Master Timothy. This is not a pretty tourist destination. There is little of historical interest here. There is no one with any reason to prevent Silence from turning into a town of ghosts and those who are soon to become ghosts. Except Fairgrove."

"True enough." Tim seemed as if he was choosing his words with particular care. "How do you intend to do carry that out?"

"Why, we have already started," Ian said smoothly. "Keighvin's clever mortal allies researched how the local fishermen and the cannery could best be supported, and found markets for the new way of fishing. We have already supplied the fishermen what they need, in the form of loaned equipment, which they may opt to pay for with a percentage of their catch. The mill was simpler; we already knew there was much wasted old-growth wood in the waters, and the mill was already equipped for minimal waste. We merely redirected the attention from cutting to reclaiming. The market was there, an avid market, may I add. And the new motorcycle works are merely an extension of the Fairgrove Industry automotive works. Racing motorcycles, like our racing cars; built a few at a time, carefully, for clients with far too much money and far too much free time." The motorcycle works were where David wanted to get a job. *And it's elf-run. God, I hope I can convince him to stick with the diner. The last thing I want to do is see him mixed up with magic and all of the crap that comes with it.*

"But fostering economic recovery for small fishing towns hasn't been a priority for Fairgrove before. Doesn't seem like there would be much money in it, never mind the fact that Fairgrove isn't exactly hurting for that. Ever."

Ian spread his hands wide. "Master Timothy, you know better than that. You know what Fairgrove's priorities have ever been. You also know that we dare not challenge the Unseleighe directly and on our own, or outright war would break out between the Seleighe and Unseleighe. You know that the last time there was such a war, the very rocks of the Land Overhill ran like water. Humankind would fare ill, caught between such a hammer and such an anvil. But when there is an opportunity to negate wrong without an outright challenge, Fairgrove will seize it. It is just as simple as that." On the rare occasions when Tim and Staci talked about elves, it always seemed to be a sticking point for Tim how they didn't take a more active role in fighting against the Unseleighe. What Ian was saying made a kind of sense, though; she had seen what the fighting could be like on a small scale. To imagine a full-blown war . . . it would be apocalyptic.

"In my experience, nothing involving the Elfhames is simple. This is a large and public move for Fairgrove. There will be ripples, ones that will reach *very* far," Tim said, leaning forward. He steepled his fingers together in front of him, waiting for a response.

"Really, Master Timothy?" Ian raised one long and elegant eyebrow. "Large and public? Your outlook has become . . . confined, and limited, with your willing retreat to this tiny, backwards, isolated spot. This is a *village,* my dear sir. Not even a town. It says as much on its very signage. The only ones who will notice are the now-decimated and ineffectual Blackthornes, whose allies have withdrawn the hems of their robes from the mere vicinity of those who lost in such spectacular fashion against a mostly-untrained halfblood and her mortal mentor."

Staci felt her heart skip a beat. They *knew* about her. It made sense; after what had happened, Tim had told her that they would be on the radar for the rest of the magical world. It was one thing to know that, and another thing for it get thrown in your face.

"I have my reasons for being in Silence. I'm still trying to get at the heart of yours, however. A nearly free chance to thumb your noses at the Blackthornes, while probably something that tickled Keighvin, still seems like it wouldn't be enough to go to all of this effort. For, as you said, a tiny, backwards, isolated *village."* He stuck a finger out at Ian, not quite accusingly. "There's some other play, Ian. It's not financial, and it's not politics. Sending three of the High Court here is indicative. Not to mention, you wanted to discuss it with me; I can't imagine my little bookstore, or my students, factoring into your plans to revitalize Silence all that much."

Ian sighed theatrically. "Master Timothy, it pains me to discover such cynicism in you. We do have an obligation to Morrigan Blackthorne, the obligation of those who provide sanctuary, to ensure that her property prospers. It is a sad thing to find that you are determined to see ulterior motives in the simple and mutual bonds of liege and lord." His eyes glittered. "Now, as host, are you not obligated to introduce your young allies?"

Tim's jaw tightened for a moment, but then he nodded his assent. "My students." He turned in his seat to face the three teens. "Wanda, our resident archer and throwing knife aficionado; she's better than I ever was, and has only been training for the last few months. Next is Seth; an excellent researcher and very handy with traps and snares. And, finally, Staci."

"Your apprentice," Ian stated. Staci started, and Ian smiled, ever so slightly. "Do not be surprised that I recognized you for what you are, my dear. It is easy enough to see your magical potential, as well as your elven antecedents." He let his eyes drift over to the other two. "You were all present at the fall of the Blackthornes, I presume?"

Tim nodded reluctantly. "They were. Staci was the one who actually destroyed the Gate. With no help and no thanks to Dylan."

Ian's eyes grew wider almost imperceptibly, and he arched one of his eyebrows again, this time in surprise. "Destroyed a Gate all on her own? That *is* interesting. Very interesting indeed."

I spiked it with Cold Iron, which is kind of cheating. But I'm not going to tell him that.

There was something going on behind Ian's eyes. Calculations, appraisal, and . . . not fear. But something not far from it. Elves were so damned hard to read, unless they were really upset. And Ian seemed to always be wearing a sort of mask; he would have made a killer politician or lawyer.

"If it would please you," Ian said, looking from Tim to Seth and Wanda, "we have some excellent facilities that might be able to assist in your training. Never mind instructors; some of our archers have been practicing since the Bronze Age . . . before it was formally called that, of course. And our libraries have some tomes that stretch back as far as the written word; I believe a few rare volumes deal with traps, mancatchers, and weapons of that nature. You would be more than welcome to make use of them, if you like." Both Wanda and Seth seemed to perk up at that; they really were getting good at what they did, but Tim was right. He was primarily a mage and a jack-of-all-trades. Decent at almost everything, a master only in magic. If they wanted to continue to grow their skills, they needed something more.

Wanda's brow furrowed for a moment. "What about Staci? Couldn't she come with us?"

Tim's composure slipped for a second, and his magical aura rippled. *Was Tim trying to avoid that question? First with holding off on introducing us . . . is he scared I would leave?* "Oh, of course. You are *all* welcome as guests. Aside from some distractions, however, I don't think we would have much to offer her in the way of training. After all, she already has a mentor. Very few mages can say they've had the . . . honor of learning under such a Master as Timothy." Ian turned his head to look at Tim. "Is this acceptable to you?"

Tim waited half a beat before responding. "Of course. They're their own persons; they can decide who and what to associate with." He looked for a moment as if he was about to say more, then thought better of it.

"But I see that we are past your closing hours," Ian continued smoothly. "I am sure you wish to lock up and return home after a long day. I will see that your names are left at the Fairgrove Cycle Works guard post so that you shall not only gain entry speedily, but be supplied with a guide for your visit, should you care to make one. I look forward to seeing you there." He smiled again. Staci could not make up her mind whether or not it reached his eyes. The three elves rose from their chairs in unison, first unlocking and then closing the door behind themselves as they made their exit. Tim quickly stood up from his chair and walked to the door, locking it behind them. He thought for a moment, then unlocked it, turning back to the others.

"Tim . . . what is going on? That was intense. Elves in Silence, again?" Staci felt like she was ready to burst at the seams with questions. The biggest among them was, *What are we going to do? Is there anything we* can *do?*

He sighed, wearily, opening the door. "Go home. Get some rest. We'll talk about this tomorrow. I have some things that I need to attend to. I think we've all had enough excitement for one night."

It was pretty obvious that Tim wanted them out of there, and all three of them had learned by now that if Tim didn't want to talk about something, there was no way they could coax him into it. Staci took the lead, saying "Night, Tim. See you tomorrow," and slipping out the door. Wanda and Seth followed right on her heels. They had barely made it out the door before Tim locked it, walked quickly to the back, and vanished into the storeroom. A moment later all the lights went out. Whatever happy mood they had all been in before had been dashed. *Elves . . . why do I have to deal with this again?*

"Oh man, he didn't even bother to clean the coffee pots!" Seth exclaimed. "He's severely not happy."

"What was your first clue? Was it when the three people with pointy ears and funny clothes walked in through the front door?" Wanda shook her head, then looked at Staci. "They did have pointy ears, right?"

"Yeah." Staci rubbed her arms; suddenly she felt a lot colder than she should have. "They have magic that keeps them looking mostly normal. Tim and I can see past it if we try."

"So weird. I mean, the Blackthornes were one thing; we didn't know about them from the start. And these are supposed to be the good elves, right? The . . . what's the word?"

"Seleighe," Seth supplied. "Those three are big-wigs, too. What they call High Court elves, like Dylan was." Wanda visibly elbowed him in the ribs, maybe a little harder than she had meant, because he winced. "Sorry, Staci. I forgot."

"No, it's okay. I'm okay." She really wasn't, but she couldn't let the others know that. Her head was swimming with memories and emotions, and she wanted nothing more than to go completely blank, to let it all fall away from her. She didn't *want* to think about Dylan, or elves. And now she couldn't help but do just that. *Why did they have to come back here?*

"Tim looked like he could have shot daggers at them with his eyes when they first walked in," remarked Wanda. "He was pissed. What do you think he's going to do? Will he go back to like he was before, when the Blackthornes were here?"

"What, go back into hiding? No way. But what about all of those things that the older one, Ian, said about him? 'Conqueror' and 'decimator' and all of that stuff? What was that about?"

"Sounds like our Tim has a badass rep, is what it sounds like." Wanda seemed more than a little proud of their mentor. "Did you catch when he offered them coffee? Now *that* would be a fun show. Elves tripping balls on some java."

The trio kept walking for a bit, passing under the streetlights. Staci just wanted to be home already, where she could throw herself into bed and sleep, and forget about tonight.

"Do you think we should go up there? To the motorcycle place? That Ian guy did offer to let us go up there and check it out." Seth sighed heavily. "I wonder what kind of books they have in their library . . . "

"What do you think, Staci?"

She shook her head, blowing out a breath to steady herself. "I think we all should go home and get some rest like Tim said. Whatever this . . . *stuff* is with the elves, it'll hold until tomorrow. I just want to put my head on a pillow and go into a coma. I'm tired of elf crap."

Wanda and Seth both nodded, Seth looking sheepish and Wanda a little concerned. "We'll see you tomorrow. Hey, call me if you need anything, okay? I'm going to be up for a little while longer; and I know Seth is going to be awake, plowing through those superhero books we won. We can hit the diner for some coffee and pie if you need it."

Staci smiled weakly, then nodded once. "It's a deal. Thanks, guys. I'll see you later."

CHAPTER SIX

Staci woke up the next morning with a start. She had been having some sort of nightmare. Again. She had lain awake in her bed for hours last night after getting home, thinking. Which was the absolute last thing that she had wanted to do. *I need sleep, damnit! Not running shit through my head like a Morrissey album on random repeat!*

Before, she probably would have pulled the pillow over her head and wallowed in misery. Not now. Instead of staying in bed and dwelling on it more, she set about the tedious business of getting up and ready to go out. She was in a daze while she showered, got dressed, and had breakfast. Her mother noticed, but quickly dropped her questions when Staci assured her that she was just tired from staying up and reading too late. This had not been one of Mom's better culinary experiments ... she'd tried for omelets and they were burned on the bottom and runny on the inside. *A start to a crap day*.... On the other hand, after a breakfast like this, she was probably prepared for the worst the day could offer. After picking through her food she said a quick goodbye, then got on her bike and started off for town.

She couldn't help herself; it all came back to Dylan and *freakin'* elves. *I knew I'd have to run into elves again at some point. Intellectually, at least. I'm a mage now, and elves are magical; no helping it. Guess I wasn't as over everything as I thought.* She pedaled harder, trying to will the thoughts out of her head. *Things were going so well, too. Things haven't been this good in forever.* Except for Dylan. It always ended up on that dead-end street. Except for Dylan, leading her on, letting her fall in love with him, then abandoning her after using her for his own ends. After implying, if not telling her, that he was in love with her. *Why couldn't things have gone differently? Why couldn't they just stay like they are now?*

Staci brought the bike to a skidding stop. "No. Not going to go there again. I'm *not* going to be that dumb girl again, whining to herself about how unfair everything is." She breathed in, holding it, and then let it all out. Some of the tension left her. She was still pissed off, and could feel the hot creep of anxiety at the back of her neck, but it was manageable again. She could have stayed there, stamping her feet and bemoaning how unfair everything is. Or, she could do something; maybe she couldn't keep the elves away from her, but she could make sure that she was ready for whatever else was coming. She noticed that she was on the last rise in the road before she would be in the town proper. Making a snap decision, she turned her bike and started off to one of the deer trails. After so much time prowling this part of the forest, she knew most of it down to the rabbit runs. Not deeper in, and certainly not close to the ruined Blackthorne Manor, but she knew *this* part the way she knew what was on the shelves at Tim's bookstore.

Time for a little solo practice. Of course, Tim would say that it's always *time for practice.*

Staci found a spot that was somewhat clear enough for what she wanted to work on. There weren't any big rocks to use for targets; she'd have to shape stuff out of dirt, which wasn't terribly hard to do. She used her hands, since she wanted to save as much energy as possible for actual magical work. Once the area was prepped, with all the proper spells in place to keep things looking—and sounding, since what she was planning on was going to be *loud*—normal, she started in. The mounds of dirt were frozen, burned, electrocuted, smashed to dust, blown up, and scattered, over and over again. Her vortex spell was still failing, spectacularly, and she felt like she was on the cusp of something with it, though she didn't know what. The frustration from that just drove her on; she poured more and more energy, focusing on all of the tiny details of the spell work, making each one perfect, then changing an aspect.

All in all, it was an hour of ferocious effort; Staci was soaked with sweat, covered in dirt, and felt almost completely drained. She wished she had brought some energy bars with her, or an energy drink; around a gallon would probably be good. Despite how tired she was, Staci smiled. It felt *good* to do something, instead of talking or just sitting and going through the same crap in her head over and over again. The piles of dirt—she had had to make more—were all wiped out. She was a little calmer, now.

Just as Staci was dusting her hands off—filthy from all of the sweat, grime, and black soil—she felt the hairs on the back of her neck stand up, and a finger of ice run up her spine. It was the same thing she had felt when she had been alone on the beach, before the others had shown up for practice. Slowly, she started to look around, and her heart began to race. *Am I just freaking myself out again?* No, it couldn't be that. Could it? She had been out in the woods plenty of times alone, and never been spooked like she was now. Tim always told her to trust her gut, too. *There is something out there.*

Now Staci really regretted expending so much energy during her practice session; she was so drained, she doubted that she could even manifest a half-decent shield even with terror fueling it. Still, she had a knife in her belt, and she knew how to fight a bit better than she used to.

Time to leave, girl, before whatever is out there decides that it isn't content with just watching, anymore. Good plan, me, she thought to herself. She turned quickly on her heel, walking back the way she had entered the woods, looking over her shoulder. She didn't see any movement, couldn't see anything obviously following her. Her eyes flicked up to the tree branches; she had been taught that threats could come from anywhere, and not to get too focused on one plane. Satisfied that she wasn't being followed, she turned her head to watch where she was walking. And nearly ran face-first into someone.

She screamed, and the other person screamed, and both of them punched at the other at the same time. Both blows missed; the other person's punch was wild and reflexive, and Staci was able to catch it and twist the person around, throwing them with their own momentum. The other person stumbled, then whirled around to face her. She started to reach for her knife when she recognized who the person was.

"Beth? What the hell are you doing out here?"

Beth had both hands pressed to her mouth, and was standing off-balance. The combat-mage in the back of Staci's mind had already noted six places she could have attacked the waitress before the thinking part of her woke up to the fact that this was her friend. She immediately took her hand off of her knife—thankfully, hidden from Beth's view—and kicked herself for being so obvious about it at the same time.

It took her friend a moment to regain her composure, mussing back her hair. "I could ask the same of you! I was out for a run before heading to Tim's; I've got a shift in a few hours, but it's nice out right now and is probably going to rain later, so I figured 'why not?' I was on the trail for a while, and . . . I don't know, I just kind of ended up here." She looked down at Staci's dirty hands and clothing, and her eyebrows shot up. "And, uh, you?"

"Working out. I started that Army-fitness-thingy," Staci replied instantly. She'd had that reply already figured out weeks ago. The regimen of bursts of running alternating with pushups and pullups and picking up logs and rocks and other exercises was the perfect excuse for her filthy condition. "I don't like doing it on the trail, I look like a dork."

Beth smiled, accepting the lie. "Well, you wouldn't need to be working out to accomplish that." She looked around, frowning. "Gosh, it was like you came out of nowhere at all."

"So did you!" Staci replied, and waved her hand at all the brush. Now she was kicking herself again; she had completely forgotten to take down the illusion spells that she had put up. If Beth had been paying more attention or looking at the right spot, it would have looked as if Staci had literally appeared out of thin air. *That* would have taken some explaining. "This's a deer trail, you can't see anything that's more than three feet from you."

"Yeah, I guess you're right. Anyways, want to get back to town? We can stop by my place to get cleaned up before we head to Tim's. That sound okay?"

Stacy groaned theatrically. "I would kill for a hot shower." She didn't mention food, although she could easily have eaten a whole pizza by herself. But Beth did. "I've got pizza in the fridge that's going to go petrified; if you're willing to let me have the first shower, I'll heat it while you're in there."

"Sounds like a plan to me!" Staci smiled . . . but still couldn't shake the feeling that something really *had* been watching her, and it hadn't just been Beth creeping up on her that had freaked her out. "Let's walk back to my bike, and we can go into town by the road."

It didn't take the pair of them very long to get back to town and make their way to Beth's place. It was a small apartment that she rented out, located above the local pizza joint. It was decorated in a very—well, not *nautical* theme exactly, more like "oceanic." Old fishing nets on the wall with old-fashioned glass floats hung on them, bowls of seashells and sand, seashell frames around several mirrors that were hung up instead of pictures, even some really pretty, big "specimen" shells on the bookshelves and end table. The curtains were unbleached muslin, edged with tiny shells; the throw rug on the worn wooden floor looked handmade, and made her think of wind-rippled sand on the beach. The colors were faded blue, sandy beige, and white—the warmth of the "sand" color made the apartment itself feel warm. There was always the smell of baking dough, which had gone up considerably in quality the last few months. Staci had expressed envy at Beth having a place all to herself as they ate pizza. "I love my mom," she said, eyeing the little two-room apartment. "But I never know when she's going to be in or out, and I don't exactly have privacy, if you know what I mean."

"It's not like I'm bringing a nonstop stream of boys here, myself. But, it's definitely a lot easier if I wanted to. And I don't have someone giving me the stink-eye and saying *Are you really going out dressed like that?* every time I change." Beth giggled. "Like, your mom should talk! The way she dresses for work? Booty shorts show way less than a micro-miniskirt!"

They quickly polished off the pizza and headed out the door for Tim's. Beth's little place even had its own separate entrance... although the outside staircase was probably a hazard to life and limb in the winter when it iced up. The town was fully awake by the time they made it to Tim's shop; people shopping, running errands, and working. Beth had been right; it looked like there was a storm coming, which probably meant rain. More than a few people were carrying umbrellas as a result. After chaining up her bike to the light post, she and Beth walked in. The bookstore was, as usual, in stark contrast to the dreary weather descending on the town; smells of cinnamon, coffee, and old books, warm lighting, and Tim doing his best to hold up the counter while he read. There was something missing, though.

"Where are Wanda and Seth?" She looked around; the pair weren't in the gang's usual spot, or anywhere else in the store.

"Good morning to you too, Staci. Beth," he said, nodding. "No, your friends aren't here. They came in earlier and waited for you, but then decided to head up to . . . the new factory. Take the tour, I guess you could say." *They took up Ian on his offer.* She felt a hollow of fear in the pit of her stomach, but it was quickly replaced. *I can't believe they ditched me like that . . . and to hang out with elves.* She knew she was being a little irrational about it; they had waited for her, Tim said. She hadn't bothered to text or call them to let them know she was going to be late, so it *was* partially her fault. That didn't stop her from feeling sore about it. She certainly wasn't about to go chasing them up to Fairgrove Industries; that was one iceberg's worth of stress that she could do without for the day.

Of course, Beth couldn't know that going there would be the last thing that Staci wanted to do. "Hey! Should we surprise them, try to catch them there?" she said as a couple of patrons entered the store and brushed passed the teens.

"No, not enough time," Staci replied, thinking fast. "That storm is coming; more likely than not, we'd get caught in it trying to reach them. I've had enough showers for one day, thank you."

"Huh, I guess you're right. I'd have to rush back to make my shift if we did that, anyways. Let's just hang here, then."

That's exactly what they did. Since Seth had most of their gaming books and all of their character sheets, they couldn't do any RPG stuff. Instead, Staci and Beth drank too much coffee and talked about this and that, picking through Tim's books and looking for something they hadn't already read. And previewing the *Goth Fashion* magazines that Tim was holding for Wanda. Soon enough it was time for Beth to head out for work; she said her goodbyes and was off, promising to stop by after her shift was over in the afternoon. Staci showed her out to the door. Looking out at the sky, she could see that heavy rain bands were quickly approaching; it was definitely going to hit the town. As a result, most of the patrons finished up their business, made their purchases, and left; there probably wouldn't be many new people coming into the shop in the middle of a storm.

Staci waited until the store was mostly empty before she approached Tim. "I can't believe Wanda and Seth actually went up to Fairgrove." She was careful to keep her voice low, without bringing it down to a whisper; whispering could attract attention, and even though there were only two other people in the store and they seemed absorbed in their own worlds, she wanted to be careful. "It's like they don't remember what happened with the Blackthornes, or—or other elves." She caught herself, stopping short before actually saying Dylan's name. "I hope you warned them, or tried to talk them out of it."

"Actually, I encouraged them to go."

Staci felt her jaw drop. "You *what?!*" The two other patrons looked up briefly, then went back to their books. She shook her head, leaning in closer. "Why would you want them to go to Fairgrove, right smack dab in the middle of elves?"

Tim closed his book, then leaned back against the wall of shelves behind him. "Before you decide to bite my head off, stop and think for a moment. Breathe." Staci consciously stopped and took a deep breath; when she had first started out, she would have taken his instructions as condescending, but now she saw that he was just trying to have her figure things out on her own. Teaching her by guiding her learning, but having her do all the mental legwork herself. "Good. First, keep in mind that you trust me as your mentor, and you trust the others as your friends. Now, with that out of the way . . . why would I want your friends to go to Fairgrove?"

"Okay. We know what Ian said about what they do up there; motorcycles and stuff like that, plus the lumber mill and the cannery. If Wanda and Seth actually go there, they can take a look at it, see if Ian is on the level. They both have good heads on their shoulders; they'll get a feel if something is up. They've got the protections you had us work up, so they won't get charmed or put under anything." One of the earliest tests that Tim had given Staci was the creation of simple magical devices that would protect Wanda and Seth from basic undue magical influence. If the elves tried to pull one over Wanda and Seth, they'd be protected and know about it. She had made the protection charms out of bookmarks; the kind that clipped onto a page instead of just sliding between two pages. That way they could be clipped into a book, a wallet, a purse, on a sleeve, someone's back pocket, a lapel, anything; concealing them might be necessary, besides. Tim already had them in stock, and they had all picked out ones they felt drawn to. Seth had one shaped like a key, Wanda one with a raven on a branch, and Staci one that was actually shaped like a sword. She had also secretly enchanted one that Beth had picked out, shaped like a trident.

"Not bad. And that is a good reason. But there's more. For starters, Ian's offer to give them facilities to train was probably a genuine one. Truth be told, I've taken Wanda as far as I can with her archery and knife throwing." He shrugged. "I can't be all things to all people, Staci. I've never been a specialist, and she's already surpassed me in those areas. For Seth, while I've got my own little library that can fit his interests, the elves have volumes that you wouldn't believe; even individuals usually have collections that make me seem like a child playing at being serious. Both of them could learn a lot there, and the more skilled and knowledgeable they are, the better for us. And for everyone."

"That makes sense, I guess." She still didn't like it. Her friends had been one of the only things keeping her sane after everything that had happened . . . and now they were off having their own adventures without her. Plus, it could be dangerous. Despite what Tim had said about them being a team, and Wanda and Seth being potentially more important in a fight than Tim and Staci, she still felt protective of them.

"There's another aspect. While the two of them are playing and learning from the elves, it keeps the elves occupied. Which I'll take any day. You know that I don't trust them; you're the same as me, in that regard. Whatever they say they're here for, there's something more to it. Something that they're not giving away. I don't know what it is, yet, but I want to find out. So, while the elves are busy showing Wanda and Seth around, wowing them and so on, we'll be doing our own work. Training you, for one."

She took a long, long breath, and calmed down. He was right. Seth and Wanda *did* need more training, and Tim was a mage, not really a fighter or a traps expert. And she wouldn't mind more one-on-one time with Tim at all. The other two were protected, and were not going to get bedazzled by bullshit—hadn't Wanda been the one to warn her about the Blackthornes? Wanda was cynical enough for five people; if Seth got a little bowled over, she'd haul him back. "Thanks, Tim, for helping me to put it into perspective. Sorry that I tried jumping down your throat before taking a second. It's been a weird couple of days."

Tim smiled. "No problem. Anyways, relax, browse, and all of that. I'll probably be closing the shop up a little early today; with this rain, we won't be doing much business. Plus, I have a few errands that I have to run before the sun goes down and everything else shuts down."

Huh? He almost never leaves the shop. "Errands? Like what?"

"Thrifting, mostly," he said quickly. "If you couldn't tell, my wardrobe doesn't change much. Hitting some of the antique shops, too, see if I can find anything that looks interesting. A lot of people bailed before Fairgrove came in, figuring that Silence was going to go belly-up, and some interesting old stuff is ending up in the second-hand stores. You never know what your ancestors were up to, especially around here." He grinned. "Besides, the first thing to go when you plan to move, if you're doing it on your own dime, is books. Books are the heaviest items for their size that there are. Nothing like being able to restock the shelves at a fraction of wholesale."

"Would you mind if I came along?" She was feeling a little lonely with her friends all off doing their own thing, despite knowing that the reasons why were good ones. Tim seemed to sense it, too; his expression softened after a moment.

"Sure. Bring Beth along, if you like. I think she'll be off of her shift by the time I lock this place down."

To while away the time before Beth came back, Tim asked Staci if she'd shelve some of his thrift-shop acquisitions in trade for two of them. Staci's response was a laugh and "Duh! Free books!" and she spent the time hauling the bargain-priced books from the back and putting them up in the right categories. Her choices were art books—well, art and fashion. A big book about Erte, and an equally fat one about Fortuny. She figured that she and Wanda and maybe Beth would have a grand old time ogling the pictures in those. Though she could not for the life of her imagine *who* in Silence would have had the money to spend on a couple of $150 books, much less have been able to appreciate them.

Time slipped by for Staci, and soon enough she saw that Tim was getting the store ready to close up. Beth showed up shortly thereafter, confused at the early closing until Tim and Staci filled her in. She seemed happy enough to come along with the pair. After leaving the shop, Staci took great pleasure in breathing in the rain-washed air; the streets and sidewalks were still plenty slick with puddles. Thus began their meandering route around town. They visited second-hand stores, pawn shops, and antique sellers; she hadn't realized how many there were in Silence. More than she would have given credit for, for such a small town. Well, maybe pawn shops. But who were the pawn dealers *selling* to?

After the second one, where she had discovered *another* fat fashion book, this time on Worth, priced at $2.50, she had asked Tim if she had permission to snatch a few before he got to them. With a smile, he'd said it was all right, and from that point on, she'd gone straight to wherever the books were piled. And when she'd caught Beth wistfully eyeing a milky pale blue glass seashell, she'd added that to her purchase.

After that, besides diving through the books—most of which were piles of old National Geographics, or volumes of Readers Digest Condensed Books—she kept her eyes peeled for *nice* little oceanic-themed things. Nice ones, not the tacky ones like cowrie shells carved with palm trees and the words "Key West." At one point, she perked up when she caught a glimpse of some magical energy slipping away from one of Tim's purchases; she didn't see exactly what it was, but approached Tim, eyebrows raised. "Just a trinket; probably has some residual juice on it. Nothing to get worked up about." Whatever the item was, it was already bagged up, and the magical signature was reduced significantly. "Let's get moving; daylight's burning."

They had done almost a full loop of the town, but were still a few blocks away from the book store. "Here, let's go this way," Tim said, nodding towards an alley. "It'll cut a little time off of our walk back."

"Walking down dark alleys at night." Beth shook her head. "Isn't this how people get mugged?"

"The city has cleaned up these last few months; crime is down in a big way, and the criminal element has all but disappeared. I think we'll be okay."

Just as Tim finished his sentence, several dark shapes crowded into the alley at the other end. They were men, but Staci noted immediately that something was . . . off about them. Their color was wrong; pale and ashen. All of them were dirty, like they hadn't showered in weeks, and their clothes were torn and caked with mud.

"Let's . . . go back the way we came, Tim." Staci turned around to see that there were more men like the others filing in behind them where they had entered the alley.

"Beth, take this." Tim shoved the bag full of his purchases into her hands. "Stay behind me and Staci, whatever you do. Try to stay calm." Beth's eyes went wide, but she swallowed the lump in her throat and nodded, moving to stay between her friends.

"Tim . . . what are they?" There was definitely a stench coming off the two groups of men; like rotting meat and plants from some sort of hellish garbage bin. She noticed that none of the men had blinked, not once; they just stared and stared as they walked closer to the trio.

"Not human, not anymore." He unsheathed a knife that he had in his jacket, holding the long blade out in front of him. "They're revenants."

CHAPTER SEVEN

The thugs—revenants, Tim had called them—started to move closer. There was no way out of the alley; the revenants had blocked both ends, and had already moved past the only two doors into buildings that might have offered an escape-route. No matter what, Staci and Tim would have to get through them to get out. And they'd have to get Beth out safely with them. Staci unsheathed her own knife from where she kept it under her baggy shirt at the small of her back.

"Where did you get *that?*" Beth clutched Tim's bag to her chest tightly, her eyes still wide with terror as she stared at the knife in Staci's hand. "What do they want from us? Money?"

"Keep quiet, and don't get near those guys." She kept her eyes on the revenants coming up behind them. "Tim?"

"We fight our way out, the way I'm facing. Make sure we don't have any of them come up from behind," he said hurriedly, seeming to read her mind on what to do. "They're strong; don't let them get ahold of you if you can help it. The knives will only slow them down. Focus on getting out, if we can't . . . then we burn them, here. Got it?"

"Got it." Staci readied herself, drawing on her magical reserves. She felt a warm glow in the center of her chest, rising and expanding. Energy flowed to her fingertips, and she sensed it concentrating there, crackling like static electricity. She was still feeling a little drained from earlier today, but she figured that she had enough energy to protect herself and Beth. *God, I hope she doesn't do anything dumb like scream or try to run. Who knows what these things would do to her?*

She didn't have time to think anymore; the revenants were almost on them. There had been four at each end of the alley; three from each group had moved forward, while one stayed back. *They can use tactics, it looks like. One left behind to catch anyone that gets past.* They moved slowly, methodically; they weren't in any hurry. Or maybe they couldn't run. Tim waited until the revenants were less than ten feet away before he called out. "Staci, flash!"

Concentrating, she traced a complex sigil in the air in front of her with her free hand, her fingers leaving glowing trails in the air. She felt the energy welling up, readying inside of her in anticipation of release, responding to the spell. When she completed the sigil, she breathed out, reciting a snatch of a prayer in Ancient Egyptian before shutting her eyes tight and pointing at the ground in front of the approaching revenants. She could feel the magical energy erupting from her, hitting the spot she had designated. She must have pulled off the timing just right; there were two thunderclaps, and she could see through her eyelids that the entire world had lit up. Tim's spell and hers had gone off at almost the exact same time; it was a downgraded version of the fireball spell that she did, with a twist; instead of setting things on fire, it created a lot of noise and flash when it went off, all of the heat going into rapidly expanding the air. It was like a magical flashbang; her ears were still ringing when she opened her eyes to see her trio of revenants. They were clearly dazed; their eyes, which had been fixed on her moments before, now stared vacantly up and to one side of her. Still, they marched forward. Their arms were outstretched now, reaching for her.

Staci darted forward, using the momentary distraction to her advantage. Getting around to the right side, she thrust her hand out, focusing energy into it and releasing it almost at once. Three bolts of magical energy shot out from her palm, one for each revenant. The bolts slammed into their chests, all perfect shots . . . but the revenants were hardly staggered. She could see that their clothing was scorched where the spells had hit, revealing pale flesh beneath. *Those bolts should have knocked those guys on their asses, easily! Tim was right, they really are tough.*

The revenants turned in the direction of the attack, still moving, still grasping for her. Their eyes were still unfocused, and they didn't seem to know exactly where she was. She ducked under the arms of the first one, slicing at the underside of its right arm as she moved away from it and back to where Beth was standing, still clutching the bag. The revenant that she had cut swung its arm in a delayed arc, slamming it into the chest of the middle revenant. She heard bones snap and a dull wet *thump*, but the middle revenant didn't even seem to notice. They were only about five feet away; she had to think fast. She heard Tim behind her; breathing heavy, the sound of a knife parting fabric and . . . something else. She wasn't as good a fighter as he was, not yet at least. She didn't want to risk going toe to toe with these things if she could help it. *Time to split them up.*

Staci sized up the middle revenant. *I don't think he'll be too heavy.* She quickly recited an incantation for the spell she had in mind, calculations and formulae speeding through her head as she concentrated on a spot underneath the creature. It took another step forward . . . and then lifted into the air about thirty feet in the blink of an eye. *A little too fast, but it did the job.* The creature had crumpled onto a levitation plate that she had conjured under it; the acceleration would have killed a normal person, but somehow the revenant was still twitching around, trying to get at her.

The other two were still coming at her, and she had to think fast. Staci reverted to a spell that she did almost every day, before she really began any sort of training; she threw up the shield illusion. One instant it would have looked like Staci, Tim, and Beth were in the alley; the next, it was completely empty. She saw both of the revenants stop in their tracks, scanning. *Whew, it worked on them. I was afraid that they would be too dumb to be fooled by the illusion, and just keep walking, or else have some way of seeing through it.* She had a stroke of genius. *So they can't see through illusions. Let's give them something to go after.* She focused, building a mental image of what she wanted to happen. When she had gathered enough energy, she traced symmetric symbols over both of the revenants in front of her, releasing the magical power into the symbols. The revenants turned to each other . . . only now, they both looked exactly like Staci. The two creatures immediately turned on each other, clutching and grabbing, trying to subdue one another. It was . . . disconcerting to watch; she knew it was an illusion, and could see the revenants' outlines under the veil of magic, but still. Two "Stacis," trying to strangle each other and haul each other down the alley. She shuddered. *Okay, that's enough creepy shit for a lifetime.*

Staci looked up at the middle revenant, still floating in the air, a thread of magical energy connecting her to the levitation plate that was under it. She concentrated, raising the plate higher, until it was close to forty feet in the air. That was the limit of how far up she could take it, at least for now. "And when the bough breaks . . . " She severed the line of energy she was feeding to sustain the plate; it vanished, and with it anything that was keeping the middle revenant aloft. It fell, and the suddenness of the fall of what looked like a person was sickening to watch. It landed on top of the two fighting revenants, and she felt her stomach do a flip as it struck. This was brutal; snapping bones, that *smack* of something that used to be a human hitting asphalt. All three of the revenants were in bad shape; still trying to move, now the third one was ineffectually trying to grab both of the others, who still looked like Staci.

She turned around, satisfied that the three revenants weren't a threat for the moment. Beth was in the same spot, wide-eyed, and staring at Staci. "Okay. This will take some explaining." Then Staci saw past Beth. Tim. He was struggling with his fourth revenant. Staci started forward, knife out, to help him, when she remembered. *Fourth . . . four of them!* She felt the cold hands on her skin, the forearm going around her neck in a choke hold, dragging her back. The dead flesh had muscles underneath that felt like steel cables, unyielding. She started stabbing, thrusting the knife above her head and into the chest and neck of the revenant. It didn't seem to notice. She started stabbing the arm that was around her neck, then sawing at it. The flesh parted, but the revenant's hold on her was absolute. The world started to go dark for her, her range of vision slowly contracting. Her eyes played over Beth, still terrorized and frozen in place. She caught a flash of Tim, still fighting with his opponent. As she was about to pass out, she thought she heard shouting, saw the flashing of red and blue lights. *So stupid. I messed up, forgot about the last monster. What a dumb way to die.* It was absurd to her, in her last thoughts. *Killed by a dead man.*

Then she was on the ground, gasping for air. No arms around her, cutting off her oxygen, dragging her to death. She heard loud bangs, like someone slamming a heavy hammer on an anvil right next to her ears. Her first thought was that it was Tim, using a spell to come and save her, maybe the flash spell or something else. Her head swam, and she felt woozy. *The revenant* . . . She twisted around while still sitting on the ground and took in the scene. A cop had shown up; the flashing red and blue lights were from his squad car. The bangs, from his gun. He had unloaded his gun into the revenant. It walked towards him, implacable, as the cop fumbled his revolver, trying to reload it with a speedloader. The revenant stopped in front of the officer, then swatted him with a backhanded sweep of its arm. The cop flew backwards, smashing into his squad car and leaving a visible dent. He didn't get back up, or even move.

Staci felt so tired. Her stomach roiled, and she could hardly lift her knife as the revenant turned back towards her and began walking. It stepped over its three compatriots as if they weren't even there, then bent down, a hand outstretched. It exploded, a brilliant cascade of purple-white energy in the pattern of an "x" radiating out from its center. Staci snapped her head around; Tim was behind her, panting hard, his forearms crossed in front of him. She could see magical sigils rapidly fading from his skin, glowing that same purple-white.

"Get up. We've still got work to do. We need to finish these things off and get out of here before anyone else shows up." Staci hesitated for a half second, then shakily got to her feet. She felt ashamed; Tim had been forced to come save her ass, *again*. This was worse than getting old, it meant she couldn't keep up. From what Staci could tell, Tim had hardly used magic during the fight. Except to save her. And the Blackthornes, the big bad menaces in town, were gone now! What if Tim hadn't been there?

She watched Tim work. He was going from revenant to revenant; first, separating their heads from their bodies with his knife. She could see an aura of magic infusing it, helping him to cut more easily. *So he was using magic . . . just not flashy crap that wastes a lot of energy, like I was.* She mentally kicked herself again. After he finished beheading the creatures, he rifled through their pockets, taking out wallets.

"Why are you doing that?" She moved closer to Tim; her legs felt rubbery, but she was recovering faster than she would have a few months ago.

"Someone went to a lot of trouble to create these things. They came from somewhere. Finding out who they were is a start." She nodded, then started helping him. "No. Drag the bodies and the heads over here, in a pile. We've got to burn them, otherwise they'll come after us again. Hurry up." His tone wasn't harsh, but Staci still felt the bite of a reproach in his words. Once the bodies and heads were together, Tim said a quick incantation. The revenants went up like logs of fatwood. Staci blinked hard, backing away from the grisly bonfire.

"Where's Beth?" Staci asked, suddenly, realizing that Beth wasn't where they'd left her.

"Over here! I need help!" Beth was at the mouth of the alley where they had first entered it, kneeling by the body of the cop. Staci and Tim ran over to her; before they were even close, Staci smelled the metallic hint of blood in the air. "He's bleeding out, I can't stop it!" Beth sobbed. The cop was lying in a puddle of water; much of it was already red. Too much. When the revenant had hit him, and he had hit the car, he must have suffered horrible internal injuries. Broken bones, organs ruptured . . . she didn't want to imagine it.

Tears streamed down Beth's face and fell on the cop's face, his chest, the puddle surrounding both of them. As the first tears dripped into the bloody water, something strange happened.

The water started to move. First a ripple, as if a nonexistent breeze ruffled the surface. Then more. Then the water lapped against them both, flowing *up*, flowing onto the cop, over him. It covered his wounds, went *into* them, and covered Beth's hands. More water from other puddles around them flowed towards and over them. The area around Beth and the injured cop, moments ago soaking wet with deep puddles from the earlier rains, was now bone dry.

The cop coughed suddenly, then sputtered out a harsh breath. Then another. His wounds had closed up; there wasn't any blood other than what had soaked into his uniform. Beth laid his head down on the pavement, backing away. Tim lurched forward to land on his knees beside the cop, checking his pulse, inspecting where the wounds had been. "He's healed." His head jerked up, looking intently at Beth. "You saved his life."

She nodded. Then threw up. Staci stumbled to her side, catching her right as she fainted and fell. "What the hell just happened?" she gasped, looking up at Tim. Tim could only shake his head.

❈ ❈ ❈

Somehow they managed to get Beth back to the shop between them without attracting any attention—though the rain, which started up again, and the fact that they kept to the alleys probably helped. Staci even had the presence of mind to retrieve the bags of stuff they'd bought, cram them all into the capacious "purse" Beth humorously called her "bag of holding," and sling it across her back before taking Beth's left arm and draping it over her own shoulders.

They left the cop in the alley to wake up by himself. *God knows what he's going to say or think—but then again, he isn't going to want to sound crazy, so maybe he'll not say anything. Or at worst, claim he slipped in a puddle and hit his head. Maybe he didn't see any of our faces; everything happened so fast.*

They came in through the back door, and left Beth on a cot Tim had set up since he'd started training the three teens. "I may work you hard enough to leave you needing a nap," he'd said, with no clue to Staci about whether or not he was serious or joking. Now she was just glad it was there.

There was a small coffee-brewer there in the back, along with the unshelved books and the office stuff. Staci had set it to brew before they'd left, and now she got cups for both herself and Tim, then dumped the bag at the foot of the cot before plopping down on the floor.

"Tim . . . why were we attacked by revenants in broad daylight? In the middle of town?" She felt so very tired right then; she hoped that the coffee would help, but at the moment the warmth of the liquid seemed to be trying to put her to sleep. Her clothes were still soaked from the rain; wasn't there a spell she could use to fix that? She hardly seemed to care at the moment.

"I truly do not know, Staci. In all the time I've lived in Silence, nothing like that has ever happened." He had changed into some spare clothes that he kept in the back office; Staci noticed that a set of sweats was folded next to her, but didn't move to go change. "This was brazen. Generally, the things that go bump in the night don't *want* this sort of exposure; humanity has all of the fun toys that could really ruin a monster's day, if they ever woke up and found out that monsters actually exist. For something to set off an attack like this . . ." He stared ahead, looking at nothing for a few moments. Absently, he took a sip of his coffee. "It's something powerful, or someone that has something powerful. Revenants are not easy to create. And to send them out like that . . . it's either desperation, or a big power move."

"It couldn't be the elves, could it?" Immediately her thoughts went to Wanda and Seth. *God, I have to call them, tell them about this. Make sure that they're safe and keeping on their toes.*

"I don't think so. Ian and his lot have the juice to pull something like this off, but it's not their . . . style, I guess you could say." He had the pile of wallets from the revenants by his foot. "I'll do some digging, find out who those creatures used to be. That'll give us somewhere to start from. Find out who this new player is."

"Are you thinking it's the Blackthornes, come back for revenge?"

"I don't know. We'll find out, I promise." Tim finished his coffee in one big gulp, then set the mug down. "What we need to figure out right now is what to do with your friend, here."

Staci glanced over at Beth. "What . . . happened? Back there?" she asked.

"Aside from you flaking out and forgetting about the fourth revenant on your side?" Tim asked dryly. "Just the diner-waitress suddenly displaying a powerful healing gift linked with water, is all. Nothing major."

Staci felt her cheeks flush red. "I'm sorry, Tim. I was worn out, and I was trying to come help you with the last revenant on your side."

"What wore you out?" Tim asked, frowning slightly. "You shouldn't have run out of juice so quickly."

"I . . . I practiced on my own, earlier today. Before Beth and I came here. I needed to work out some frustration, I guess you could say." She looked down into her mug, swirling the coffee around. "I overdid it a little." Staci looked up suddenly. "Wait, that reminds me. After I finished practice this morning, I had the strangest sense. That something was watching me, in the woods. I've had it before, down where we usually practice."

"And you're only telling me *now?* Staci—" Staci held up a hand, placatingly.

"I know, I know, I'm an airhead. I got freaked out, and actually ran into Beth while getting out of there."

"In the middle of the woods? How did that happen?" Tim glanced at Beth briefly, his brows furrowed. "Quite the coincidence."

"She was out running, and went off of the path she was on." Staci shook her head. "I know. Now maybe...I dunno. Not a coincidence?"

"While you were doing magic. This is starting to make a little more sense." Tim nodded. "Well, we know her healing power seems to be related to water. That gives me some more data. Huh. Maybe the Blackthornes locating here *wasn't* just because there was a Gate-node here...."

He didn't get a chance to say anything else, since Beth chose that moment to groan and open her eyes. "Ow. My head," she said, wincing at the light. Staci got up and got her a cup of coffee, loading it down with creamer and sugar. Setting down the cup of coffee seemed to snap Beth back to reality; she blinked hard, then quickly sat up, pushing herself back to the edge of the cot and away from Staci and Tim.

"Hey, it's okay Beth, it's okay! It's just us. Try to stay calm." Staci didn't make any sudden movements, or try to get closer to Beth. *Poor girl is freaked out. Kind of like I was when I first got into this stuff.* Unbidden, an image of Dylan flicked through her mind.

"Were you bitten? Were either of you bitten?" Beth's eyes were wide, flitting back and forth from Staci and Tim, looking at their arms and necks.

Staci shook her head, confused. "Bitten? No, we weren't bitten. What are—"

"Are you sure that the zombies didn't bite you? If you're infected, then you're dangerous! Right?" She clasped her hands on the top of her head, looking frantic. "Oh my god, and to think I used to make fun of Seth saying the zombie apocalypse was coming and he was right all along! Oh my god! Seth and Wanda! We have to get hold of them! Are the cell phones still working? We've got to warn them, and get them here so we can barricade the front of the building! No, wait, we should go to my place, we can barricade the downstairs and block off the stairway and eat pizza for months—"

"Beth. *Beth.*" Tim held up a hand, cutting her off. She closed her mouth so fast that Staci heard her teeth click. "There wasn't a zombie apocalypse. Those things weren't zombies. Wanda and Seth are fine. And you couldn't pay me to eat nothing but pizza."

"Then...what were they? Liches? There's such a thing as liches?

You're wizards, right?" Her hands were still clasped on the top of her head, as if she was trying to hold it onto her neck, and her eyes were so wide Staci could see the whites all around the irises.

"One question at a time. They were what's known as revenants; reanimated dead bodies. Those ones were servants for . . . something. We don't know what." He let that sink in for a moment. "Staci and I are, technically, mages. A little bit different. But for practical purposes, the same. We perform magic, through the use of spells and certain items. Staci is my apprentice." He coughed. "Now, I know why I can perform magic. And I know why Staci can. The question I have right now, is how and why *you* can."

"Why *I* can?"

Tim looked at Beth sternly. "Don't play games with me, Elizabeth. There was an almost-dead cop back there. Now there is a live and uninjured cop back there. That was your doing. So what are you?"

"I—I don't know! I don't know how I did that, I—" Her voice caught on a sob. "—just wanted to help him, okay? I didn't know how to help him, and he was dying, and . . . " Her voice trailed off, and the tears finally came in earnest. Beth seemed to shrink in on herself, pulling her knees to her chest and hugging them.

"Nice, Tim," Staci whispered. He shrugged in response. Slowly and carefully, Staci moved over to sit on the cot next to Beth. When she wasn't rebuffed, she put her arm around her friend's shoulders. "Listen, I know this is scary, and a lot to take in. Trust me, I've been there. Not long after you met me I got caught up in all of . . . this," she said, waving at the room. "But we need to figure some things out. It's for the best; please answer our questions, okay?" Beth's eyes, red and teary, met Staci's. She nodded once. "Have you ever done anything like that before?" she asked.

Beth rubbed her eyes with the back of her hand, and sniffled. "Maybe? Sort of? I rescue fish. . . . "

"Explain," Tim said flatly.

"When I find fish washed up, I . . . I pick them up and I ask them to live and put them back in the water. And they always swim away. . . . " She sniffled again. "I always thought I was just lucky about that, getting to them before they died."

"I'm beginning to think I know what's going on here, with you, Beth," Tim replied, finally giving just a hint of a smile. "Let me guess.

You've always loved being in the water; oceans, pools, lakes, rivers, whatever. Mostly the natural ones, though. You love it when it rains. And you always seem to get drawn to strange things, and you don't know why."

"Yeah, not so much pools," Beth admitted. "Chlorine is gross. But all the rest, yeah."

"You became friends with Staci fairly quickly, even though she was a new girl in town and somewhat oddball, right?"

"Hey! Tim!" Staci said, indignantly.

"Bear with me, Staci." He looked back at Beth. "Staci told me about how you ran into her this morning. What made you wander off of the trail you were running on?"

"I don't know. I just . . . wanted to go that direction." Beth bit her lip.

"And the Blackthornes. How did you feel about them?" Tim continued.

Beth flushed. "You'll think I'm nuts," she muttered, dropping her gaze to her knees.

"Beth, we all just fought magically animated creatures, and you healed a dying man. Why would I think you're nuts?" There was a chuckle in Tim's voice this time. Beth managed to at least smile at that.

"I—I could always tell when one of them was coming around. And when they did, I hid. Thank God the diner was too low-rent for them, or I don't know what I would have done if they'd come in. But anyplace else—if I couldn't get away, I hid, and if I could, I left, and got at least two blocks away." She looked back up to judge their reactions to that statement.

"Wish I had," Staci muttered.

"Beth, the reason you felt like that, the reason why you were doing those things . . . it's because you're attuned to magic. Attracted to it, if it's being used properly, and repelled if it's being used for evil. Which means you're more than you seem." He paused for a moment, thinking. "I've got an idea. Wait here." He got up and went to the sink, filling up a glass of water. He walked back, kneeling in front of Beth on the cot. "I'm going to turn this glass upside down. When I do, if you can't keep the water in it, it's going to dump all over both of us. You might not mind getting wet, but I'm getting old and I might catch pneumonia. So keep it in the glass." He didn't give her a chance to react to that statement, he just inverted the glass.

Beth gave a strange little gulping gasp.

The water remained in the flipped glass, in resolute defiance of gravity.

"That is so cool," Staci breathed, moving closer to get a better look. "Wow!"

The water started to tremble on the surface. Tim flipped the glass back over—a bit escaped, splashing all three of them, but most of it stayed in the glass.

Tim smiled in triumph. "Well," he said. "Staci has elven blood in her. You clearly have one or more ancestors that were magical water-creatures. Now all we have to do is figure out what kind." He raised an eyebrow at Staci. "Your mother came here on her own, and stayed, even though Silence wasn't her kind of town. Beth stayed here, even though she could have left. And . . . yeah, I came here and stayed too. I don't think that's any kind of coincidence."

Staci bit her lip. "And now . . . Fairgrove's here. You're right, Tim. I don't think it is, either."

CHAPTER EIGHT

"Wait—" Beth said, interrupting them before they could say anything more. "What? I'm what? What are you talking about?" She was looking . . . a little frantic. "How did you do that? What do you mean, I did it? Are you nuts?" Tears filled her eyes. "Am I?"

"It's okay, Beth, it's okay. Again, I've gone through this, too. You're not insane. The world isn't crazy—well, for the most part." Staci refilled her own cup of coffee, but decided to get Beth some tea instead. *The last thing that she needs right now is another mega-dose of caffeine.*

"Beth," Tim said, slowly. "You're not crazy. You've just discovered the hard way that there is magic, real magic, in the world, and that you have some of that magic. Staci, show her something simple, while I do the same."

"Simple? Sure." Staci brought the cup of cold water and the teabag over to Beth. "Stick your finger in. Cold, right?"

Beth nodded.

"Okay, now watch." Staci used a simple cantrip, and traced a couple of runes over the top of the water with her right index finger. A moment later the cup was steaming, and she handed it and the teabag to Beth. *"Don't* stick your finger in it this time," she warned, as Beth cradled the hot cup in her hands. Staci had some of her energy back; coffee with *lots* of cream and sugar helped. Still, she didn't want to overexert herself again, so she was keeping her magical expenditures small. "Your turn, Tim."

Tim picked up one of the coasters on the table, holding it out in front of his face. "Magic, the kind that Staci and I do . . . some of it is inborn. The rest of it takes a lot of study, and a *lot* of practice." Slowly, he opened his fingers . . . and the coaster was left hovering in place. "Formulae, mathematics, physics, and all of the usual hocus pocus crap go into it. Some rules get bent, others get broken," he said as he used his other hand to swipe the outside of the coaster, causing it to spin. "Concentration, forcing your *will* onto the world . . . that's the biggest part. And that takes energy." The coaster, still spinning, started to float down to the table. It spun like a top for a few more seconds, then stopped, still standing on edge. "You saw a little bit of that tonight. And you also saw what happens when that energy runs out." Casually, he flicked the coaster, and it clattered across the table.

Beth's eyes were as big and round as a cutesy anime critter's. "But . . . but . . . but . . . " she stammered. "You said *I* can do that . . . "

"You can. You did," Staci told her. "You are the one that kept the water in that glass just now, and you healed the cop back in the alley. Tim is pretty sure it's because you've got some magic creature back in your family tree somewhere, just like I do. Mine's probably an elf," she added. "We haven't figured out what yours is." Then an idea bloomed in her head like a light going on. "Tim, Beth's place is all . . . watery-decorated. Not nautical, more like the sea or rivers and lakes and ponds. Natural stuff. Is that a clue?"

"It's a part of the puzzle, that's for sure." He frowned, looking from Beth to Staci. "I need a book." He stood up suddenly, retreating through a door marked "Private"; his personal office, where he kept all of his non-mundane books and supplies. Staci noticed that Tim had already drained his coffee mug, again. She set about fixing him another mug, talking while she worked.

"It's a head rush, right? Everything changes. One moment, you're worrying about what's on reality TV, what to wear, whether the cute boy at school likes you. The next, you're worrying if he's a soul-sucking dark elf with a penchant for mass murder." She smiled over her shoulder at Beth. "One of life's little funny twists, I guess." She made her way back to the cot and the chairs, setting down Tim's mug. "It'll be easier, though. It'll get easier. When I went through all of this . . . well, I was alone. For the most part. Seth and Wanda helped later on. And Tim, after that. But the hardest part is the beginning. I'm here for you, Beth. And hey, look on the bright side. At least you don't actually have a soul-sucking dark elf with a penchant for mass murder trying to make you his girl."

Beth nodded mutely, then her eyes went big again. "Oh. My. God. The Blackthornes? And Sean Blackthorne? And that was why the Blackthorne estate exploded? Ohmygod . . . " She shook her head, making the connections.

Crap. I just had to bring up ex's, Staci thought . . . never *a good idea.*

"It got way, way more complicated than that," Staci said weakly. "But . . . yeah, that was all part of it."

"Any time I saw one of them I used to feel like I had to go hide! And then it was so bad I *would* go hide, or just get out of where they were!" Beth babbled, clutching her teacup, her eyes starting to fill again. "All I could think of was that it was a good thing none of them would ever be seen dead in the diner. Oh my god, I thought I was crazy."

"No, you weren't crazy, you just had really good instincts. Better than mine," Staci added sourly. "If it hadn't been for Wanda and Dylan, I probably *would* be the girlfriend of a mass-murdering dark elf right now, and . . . well, let's not go into the rest of it."

Beth cocked her head to the side. "Who's Dylan?"

Double crap. His name just slipped right out. "Well . . . "

Luckily, Tim chose that moment to rejoin them. Staci did not want to dredge up her history with Dylan if she could help it. Under one arm, Tim had three very thick leather-bound books; under the other, some sort of wooden chest. It looked weathered and old, with iron fittings and hinges. He set everything down on the table; Staci cleared a space for him without needing to be asked. He cracked open all three books, but left the box closed for the moment. She handed him his mug of coffee, and he took it without looking up from the books, sipping it as he read. "Thanks, Staci. Okay, let's see what you are, Beth."

Tim asked Beth dozens of questions, mostly about her history. Some of them seemed completely random; asking her to guess what number he was thinking of, to name a place randomly off the top of her head, or to run through the Celtic alphabet backwards (she couldn't, and neither could Staci for that matter, even though she had been trying to study it). Finally, he opened the wooden chest. Staci noticed that it had trays inside of it that folded out, kind of like a toolbox. On the trays were all sorts of vials, bottles, beakers, and jars; some were made of colored glass, others were clear, and some were completely opaque. She couldn't identify any of the jars' contents. Tim removed three squat jars, stoppered alternately with cork, a glass plug, and one that seemed to have been made without an opening yet was still filled. All had the same colorless substance in them; it looked viscous, like some sort of heavy oil. He set all three down in a row in front of Beth.

"Now for the last part. Beth, when I tell you to, I need you to place your hand over each of the containers in turn." She nodded once. Tim took a deep breath, then closed his eyes. Staci watched as he started saying incantations under his breath, tracing complex sigils and runes in the air above the three jars. She watched as tendrils of magic flowed down onto the table, encircling the jars, then flowing into them. *I wonder if Beth can see magical energy yet, the way that I can? It took training for me to be able to do it, but maybe she's different.* If Beth could see what Tim's spell was doing, she made no indication of it. Finally, the spell completed; Tim slowly opened his eyes, still concentrating. "Okay, Beth. Move your hand over each of the containers, if you please."

Beth did as she was asked. Hesitantly, as if she were afraid the jars would leap out and bite her, she hovered her hand over the first jar. The substance within reacted almost immediately; it swirled around violently, then darkened. It looked like ink, now, except more... sinister, somehow. Staci heard a sharp intake of breath from Beth. "Is that... normal?"

"Yes. I sort of expected it. Keep going." Tim didn't take his eyes off the jars, still concentrating intently.

Beth moved her hand over the second jar. This one didn't change as quickly. It looked like there was a small spark buried in the substance. It glowed brighter, flickered, and then became *much* brighter, very suddenly. The substance lit up like a flash bulb, leaving spots in Staci's vision and eliciting a yelp from her and Beth both. The interior of the middle jar was blackened, now; whatever the substance was, it had been used up with the flash.

"Okay... *that's* interesting." Tim licked his lips, nodding his head ever so slightly. "The final one, please." Staci and Beth traded a look. Beth took a deep breath, then placed her hand over the last jar. This one slowly started to glow; first, a soft blue light, then brighter and brighter, until it was a scintillating electric blue; it looked like motes of energy were dancing in the jar, turning in complicated patterns. Tim smiled. "You can drop your hand, now." He looked up from the jar, and the effect faded until the jar was back to normal. "That settles it. You're part Selkie, Beth. Did you ever see the movie, or read the book, *The Secret of Roan Inish?*"

"You mean the book, *The Secret of the Ron Mor Skerry,*" Beth corrected automatically. "That's the name of the book. Oh!" She brought one hand to her mouth. "You mean the seal people? They're *real?*"

"As real as you are." Tim put the jars away, locked up the box, and took it and the books back to his office, leaving Beth to stare at Staci.

Staci shrugged. "Don't look at me. I don't know what you two are talking about."

Beth stared at her mug of tea, shaking her head slightly as she talked. "The Selkie . . . Dad used to tell me stories about them when I was little, before he and Mom died. He's the one that had a copy of the book. I still have it. They're, like, magical creatures. Most of the time they look like seals, but they can take off their skins like a coat and then they look like humans. Sometimes they fall in love with humans and marry them, and the kids can turn into seals too. You can keep them on land with you if you hide their sealskins. In the book, this girl's little brother disappears, and her grandfather tells her he's actually got a big dose of Selkie blood, and he didn't drown, he went to join them."

"That's pretty cool. Trade you? Elves seem to be nothing but trouble." Staci was trying to lighten things up, but at the moment Beth wasn't having any.

In fact, her eyes just got big again. "But if I'm half Selkie, or part Selkie . . . that explains why weird stuff kept happening around me. Why didn't I see it and remember about the Selkie? Me falling off the dock as a kid and just being able to swim, like magic—seaweed and seawater always getting into the house, and no one knowing where they came from, gulls always coming around me like they were pets—that's why when my foster family wanted to move, and I didn't; they were so happy they set me up in my apartment without even trying to talk me out of it! I mean, I was just barely seventeen, and they set me up with the place for a birthday present, even paid for a whole year of rent, and practically ran out of town!" Tears started to trickle down her face. "They kept saying they didn't want to take me away from where I was born, but now—maybe more weird things happened around me they never told me about and they were freaked out by me!"

Staci was silent for a few moments. "Beth, I'm sorry, I didn't mean—"

Beth broke down, crying openly now, and Staci feared that she had really messed up. Then Beth threw her arms around Staci's neck, sobbing into her shoulder. "Thank you! I never knew why things were so different for me!" Staci held her friend, rubbing her back as she cried. "I always try to put on a happy face, and . . . it's not an act, not really, but it's not everything. I've always been so confused about *why*. I thought I was broken, poisonous or something, and, and—"

"It's okay, Beth. I totally get it." They sat there for a minute, and slowly Beth's sobbing grew quieter and tapered off. "My mom is the one with the elf blood, and when she found out all the things she'd been seeing were totally real and not drug flashbacks or something . . . it was being told that even though she thought her whole life was messed up, and she was crazy, she was all wrong. And she'd been living that way twice as long as you. I think she must have been drinking and doing shit to keep from seeing the things she was seeing."

That just set Beth off again for a while. Staci could almost feel the relief pouring off of Beth; this was cathartic for her, and Staci only wished that her own "awakening" had been as comforting. After a time, Beth gently pulled back from Staci. Her eyes were red and still tear-filled, and she sniffled a little as she smiled. Staci handed her a napkin from the table to dry her eyes with. "Thanks," Beth replied weakly, then laughed. "Oh, wow. Glad I got that out. Although my makeup must look horrible, now." Both of them chuckled at that.

"No more than usual, actually." Staci dodged a mock punch from Beth.

"Jerk." She sighed, looking around. "So . . . now what? What do I do now that I . . . well, kind of know what I am? Who I am?"

"That's up to you." Tim stood in the doorway to his office, leaning against the frame with his arms crossed in front of his chest. "Sorry,

I thought that you two could use a few moments alone. Anyway," he said, walking over to sit back down in his chair. "The choice really is yours, Beth. You could just go back to living your life the way you always have. Just with a little extra knowledge that there's more to the world than most people give it credit for. Things probably won't change much for you, though I do have to warn you; magic attracts magic. It's why you were drawn to Staci, and to Silence. Magical creatures, people, and energy will always be around you, for better or for worse. Silence in particular seems to have more than its fair share of magic, for some reason."

Beth nodded, straightening in her seat as she did so. "Okay. You say that like there's an option 'B.' What is it?"

"Well, *one* of the other options is that you embrace your magical heritage. You've got a natural healing ability, and a damned strong one, by my estimation. What happened with the cop earlier . . . that was a sort of 'burst' of magical energy, kind of a pent up reserve that you didn't know you could access. It'll take a while for you to pull off something dramatic like that again. And some training." He leaned forward, steepling his fingers in front of himself. "Training that I can help you with, if you want."

"You mean you'd make me a mage, like you and Staci?" Beth looked back and forth between Staci and Tim, her eyes lighting up.

"Not quite. It'd be more like helping you to develop your natural talents. It'd still be difficult, but in a different way than the training that I'm giving Staci. Basically, putting you in touch with what you can do as part-Selkie. Healing, controlling water, attuning yourself to the sea and other natural bodies of water. I'd have to research a little further, maybe contact some old friends for some information. But it's completely doable, and probably won't even cut too much into your leisure hours."

"I don't think you want to be a fighter-mage like me anyway," Staci said. "It involves a lot of pushups."

"I wouldn't mind the pushups but . . . " Beth shook her head. "No, I can't see myself fighting anyone."

"That's clearly not where your natural gifts lie anyway, Beth," Tim said, quickly. "I take it that you're interested in—"

Beth didn't even let him finish. "I want to find out what all the weird stuff that happens around me means. I don't care if it's weird, as long as I know there's *reasons* for it. And if I can help people, like that cop, I *have* to learn how to do that when I need to."

Tim and Staci exchanged a surprised look. "I've got to say, I love her enthusiasm." Tim smiled, stood up and stretched. "All of that can wait until tomorrow, though. It's been a hell of a night, and I think we all need some rest. I'll drive both of you home; until we know more about what's going on, I think it's best if you two don't go running around alone."

Staci and Beth collected their treasures from the thrifting haul, and Beth piled into the back seat of Tim's battered car while Staci took the front and Tim hung the bike on a rack on the back. "We really need to tell Wanda and Seth about this, as soon as we can," Staci told Tim, as he climbed into the driver's side.

"Wait, Wanda and Seth—" Beth began, then shook her head. "Of course they know. Are they magic too?"

"Nope," Tim told her cheerfully. "They're just lucky that way, I guess." Staci looked back at Beth and rolled her eyes. Beth clutched her bag to her chest and giggled. "Still, they're important parts of our ... team, I guess you could say. And they have their own talents. We'll talk about this later; let's make some tracks."

They dropped Beth off first; Tim carefully made sure she had gotten up the stairs and inside her apartment before he drove off. Staci noticed him doing a covert magical scan of the apartment when they first arrived. *Doesn't hurt to be too careful, especially after our day.* The pair were silent for the entire ride home; Staci was too tired, even after all of the coffee, to come up with anything to talk about. Tim broke the silence when they pulled up in front of her house.

"You had a few slip-ups today," he said, putting the car in park.

"I know, I know. I messed up—" she said hastily, trying to head off the tear down.

"—and you also showed some genius."

Staci blinked hard. "Huh?"

"Low on energy, outnumbered by foes that you didn't fully understand, and trying to protect a mundane, you sized up the situation and were able to use what reserves you had masterfully. The trick with the levitation plate was pretty nifty; yes, even during the fighting, I was keeping an eye on you." He turned in his seat so that he could face her better. "You fought smart ... for most of the encounter, at least. It made me proud. And I'm hard on you because, even so, you need to be better. There are no training wheels out in the real world; even if you do everything perfectly, you can still end up dead for no good reason at all. We train the way we do to try to stack the deck in our favor, as much as we can."

"I understand." She hesitated for a moment. "Thanks, Tim. I promise I'll do better in the future."

"I know you will, apprentice. We're in unknown waters, here, so things are going to change a bit. All of that can wait, though. Get inside and get some rest. I'll see you tomorrow."

Staci felt almost as if she ought to kiss Tim for that—well, a "daughterly" kind of kiss—but she kept it to "I will, thanks Tim. Remember we need to get Wanda and Seth in on this ASAP," as she hopped out, and started to close the door.

"I know, I know, don't remind me." Tim half-groaned good-naturedly. "Get. I have a hot date with a late dinner."

"Right. So do I," Staci replied, got her bike, locked it to the railing, and turned and ran up the stairs, already planning what she was going to wolf down while she leafed through her new books.

Staci slept in later than usual the next morning. With all of the training she had done, the fight, discovering Beth was part-Selkie, and just the emotional rollercoaster of the day had left her completely depleted. After showering and getting ready, she went downstairs to find that her mother had already left for work. There was a note on the fridge, however, telling her that her breakfast was in the oven, still warm.

Mom, you're a godsend. And as she thought that, it occurred to her that a few months ago . . . she'd have been peering in the fridge at zombie-pizza and a half bottle of cheap tequila. She wolfed down the food and chased it with two glasses of orange juice; there would be coffee at Tim's shop, better than what they kept in the house, at any rate. Then she was off on her bicycle, making the ride into town.

There was something different this morning. She was paying much closer attention to the woods. She didn't get the creepy feeling she had the other day, or when they had been down training at the beach. But she couldn't shake the idea that *something* was out there. Logically, she knew that there *always* was something out there; just the nature of the world, especially when you took magical creatures into account. This was different in that, whatever was out there ... it was *actively* targeting her. The sense of *déjà vu* from just a few months ago was overwhelming; was this what it was always going to be like? Some horrible beastie or another deciding that she was exactly what they needed to hang up on the mantle, or have for a snack? Staci pedaled her bike harder, willing the thoughts away with the promise of coffee and her friends.

When she arrived at the shop, Wanda and Seth were already there. There was no sign of Beth, however. *Either she's working, or she needed the extra sleep as much as I did.* Or both, of course, but Beth was good at powering through exhaustion, like the times she'd had to pull double shifts. *I wonder how much of that was "powering through," and how much was unconsciously pulling on her magical reserves?*

"Hey guys!" she greeted them. "Uh, has Tim filled you in yet?" She glanced around the store; there was no one else there for the moment, it seemed like a good time to drop the bomb.

"Tim has been waiting for you," Tim said, flipping the sign in the door to "Closed for Coffee" and gesturing to the three of them to follow him into the back. "Come on, you lot. Staci and I want to hear about your Adventures in ElfLand, but first we've got some news of our own."

"She's a *what?*"

It took almost an hour to get through everything, from the attack, Beth's magical "reveal," the weird feelings of being watched that Staci had been having the last few days. Wanda and Seth had a lot of questions, naturally; Tim and Staci did their best to answer them. Towards the end of the explanations and answers, there was a knock on the front door. Beth was there, her hands cupped around her eyes as she tried to peer through the glass. Tim got up to let her in.

"Well, if it isn't the Magical Seal Girl herself. Oh, god, that sounds like an anime that I might actually watch," Wanda said, shaking her head.

"Oh! They already told you? Crap, I wanted to get here in time for that. But, uh, yeah. That's me, I guess!"

Seth turned to Tim once he and Beth had returned to the coffee table that everyone was seated around. "Tim, I've got a question."

"Another one about Selkies? Or Beth?"

"No. Not quite." He took a deep breath, then leaned forward. "Do Wanda and I have magical backgrounds, but you're not telling us because we're not ready for the information yet? We haven't come of age, completed a great quest, or something? Because, I'm totally ready."

Tim made a face. "Well, now that you mention it . . . " Staci noticed Seth holding his breath. " . . . no. This is not an anime. It's not a book. It's not an RPG. Most people in the world aren't the products of a magical one-night-stand. So, no. Sorry. Halfbreeds are rare, and you've got better odds of winning the lottery."

Seth deflated slightly at that, and Wanda nudged him with her shoulder. "Guess we'll just have to be awesome norms, right?"

He sighed. "Yeah, you're right. But it would've been cool to be part dragon or something."

"Not as much as you think," Tim said, then quickly changed the subject. "Now that we have the update with Beth out of the way, you two said that you had something to share. About Fairgrove."

Seth brightened at that. "Yeah! First off, they want you and Staci to come up there and get the grand tour. Second, they are totally down with helping me and Wanda train, and you should *see* the building they're setting up to do training in! They said everyone at the plant that knows about what they are gets an hour or more training time, every day. That's so *cool!* I'd totally take a job with anyone who did that!"

"The people at the plant know that they're *elves?*" Staci was on her third cup of coffee at this point, and sat down again with a fresh mug.

"Some of them. Mages, like you two . . . well, kind of. Apparently, most of them aren't as good as you two; just 'minor' mages, or whatever. And some people they call 'family,' and I have *no* idea what they mean by that, cause my gaydar totally is not going off with them. They've got regular folks that work there, for the most part, and they have stuff in place to make sure that no one lets on about all the wizard stuff." Wanda cooled her own mug of coffee with her breath before taking a sip, and continuing. "It sounds like it'd be hell juggling all of that, but it seems to work well enough."

Tim mulled this over for a few moments. "When do they want us to come for a 'visit'?"

"Oh, whenever you want," Seth answered. "They were insistent that we make that clear; open door policy and whatnot."

Staci watched Tim. She knew how he felt about elves; given her experiences with them, she felt largely the same way. There was something going on behind his eyes as he pondered what to do; she could never ask him what he was thinking, of course. He would change the subject or otherwise dodge the question. And, right then, she really wanted to know how he was working this over in his head.

"We'll go tomorrow. I'll close the shop early, and we'll all head over together." He glanced over at Beth. "You're diving head-first into magic, girl. Hope you brought nose plugs and swim goggles. If in doubt, don't touch it, and ask me or Staci if you have any questions."

Okay, that's *not what I expected.* Tim was always on edge whenever elves were involved; for him to agree so quickly to right into the heart of Fairgrove Industries . . . it surprised her. *He's got something else going on, something that he wants from them. Get a peek at their operation, see how they really work, right?*

She didn't have time to work it all out on her own.

"So, who wants to tell me what the hell we're going to do about zombies attacking you three last night?" Wanda had set her mug down, looking around the group with her arms crossed in front of her chest. "I mean, cool that Beth is a seal-girl and whatnot, but are we under attack?"

"I have some ideas, but first, I want to hear what you think, all of you." Tim pointed at each of them in turn. "All of you. I won't be around forever, or even necessarily when you need me most. Shit happens. I could get sick. I could get run over by a bus. I could be out fighting something else alone. You're going to have to rely on each other, and yourselves. So, think this through. You're under attack; what do you do?"

"Well, we have to know more, obviously." Seth leaned forward, steepling his fingers as he propped his elbows on his knees. "We don't know who or what is behind this attack; if it's a group, or one being. We need to figure out what's capable of this sort of attack, first off, and then work our way down from what's the most likely culprit to the least."

"So, whatever can raise zombies—"

"Revenants!"

"—whatever!" Wanda replied. "Whatever can create those. Then we have an idea about what we're fighting. So then . . . well, I guess part of that would be actually asking Fairgrove."

Tim nodded sharply. "Good. Keep going."

Wanda licked her lips, working her way through the idea as quickly as she was speaking. "Well, they're major players in the magical world. They've *got* to have some information on whatever it is we're up against, whether it be something we could research or some sort of elvish scuttlebutt. Even if they don't, letting them know that something is up couldn't hurt."

Staci saw Tim frowning at that last part, but he didn't say anything. The others looked to her, finally.

Well, there was one thing she could see that needed doing. Because when she and Tim had been dealing with the zombies—revenants—whatever—they'd been working as two individuals, not as a team. She vaguely remembered something about how the reason the Vikings never became a major force in the world was because they fought as a bunch of soloists who just happened to have been brought to the same place on the same boat, and not like a real army. "We need to train. Not just like how we have been. But group training; how to work together when the shite hits the oscillating blades. It's something we've tried before, but haven't focused on. If we're going to be getting into the thick of it, and soon, we need to know we can count on each other when it gets hot and heavy."

"Full marks, all of you," Tim said, finishing his coffee. "All prudent ideas. In addition, we're going to up our protections; extra wards on your homes, making sure that you travel together as much as possible, and ways for us to communicate in an emergency. So, that brings me to homework; all of that stuff that I just mentioned is going to take up the rest of today, if we bust our asses. So, grab another slug of coffee, because you're going to need it." This elicited collective groans from the group, save for Beth, who looked excited. "We'll get the necessary stuff done first. After that, we're back on the beach for a specialized training session. You will have Beth working with you for the first time, so it ought to be interesting. Let's get moving, folks."

CHAPTER NINE

The entire gang—Beth, for better or worse, really *was* one of them, now—met up at Tim's as planned around three o'clock. It was a nice enough day, so instead of taking a car for the short drive Tim volunteered the idea that they walk. Without needing to say it, Staci took a position on one side of the group, while Tim mirrored her on the other. Wanda and Seth were keeping their heads on a swivel, as well. Beth was the only one that didn't seem to notice that the group was being extra vigilant; everyone talked casually and joked as they normally would. After the attack the other day, they weren't going to take any chances, even in town.

Fairgrove had taken over an area of about ten acres on the edge of town that had once supported several now-defunct canneries. Among other things, the spot was on the waterfront and had had its own (dilapidated) wharf. When Fairgrove had first taken over the property, they'd put an eight foot tall fence around it and hired a local crew to demolish and haul off everything inside the perimeter. The buildings were turn-of-the-last-century, not attractive enough to be considered "heritage," and mostly considered to be hazardous eyesores, so no one had objected. The town council was happy enough having money coming in for the local work crews, so the permits were pushed through with a minimal amount of fuss. What had gone up in their place *was* considered attractive, at least to the town council, which had issued gushing reviews of the "sleek, modern facilities" that were "ushering Silence into the Twenty-First Century."

Staci had to admit, as they made their way towards the guard-booth at the gate, this was a pretty nice looking facility, if you favored the "google-plex" look. Lots of beige brick with some sort of glazed finish, lots of aluminum, lots of windows. Behind the beige-brick buildings were standard industrial metal buildings made with aluminum panels in that same beige. Of course, if you knew, as she and the others knew, that elves worked there, the reason for that type of architecture was obvious.

No iron. No steel. She was pretty sure that even the internal supports for the buildings would be something other than iron or steel. *I wonder if even the shape of the building is part of some sort of magical feng shui, or something. I'll have to ask Tim about that later.* She didn't know enough about building design to say anything other than that it looked almost exactly like the sort of place owned by the high-dollar corporate types served by her father's law firm.

"This place looks like someone dropped an oversized sculpture on its side," Wanda breathed. "It's kind of cool, right?"

Beth shrugged. "Too modern-arty for me. Anyways, we're here. Do we just walk in, or . . . "

The front doors swung open, and a young man strode confidently towards them, smiling. He was wearing a green and yellow racing jumpsuit; it was covered in patches, with a prominent "Fairgrove Industries" patch over the left breast. "Hello! Welcome! My name is David, and—" He stopped just as his eyes met Staci's. Everyone was holding their breath, and Staci felt the world drop away beneath her.

What. The. Hell! David, too?

"Staci . . . you're with—oh, of course. I'm an idiot." He slapped his forehead with the palm of his head. "So, uh. Yeah, this is awkward."

Tim's only reaction was a raised eyebrow, keeping his arms crossed in front of him. Staci was thankful for that; the last thing she needed at that moment was his take on her love life.

"No shit, Sherlock," Wanda breathed. This time Seth elbowed her in the ribs, eliciting a slight yelp. "Hey, wait a second. Seth and I have been coming here for a while now; why haven't we seen you before?"

"I just started working here; yesterday was my first day. Helping to greet all of you is part of my training, or so I was told."

Staci could feel her cheeks burning. *I told him not to come work here! I didn't want him getting caught up with elves and magic, too!*

Maybe he's just part of their normal stuff. Still! Is this going to be what it's like every time I take some sort of interest in someone?

"So . . . can we come in? Or just stand out here and be all uncomfortable?" She very briefly looked up at David, but couldn't bring herself to focus on him for too long.

"No, no, you're right! Please, come inside. Uh, welcome to Fairgrove Industries." David made an elaborate welcoming gesture that was half bow and totally comical, and they walked past the amused guard in his booth and up the driveway towards the main building.

"So, uh, this is the main building," David said, a little flustered. "As you can probably see, we've taken a lot of care with the shielding so nothing magical leaks to be detected outside. Magic is one place where it never pays to advertise, or at least that's what they tell me."

Staci had to work to keep her jaw from dropping. *He knows! He knows! How in hell . . . why is it that every guy I like is a magic magnet?*

"And you are a—?" Tim raised an eyebrow.

"Plain old garden-variety human magician." David grinned a little shyly at Staci.

"Wait, *what?* How? Why didn't I notice earlier that you're a mage?" she demanded.

"There are ways to hide your magical signature. It's one of the first things I learned, and it's something I practice quite often. Better to keep a low profile than to stick my head up, only to get it chopped off. Not trying to be a jerk, but you stick out like a sore thumb, magically. The first time I saw you, your wards left spots in my vision."

"You knew I was a mage, too . . . and you didn't say anything?" She had gotten over the shock of finding out that David was just as deep into magic as she was. Now she was building up a righteous anger.

David seemed to sense that he had misstepped. "Well, it's none of my business. It's like outing someone. It's not cool. If you wanted to stay in the broom closet, that's your business, not mine."

Staci fumed, looking away from him and biting her lip to keep from shouting at him and getting into an argument right there on the front steps of Fairgrove. She knew that he was right, at least a little bit. But she was too angry to really admit it right then. And certainly not to him.

"Maaaybe we should move the dime tour along, Romeo," Wanda said.

Beth leaned in close to Staci, whispering. "So, David is a mage, too? How many more do you think are in Silence? Do you think—"

Seth was the one that saved her, tapping her on the shoulder. "Questions for another time, I think. Let's keep moving."

Flushing with embarrassment, David took them in past offices that looked perfectly normal, complete with receptionist and secretaries and computers, and down a hall that ended in a beige wood door. "Okay, past this door we don't talk about magic, all right? Some people in the assembly area know about it, but some are from Silence and don't. So—this is the assembly building for the superbikes."

When he opened the door, there was noise, but nothing like as loud as Staci had expected. There were about twenty bikes in various stages of construction, and a half dozen lined up, apparently finished. The unfinished ones had one to three people working on them.

"All of the bikes in here have owners," David said, proudly. "In fact, we have a one-year waiting list. Some of them are going straight to the track, some are going to collectors, and the rest are going to people who want a superbike that you don't have to be the Incredible Hulk to pick up when it goes down."

Staci noticed how much these motorcycles looked like Metalhead, Dylan's elvensteed. Had the elvensteed copied the styling of the bikes, or had the bike designers taken their cue from elvensteeds? She wanted to ask that, but they weren't supposed to talk about magic here . . . plus, she was still miffed at David.

"How much do these babies run? Last time we were up here, I've never really had a chance to find out," Seth asked, pure lust in his voice.

"It varies by how overclocked they are. Low end of a hundred k, high end of about five hundred," David said casually.

Seth choked. David grinned. "We're only middle of the price range for superbikes, you know," he said. "You can pay as much as a million and a half for a high end purpose-built racing superbike."

Seth choked again. "Is there a big market for this stuff? Should I start looking into where I can sell organs?"

"It's a very specialized market, and no, it's not big," David told him. "It's about one third people buying these bikes as an investment and storing them somewhere in pristine condition, one third serious, professional racers, and one third people who want a dangerous toy. The trick is to keep your product rare enough to be desirable, yet priced to be attractive to that market, and keep your supply just a little short of demand so you can keep the business solvent. Like Shelby Cobras." He lowered his voice some. "Of course, *we* don't have to worry about keeping the business solvent, since we have other sources of income."

Tim smiled cynically. Staci remembered Dylan creating a handful of gold chains to take to pawn shops. A place like this, she supposed, would have owners whose sales of Krugerrands or gold bullion wouldn't even raise an eyebrow or gain the attention of the law.

"Anything you want to see here?" David asked. Staci took a good look around. She thought she recognized about half the people working here, at least vaguely. Maybe more.

"Oh! I know! You guys also do jet skis, right?" Beth was raising her hand like she was in a classroom, all but bouncing with enthusiasm.

"Not yet," David smiled. "We plan to start production in about six months, when we've got all the data from the prototypes and we've got the tooling and assembly building set up. My bosses are pretty sure the jet ski business won't be self-supporting for two years at least; we need to get a rep in racing circles before they are as in demand as the bikes and race cars are. But that's one reason why Fairgrove expanded here; we've got lake, open-ocean, and protected bay test areas available to us." Beth deflated slightly, but nodded along anyways. "If it makes you feel any better, the prototypes are done and ready to start testing some time next week," David added.

Staci was having a little bit of a hard time holding in her temper over the way David kept saying "us" and "we," as if he was already part of the "Fairgrove family." *So these outsiders just waltz in, and take over the economy!* she thought resentfully. *It's like the Blackthornes never really left!* Now she could see why Tim was so annoyed. Couldn't she and Tim and the rest of Silence just have been left to work out their own destinies without these rich elves coming in like a bunch of millionaires looking to adopt a third world child as a kind of trophy? She realized that some of that was probably her being pissed off at David bleeding over, but she couldn't help it. *Where do they get off pulling everyone into their games?*

Wanda hung back from the others, waiting until she was abreast of Staci before she started walking again. "Hey, listen, I know you're mad," she whispered, leaning in close. "But none of us knew about David, either. He's not a bad guy. And look at it this way. You don't have to hide magical crap from him, now. Maybe you could even study together, what with your dead languages and musty scrolls, and all of the other geek stuff that Seth loves."

Beth had caught on to what Wanda was doing, and joined the pair, apparently having heard at least a little bit of it. "It's really not all that bad. It's just a different sort of relationship now; not better, not worse. Different."

She supposed they were right, at least a little bit. But couldn't they see? She wanted something *normal* for a change. *Someone* normal. She couldn't tell them that right now, though. Instead, she nodded, took a breath, and put on her best "I'm totally cool with this, see?" face. She regretted this entire trip; not coming wouldn't have changed anything, but she still didn't want to be dealing with this. If she had found out later, she could have met up with David and confronted him about it alone, with just the two of them. Now, she was stuck here, dragged along with the others for a tour that, while instructive, was starting to make her want to scream. David was still rattling on about jet skis, emerging markets, even the beaches of Silence and how their potential was "untapped." She tuned him out for a while, consumed with her thoughts.

After working their way through another workshop, they came to a wide set of double doors that looked to be made of dense hardwood. The doors were *thick*, too; at least six inches. On the right hand side was a small pad of some sort. Outwardly, it looked like a digital lock with a keycard reader. Staci let her mage-sight focus in on the door, then the lock. She almost gasped at what she saw; layers upon layers of powerful magic, stacked and inter-linked so intricately that she could scarcely tell where one ended and another began. The wooden doors were completely infused with magic, as was the surrounding wall; she doubted a tank would be able to get through either. The keypad was some sort of false faceplate; it wasn't even hooked up to any electricity other than maybe a battery, from what she could tell. David removed a keycard from his pocket; it, too, glowed with magic. When he pressed it to the card reader, she saw the layers and threads of magic in the door change; it looked almost like the gears of a clock, suddenly coming to life.

"Hurry up, the door only stays open for few seconds," David said, as the door swung open. He squeaked through last, and the door practically closed on his heels. They were in a small connecting room, with another pair of doors in front of them. After the large doors behind them closed, the ones in front opened on their own and she felt a small thrill run through her. *Okay, I'm not completely jaded yet. Magic can still "wow" me.*

"This is Research and Development," David said from behind Staci now. "Go on through. It's pretty cool. We do prototyping in there; those jet skis that Beth was asking about are all in there right now, plus the next generation of superbike. We figure we'll price that around $750k."

Seth was first through the doors, and stopped dead. Wanda and the others had to give him a push to get him moving. Staci looked at his face before she looked around the room; he looked exactly like a toddler on Christmas morning. "I can die happy now," he breathed, scanning the room slowly and taking it all in.

At first glance, it didn't look all that different from the assembly room they'd just left. There were jet skis and one motorcycle up on work stands; the bike was only partly assembled, the jet skis all looked finished, but had their cowlings off while people tinkered with them. All the work stations were surrounded by rolling tool chests and various pieces of diagnostic equipment.

Except that some of the diagnostic equipment was constructed of crystals, still-living tree-branches and vines, various bits of artifact, and jars full of seaweed. And one of the techs working on a jet ski was a mermaid in a wheelchair, her upper torso covered with the top half of a racing mechanic's suit. And some of the techs were clearly performing magic, either with their bare hands or the assistance of daggers or wands. There was something that looked like a tiny lizard encased in fire doing a delicate bit of welding on the bike.

They paid no attention whatsoever to the newcomers.

"Simon, no," one of the techs on the bike said. "Don't do anything the mundanes out on the floor can't do. Unweld that, and reweld it, please."

The lizard made a snorting sound, but obeyed.

"Quite the operation Fairgrove has here," Tim said, nodding as he surveyed the room. High praise for elves, especially from him. And, Staci had to admit; it *was* impressive. She could recognize some of the magic that the—were they technicians? Fellow mages?—people were performing, but other parts of it were so exotic and foreign that she wasn't even sure *what* effect they were attempting to produce. And, holy crap! A real life mermaid! She knew from reading Tim's books that they existed, but she had never expected to see one. Especially one that looked like it was fine-tuning a carburetor on a jet ski.

David saw where she was looking. "Melody is fine-tuning the flow on the intake manifold," he said. "She has an instinctive understanding of laminar flow. She's never wrong, at least that's what they tell me."

Seth turned and gave him a funny look. "How do you fine-tune a manifold?"

"In this case, she's removing material on the inside. I watched her do it earlier today," David replied. "Magically, of course. That's why we can't have any ferrous metals in the prototypes or too near the working area. Speaking of which, I'll have to ask you to put anything with iron or steel in it in the vault there." He pointed at a thick-walled container on the floor right by the door. "You can pick it all up when you leave."

Staci and Tim shared a look, but he shrugged. "Their house, their rules." That was true, Staci supposed. Staci, Tim, Wanda, and Seth all began to remove daggers, throwing knives, specialty metal knuckles with arcane symbols carved into them, and all manner of other iron or steel weapons from their bags and persons. Beth had gone completely wide-eyed, her mouth coming slightly open in surprise as she watched the pile of weapons grow.

"I didn't even know you guys had any of that stuff!"

"That's the point. Better to have the element of surprise, if you need it," Tim said, patting the outside of his jacket and pants as a last check for anything he might have forgotten. Even with their iron and steel weapons and tools locked up, they still had magic if anything happened. Not that she expected anything to happen here, in the heart of Fairgrove Industries . . . but then again, a lot of things she had never expected had come to pass in the last year.

"This is for your own safety as well as ours," David reminded them. "If any of you have short-circuited magic with the use of Cold Iron, you know how explosive that can get. And I won't go to bail for your safety if you screw up what one of our techs is doing. They'll probably turn you into a newt." Beth looked over to Tim and Wanda at that; Tim shook his head "no," while Wanda was vigorously nodding "yes." Staci remembered what had happened when she had destroyed the Blackthornes' Gate; she certainly didn't want something like that happening anywhere close to her.

"In fact," said a new voice, "that very reaction forms the core of our first-line defense against dark magic. Let it never be said we cannot adapt."

Coming in through the door behind them were two of the three elves that had turned up at Tim's store, Caradoc and his sister Branwen. Caradoc was the one who had been speaking. Tim actually lost a tiny bit of his glowering suspicion at that, and looked interested. "And just how does that work?" he asked.

"Pure Cold Iron rods in silk-lined sheathes underground buried six inches inside our perimeter," said Branwen, readily enough. "The system can be activated from in here, and the rods rise out of the ground. But there is a fail-safe; if the power is cut here, the activation is automatic, and it runs on its own battery."

"Fairly ingenious. I imagine that the construction crews were a little baffled at the inventive 'lightning rod' system." Tim's tone was neutral.

"That, wizard, is what we have human allies for," Caradoc said lightly. "The system was created by a pure, non-magical human engineer we recruited in Savannah. It's fairly straightforward to install. We brought the same crew up from Savannah that did the initial installation at the original facility. Had anyone asked—no one did, by the way, the locals were exceedingly incurious about the holes we were digging and electrics we were burying—we were going to say it was a security system."

"Human allies?" Staci perked up at that. *I wonder if that's how some people get some elf in their bloodline.* "How do you mean?"

"Very occasionally we find someone with an open mind and skills we need that we recruit as an adult," Branwen replied evenly. "Tannim Drake and Sam were two of those. They are more often than not mages and wizards in their own right. Sam is one of the exceptions, but his engineering skills seem quite magical to most of us." She smiled. Staci found herself smiling back. "But for the most part, our allies are our fosterlings."

"What are fosterlings?" That was Seth; he was listening in to the conversation, but his eyes were fixed on the fiery reptile on the motorcycle. The tech seemed to be having a conversation with it.

"Elves have a very, very long tradition among you humans of *stealing children*," said Caradoc. "That is not . . . exact. Yes, we do take human children away from their parents, but only if their parents are abusive. In the past, we have kept them Underhill where they can live unchanged for centuries. That . . . as some of your human legends will attest . . . is often a practice that ends in tragedy, when the human longs to see his or her home again and passes the Gate despite all advice otherwise. Their years come upon them all at once, when they have passed the protective confines of Underhill. They age, and generally die, within moments of returning to the World Above." Beth gasped, but Caradoc carried on. "So, now, we allow them only intervals Underhill, short ones at that. Generally a period after we have taken them, so hue and cry can die down, or the changeling we left in the child's place dies. Then they foster in the World Above with us, a practice that is much easier with the internet, since they can receive a fine education that way, and decide what they wish to make of their lives. Though generally they stay with us, going from fosterling to employee and ally."

"Nice and self-contained." Tim was stone-faced, not giving anything away. Previously, he had told Staci exactly what he thought about the elves' practice of taking human children, and his doubts about it. Still, this wasn't the time or place to get into that sort of thing. They were here for a different purpose than to get into a moral argument with their hosts.

"The rest of the facility is far more humble than this. Your friends Wanda and Seth have already seen our training rooms, our libraries, and the cafeteria." Caradoc seemed to have picked up on Tim's skeptical disapproval though.

"Perhaps our visitors would like to speak with some of our fosterlings at some later date . . . so they can be sure we have not somehow englamoured them." Ian Ironoak now came striding through the door—though he seemed more amused than irritated at Tim's attitude. "However, let us repair to my office, where we may speak in a less public surrounding."

When Staci had first visited the Blackthorne mansion as Sean's guest, she had thought that it was all so gorgeous and opulent. It wasn't until walking into Ian's office that she saw what it looked like when "rich" and "good taste" came together; the Blackthorne mansion's appointments all seemed forced and gaudy by comparison. The room was entirely paneled in wood; whatever kind it was, it had a way of catching the sunlight in its grain that was entrancing. The desk, a simple but refined affair with rounded corners and a black top, was made of the same wood. The only things on it were two trays for papers, an expensive looking fountain pen, and a short stack of books. The chair behind the desk was old leather and looked well used, and very comfortable. There weren't many knickknacks or other furnishings; a few seats for guests and a small couch against the wall, but no pictures or framed degrees. Behind the desk and chair was a set of cabinets bookending another stretch of desktop, also with rounded corners. There was a closed laptop on the desktop, along with models of motorcycles and a jet ski; they looked like production models, used by the designers, rather than commercial cast models or completed model kits. Behind this were wall-to-wall windows. The real standout was the view; the windows gave a perfect panorama of the sea, since the office overlooked the bay and the docks, and somehow it all appeared as if it was something out of a painting. The lighting was all recessed into the ceiling, and bathed the room in light identical (so far as Staci could tell) to sunlight.

"Are you guys adopting? Because if this is how you live, sign me up." Seth gulped; maybe he realized that that might be a thing they could actually take him up on.

"Might I offer something to drink or to eat while we talk? We have a very wide selection of herbal tea, hot chocolate from Venice, or coffee, if you prefer." Ian casually moved through the room, coming to rest in the leather chair. He was completely at ease here, and why shouldn't he be? This was a seat of power for him in the World Above.

Almost at once, Staci, Seth, and Wanda all said, "Coffee."

"Um, hot chocolate please," Beth said, raising her hand sheepishly.

"Nothing for me." Tim was the standout, still appraising the room.

"Of course. David, would you please fetch our guests refreshment? And something for yourself as well, if you'd like." David nodded and quickly exited the room, closing the door behind him. "Please, be seated, make yourselves comfortable." Branwen and Caradoc stood behind the desk and Ian's chair, flanking him on either side. Staci and Tim both sat in the chairs immediately in front of the desk, while the other three plopped onto the couch together.

It wasn't long before David returned with their drinks on a small tray. Staci noticed that he had brought a mug of coffee for himself, too. Once everyone had their drinks, David stood near the door, quietly blowing on his mug and occasionally sipping it. *I suppose he isn't sitting down because he's still on the clock.* Staci took a tentative sip of her own coffee; it was good, but it wasn't the same as the stuff back in Tim's shop. She couldn't tell if she didn't like it as much because it was the elves that had offered it to her—as silly as that sounded—or if Tim's coffee was actually better. *Maybe it's just the setting; Tim's shop is home in a way.*

Another sip, though, convinced her. Tim's was better. This wasn't "diner" coffee, but it was more like her mother's coffee. Nothing *wrong* with it, just nothing outstanding either. *Wait, though. Elves don't drink coffee, they have a problem with caffeine, it acts like instant morphine on them. I guess if you never taste something, you don't know how to tell what the good stuff is.* Whereas she knew for a fact that Tim not only bought only coffee he himself had tried, he ground it himself fresh every day. She hid her grin in her cup. *So, money can't always buy good taste.*

"I'm glad that you decided to come here today. I feel that we can help each other quite a bit, if we work at it." Ian leaned back in his chair, steepling his fingers in front of his chest.

"Thank you for the invitation. You have a lovely facility, and it looks like your products are going to be just as wonderful." Tim was still playing things close; he was assessing the elves, that much was certain. But Staci also got a sense from him that he was waiting for something. She didn't have a clue what it was, but she figured that she would know when it happened.

Ian paused for a moment before continuing. *Tim's not the only one sizing things up.* "When I said that we can help each other, I meant it. I think that we all want what's best for Silence, even if our . . . methods might be different."

"That's one way of putting it, certainly." *What Tim means to say is, "At least we actually get off of our asses and take the fight to the bad guys instead of playing wait-and-see all the time."* Staci had certainly been converted, by her own experiences if nothing else, that evil left alone doesn't just go away or get better; it gets worse. "Before, when you paid us a visit at the shop, you mentioned that a 'darkness' was coming. Is this what you want to work together for? Fighting against whatever this 'darkness' is? And how do you know about it?"

"All pertinent questions, to be sure. Yes, it is the reason we want to pool our resources and talents. In normal times, we would be content to allow you to maintain things on your own, and continue with our own work individually. Unfortunately, these are not normal times." Staci bristled at Ian's choice of words. *"Allow" us? He sure does have a high opinion of how much sway he has over us. Well, at least Tim and myself.* "Things are changing more rapidly than we had anticipated; it's a failing that our kind sometimes falls prey to."

"I'm aware." Tim leaned forward in his seat, his eyes never leaving Ian's. "Why now?"

"We are not sure. There are so many factors and things that can affect magic here in the World Above, so many complicated systems within systems. Is it one thing, or a large number of different causes? There's no way to be sure. What we are sure of, however, is that it began with the destruction of the Blackthorne clan here, in Silence. And that it is clear that something inimical to humans and our kind alike is behind it."

"And the 'darkness'?"

"I'm sorry, but I don't have any answers as to what it is, nor who, or what, is behind it." Ian actually looked a trifle frustrated. "What we have is the equivalent of smoke, where there should be no smoke, and it is getting thicker. So we know there is a fire hereabouts. Where exactly, and what caused it, we don't know. But it is in a place where there should be no fire, where fire can only cause harm. As to the 'how' of our knowledge about this impending danger, we have always kept close watch over the World Above. Through magic, and information supplied to us by our human allies, we were able to sense that there is something ... gathering here. It's impenetrable to our sight, but we can still sense its presence, and we can tell it means nothing good. It is building, day by day. There can be no doubt of that."

Staci turned in her seat to look at Tim. He noticed her, then frowned and nodded. "I think," she said, diffidently at first but gaining more surety as she continued, "that Tim and I have seen some of that darkness."

"Or at least evidence of it," Tim added.

Ian arched a single eyebrow. "Oh?"

For the next ten minutes, Staci and Tim laid out all of the weirdness that had been happening lately; how Staci had felt as if she was being watched when in or near the woods outside of Silence, the broken trees in the clearing, and finally the attack in the alley.

" ... and that's how we found out that Beth is part-Selkie, too," Staci said, taking a deep breath as she finished.

Tim picked up where she had left off. "I used some friends to run the information on the revenants that came after us. They have some commonalities that are interesting and might lead to wherever they came from." He held up a hand and started ticking off fingers. "One, most of them are from Silence. Two, all of them have criminal records, some of which are pretty extensive. And three, all of them have either been declared 'missing' or their whereabouts have been unknown for the last three or so months."

Ian was silent for several long moments, absorbing all of the information. "I see."

Tim shrugged. "I hope you see more than I do. What we have is a bunch of different threads. The next step is to pull each one, see if we can follow it to something bigger. I had some ideas about that." He looked to Staci, then to the rest of the gang on the couch. "Might as well tell all of you now, since we're together. Whatever is going on, it seems to be connected to the woods, somehow. If we're going to find out what it is, we've got to go into them. Now, that's a lot of ground that would need covering, and I really don't like the idea of us searching through a forest randomly, stumbling around until we bump into something ... or something bumps into *us*."

"What do you propose then?" Caradoc was leaning against the counter behind the desk, his back to the windows. He and Branwen had listened silently for the entire meeting, allowing Ian to take the lead.

"That we, my group, go to Blackthorne Manor." Tim was watching Ian's face closely, and it seemed that whatever he saw there encouraged him to continue. "It was condemned and abandoned after its destruction. It's far enough out from the town and deep enough into the woods that it would make a good base of operations for someone, or something. Plus, there's still enough residual magic in that area that it might attract something nasty. Whatever we find there might give us another thread to pull; if there's nothing, then at least we have one big place checked off the list of where to look."

Staci didn't relish the thought of going back to the Blackthorne mansion, even though she saw the logic in Tim's plan. There were too many memories there, all of them bad, and some stained with blood.

Ian, Caradoc, and Branwen huddled together, conferring for a moment. They weren't whispering so much as speaking low, and she recognized that they were using Elvish. She didn't know enough and wasn't fluent enough to interpret what they were saying on the fly. Ian nodded, turning back to face Staci and Tim. "It's a sound idea. In the name of cooperation, I would hope that whatever you do find there, you'll inform us after your safe return?"

Tim nodded once. "That's reasonable."

"There's also one key facet of this situation that may have escaped your notice."

For the first time during this meeting, Tim showed a slip in control, bristling at the statement. "And that is?"

"That there is a single thing that ties everything, from beginning to end, together. From the destruction of the Blackthornes, to the happenings in the woods, the revenants, even your coterie." Ian's eyes snapped to Staci. "Her."

CHAPTER TEN

Tim kept glancing over at Staci, with his brows furrowed. Finally she glared back at him impatiently. *"What?"* she snapped.

"You. I can't make up my mind if you're angry or frightened," he admitted. "But in either case, apprentice, get your head in the game. We might not find anything up at the Manor, but if we do, we need to be ready for whatever it is."

Staci took a deep breath. He was right; her head had been elsewhere. Specifically, on the meeting with Ian yesterday. Much as it disturbed her, she did have to agree on one thing. Ian was right, at least on the face of it. Things in Silence had been pretty much in a state of stasis until she moved there. For whatever reason, that had changed after her arrival; *she* had changed with it.

But the accusation had also been profoundly unjust. *Dylan was already zeroing in on the Blackthornes,* she seethed, as Tim's little car wheezed its way up to the Blackthorne ruins. *Even if I hadn't moved to Silence, he'd still have stirred things up.* And it wasn't like Sean's plan only materialized after she had come into his life; he had been working towards torturing the town to death with a magical plague for months or maybe years. Decades, even. *In fact, by the time I got there, the only difference my being in town made to him was that he figured on making sure I was up in the mansion when he closed off and infected the rest of the town. To keep his "plaything" safe, the sick bastard.*

She realized that they weren't saying that she was the cause of any of it, not intentionally. Only that there was something about her that acted like some sort of magical crap magnet. *Like I didn't already feel like a crap magnet.* She had been so concerned with the world leaving her behind, when she had first moved to Silence. Afraid that she might actually be bored to death. Well, it just went to show what happened when you wished for something.

Staci had spent the rest of the day after the meeting in a funk, consumed with her thoughts. Tim and Ian had discussed how or why Staci might be the center of all that had been happening in Silence, but she had tuned them out, partly out of shock. The walk back to the book shop had been quiet; she felt everyone's eyes on her. She knew that it wasn't because they were afraid of her, or anything dumb like that; they just didn't know what to say after such a bombshell. Once they were back to their bikes, the group had split; Seth, Wanda, and Beth saw each other home, and Tim gave Staci a ride back to her place, with her bike in his car's trunk. Even with the revelation that whatever was going on now probably had something to do with her, *all* of them were being careful not to travel alone.

But Tim was right. She needed to get her head in the game. She stared out the window, looking at the woods, wondering what, if anything, was in them. There sure had been plenty when the Blackthornes were in residence. Those Huntsmen, for one thing. The Hounds that the Huntsmen used, and the Wendigos. The . . . what had Dylan called it? Leannan Sidhe? Had any of them been left behind? That wasn't even counting whatever might have moved in with the Blackthornes gone.

All the same, the accusation weighed on her. And finally she'd just had enough of it. "Goddamn it," she burst out. "I am *not* a supernatural crap magnet! Dylan was *already* here and getting ready to take on the Blackthornes alone before I even moved here!"

Seth was the first to react to her outburst. "Uh, okay, but how do you know that?"

"Because Dylan was already on the police watch list," Tim said casually, his eyes on the road now. "I have a little bird in the Sheriff's Department. Good, Staci. Don't let that elvish overlord rattle you. Their truth oftentimes is just enough to suit their purposes; doesn't mean that it's the whole thing, not in the slightest."

Whatever happened at the mansion today, she hoped that it would provide them with some answers. This whole "wandering around in the dark" stuff had been old back when she first found out that she was part-elf. She wanted to know what was behind all of this crap; once she knew, she'd have something that she could focus on, something that she could fight.

The car came to a stop, pulling off the road and behind a stand of trees and overgrown bushes. They had arrived. Tim had decided that the group would approach from different directions, starting at the foot of the main drive into the mansion. Tim, Staci, Beth, Wanda, and Seth; it was a good little strike group, despite Beth being green. She wouldn't be a frontline fighter, besides; her job would be to help heal up anyone that got into a scrap, keep them upright. That said, this was a real test for Wanda and Seth, too; neither of them had been in much of a fight since the last time all of them had been at Blackthorne Manor. This would be their first time putting their training to a practical use. *I'm going to make sure that I don't make the same mistakes that I did in that fight with the revenants, that's for sure.*

Everyone got out of the car, gathering up their weapons and tools; daggers, short swords, throwing knives, and other sharp implements, all made of iron. Wanda had her bow and arrows. They all had FRS "family band" short range radios, little things that looked like kids' walkie-talkies and hooked to a belt loop. Beth looked unsure with her short sword; Staci had determined that she was going to make sure that Beth never had a chance to use the sword, at least not today. Seth had a few more specialized items that he could use, some that he had come up with on his own. And he had an entire bag of those steel jacks that they'd all used to such good effect the last time. Staci was a little chagrined she hadn't thought of that. They were all in their "fighting clothes" as well; Staci in her brown and green turtleneck, cargo pants with a leather belt adorned with pouches, and leather boots. The others had variations on the same theme; all earth tones, close-fitting, and hardy. Tim . . . looked like himself. Leather jacket over a blue and white plaid shirt, dark jeans, and brown leather work boots, worn with age and use. They all had spare clothes in gym bags in the car, a jug of water and some junk towels from the thrift store; crawling around a forest, or getting into a fight, tended to get messy. It wouldn't do to go back into town covered in mud and— hopefully not—blood.

Tim gathered everyone together once they had finished with their gear checks, waiting for them to form into a huddle.

"This is the real deal, folks. No more playing around, no more training. You're in it, starting now. Keep your heads up and your eyes moving. Watch each others' backs. If you get into trouble, use your radios. If you get magical interference or the radios go down for any other reason, use the whistles you have. Remember, last resort on those; if you can handle it on your own, do so. We're going to try to be a little bit more stealthy than you all were when you were last here. Any questions?"

There weren't any. The group had spent the entire morning planning this excursion, discussing backups and contingencies, everything that might go differently or wrong. They were as ready as they could be.

"Staci, you're with Beth; keep an eye on her. Seth, Wanda, you two have been working as a team all this time and I am not breaking you up when this one isn't a training exercise. Staci, you and Beth head in towards the objective from the southeast. Wanda, Seth, from the northwest. Remember your routes of retreat. This is old ground, but that doesn't mean it won't hold new surprises." He looked each of them in the eye before nodding. "Okay, let's move."

Staci turned to Beth, lightly touching her elbow. "You're with me. Stay close, stay quiet, and follow my lead, just like we talked about this morning."

Beth nodded, her eyes wide and her lips set in a tight line. She looked both excited and scared to death. *Is that how I looked when I first got into all of this crazy magic stuff? No . . . it's different for her, isn't it?* For Beth, finding out about why she was different from everyone else had been affirming, and positive. Cathartic, even. For Staci . . . hell, she was still trying to decide. So far, discovering magic had meant more homework. She loved magic, no doubt about it, but damn if it wasn't a lot of drudge work. Discovering what she was had also given her a lot of heartbreak. With that thought, a powerful urge rose in Staci. She wanted to protect her friend more than ever, to keep her from going through the things that Staci had already. It was sudden and unexpectedly strong. She had to take a moment to breathe and clear her head yet again before pressing on. Emotions, as Tim had said over and over again, were powerful, but you couldn't let them control you. Your head had to be in charge.

"People who say that they feed off their emotions in a fight . . . are

fools. Plain and simple. You shut down reason, you start letting your heart control your head, and you're screwed. Doesn't matter if it's in a fistfight, knife fight, gun fight, or mage fight. You lose control, you lose. So . . . make your opponent lose control. Antagonize them. When people get nervous, or angry, they slip up. That's an opportunity, and you need as many as you can get in a fight for your life."

She nodded her head in the direction of the remains of the mansion. "Come on," she whispered. "Let's go. Stay behind me, especially if we have to fight something. Remember to concentrate on me; I'm going to use magic to make me stealthy, but *you* have enough power in you that I bet as long as you will yourself to see me, you won't lose sight of me."

Beth swallowed, but nodded again. Staci found a game-trail at the edge of the woods going in roughly the right direction, and they plunged in.

The Blackthornes had never done anything like landscaping this far from the mansion, and right at the edge the underbrush was thick. But as soon as they got past the zone where sunlight really penetrated, the going got easier. This was definitely old-growth forest; it didn't look as if anyone had felled one of these trees since Colonial days, and maybe not even then. The trees were huge, and pretty much blocked most of the sun, leaving only a few places where moss and ferns and other shade-loving plants grew. There was a very clear path, not so much laid out on the ground, as defined by the place where the space above the ground was clear of the hundreds of spindly little bare branches protruding from the trunks of the trees. Most of those branches looked (and were) dead, easy to snap off. So anything moving along this path that didn't care about moving silently would have broken them.

Only a few things I can think of that didn't care about moving silently; the Huntsmen and the people they were hunting, for starters. They loved making a lot of noise; driving their prey in front of them, getting off on the fear. Sick, sick, sick.

Well the good news about this was that you could see for a long distance under the trees. And it wasn't all that far to the mansion, or at least, the area around the mansion that the Blackthornes had kept groomed. Still, just because she could see, that didn't stop her from moving as quietly as practice and magic would allow. For all *she* knew, there were critters that could look like tree trunks. Or ents were real; they probably wouldn't be as cool as the ones in the books, either. Or there were things that could press themselves up against a tree and blend in, like some owls could.

Progress was uneventful—if slow, due to keeping watch over Beth as much as the environment—until they got to the part of the property where the Blackthornes had taken a hand in taming nature. And conversely, that was where the going got tougher, because one of the things they had done was to thin out some of the big trees, allowing more light to get down to the forest floor. So there were all kinds of things growing at the foot of the trees; bushes, tangles of brambles, blackberry and raspberry vines, all of it stuff that might just as well have been created in order to snag anyone trying to pass through it and slow him down.

It suddenly occurred to Staci that might have been the Blackthornes' intent in the first place. Start your prey running from the mansion; give him an easy start through the meticulously landscaped area around the grounds, with all the brush pruned and a manicured lawn giving him an easy run. And then, *wham,* he hits the tangles, just as he thinks he's going to get away. Easy to predict what the result would be then—panic. Maybe he decides to double back, which is fine by the dark elves, since that's going to bring him back to the Gate in the maze and they can send him through to Hunt in Underhill at their leisure. Or if he doesn't, he struggles through, tiring himself out, and when he gets under the more open, deep forest, he just runs blindly. Tim had told her that when people ran in a blind panic, they generally ran in circles. And even if the person they were hunting *did* run in a straight line, when he hit the tangled undergrowth near the roadway, he'd automatically assume he'd gone in a circle and run in the opposite direction. That would make for a very entertaining Hunt, with very little chance the quarry would reach the road.

The trees being a little more spread out seemed to be the only evidence of past care left. The months of neglect since the Blackthornes' destruction meant that the grounds had gone to pot. Waist-high grass extended beyond the mass of bushes, and beyond that there was the outer wall of the mansion; it was completely covered in vines and its own set of bushes, all of it wild and unkempt.

Six months was all it had taken for the forest to reclaim the manor; she suspected that residual magic had something to do with the aggressive growth of the plants. Staci wasn't here to conduct a botany study, however. *First things first; try and find out what's ahead, if I can.* She held up a hand, signaling Beth to stop.

"Going to take a reading," she whispered, keeping her eyes scanning ahead. "Try not to move around a lot." She paused for a moment, then started working the spell. Her hands worked through the patterns, fingers contorting into joint-aching shapes, as she breathed the incantations. She was enhancing her senses; it wouldn't last more than a few moments, but it'd give her a better picture of what was ahead of them, if anything. It was a risky spell, too; if there was anything too jarring, she could get overstimulated in a hurry; there was a chance she could be stunned if there was anything too loud or bright, for example. Bringing her hands together in a slow-motion clap, the spell was completed, and she opened her eyes. The world was incredibly more vibrant, now; she could see shades and depths of colors and light that she would've never guessed were there, could smell *everything* from the leather of her boots to the moisture collecting on leaves, and hear the smallest movements. *Focus; you can marvel at the beauty of nature or whatever some other time.* Immediately she pinpointed Seth and Wanda, approaching the mansion from the northwest, just as planned. They were doing a good job of being sneaky; even with her enhanced senses, they were barely registering for her at this distance. Knowing where to look for them had been the only reason she had found them so quickly. Ahead, she felt that the grounds around the mansion—the pool area, the lawn, even the maze—were all empty of anything concerning. Just an errant squirrel and a family of hedgehogs doing animal things. She reached out a little more, into the mansion itself, and that's where her first surprise was waiting for her. There was *something* in there...

Just like that, the spell fizzled. It was only good for brief glimpses, kind of like a sonar "ping" from a submarine. She didn't dare try to use the spell again; it took a lot of energy, for starters, and left her vulnerable while it was active. *Funny, I didn't get any "hits" from Tim. He must be hanging back.* It occurred to her that he hadn't mentioned which group he was going to be with during this excursion. Probably another test; watching both groups, making sure that he was there to help if anyone got into trouble. Staci often wondered how he did it; taking so much on and still being able to do everything, as if he was inexhaustible.

"We've got something in the mansion," Staci said, turning to Beth. "I don't know what it is, but I definitely felt something moving around in there with my spell. All the same, we're going to be careful as we get closer; no clue if whatever it is has some sort of early warning system."

Beth pulled the little "family band" radio off her belt and held it up. "Should we let the others know, too?"

Staci mentally kicked herself. *She's learning quick, and I'm asleep at the wheel.* "Good idea." She waited a moment. "Thanks, by the way. I'm glad you're along with us on this." That took some of the fear out of Beth's eyes, and she smiled. Staci took the radio and keyed it on. "Goon Squad 2, do you copy?"

Nothing but static. She frowned and made sure the radio was set to the right channel. It was. She had *seen* Seth and Wanda, they were well within the one-mile reach of the radio. And they had checked and double-checked to make sure that the batteries were fresh and everything was working when they were packing the car. *Must be the leftover magic in the area; it's definitely not anything coming off of me.* She could feel magical energy humming in the ground; it wasn't nearly as strong as it had been the last time she was here, but whatever was left seemed to be enough to disrupt their radios.

"Can't raise them; magical interference. We can't give our hand away and use the whistles, either; might scare off or alert whatever is in the house, making this entire trip pointless. We'll just have to trust that they know what they're doing. Let's keep moving."

They crossed the distance from the edge of the forest to the outer wall, Staci still in the lead. When they reached it, Staci held up a hand again, signaling Beth to wait for a moment. She grabbed the edge of the wall and pulled herself up just enough so that her eyes were over the lip. It took her a moment to take in the exterior of the manor. Weeds and wildflowers were everywhere, the grass was all over waist height, and she could make out what had once been well-tended plants now gone rank and either being choked out or overrunning sections of the garden. There were pieces of broken furniture out on what had been the lawn, here and there, some of them scorched. The maze itself had run completely wild, the hedges no longer in any sort of recognizable pattern, and the pool was green with algae and duckweed.

Recognition hit Staci like a gut punch, and she almost gasped aloud. *This place is a perfect picture of that training illusion that we did a while ago. How could that be?* She knew that magic operated on a set of laws; some could be bent, others could be broken. One of those was the Law of Contagion; had the spell Tim used picked up something from the real world, made itself fit this place? Or had Tim been here since the fight at the mansion, and crafted his illusion around what he had seen? Why would he come here on his own, especially without telling Staci or the others?

Those were all questions for later. She had to focus on the task at hand. She dropped down, landing silently. "Okay, Beth. Once we're over the wall, stick to me like glue. We're going to get inside quickly and quietly. If anything happens, get behind me and find some cover." Beth nodded, gulping. Staci went over the wall first, pulling herself up and on top of the wall in a single smooth motion. She glanced around the yard, making sure that nothing had changed, before straddling the wall and reaching down to help Beth up. It took a moment and a little bit of effort—Beth, while in decent shape, wasn't quite caught up to Staci in terms of strength—but finally both of them were over the wall and on the other side. Unconsciously, Staci took nearly the same path she had when they had been training in the illusion of Blackthorne Manor; obviously, she hadn't sprung any traps or alarms, and was much more cautious this time.

Nothing happened; no arrows raining from the sky, no traps or alarms. Aside from the background magical signature of the place, she wasn't getting a blip of energy. They reached the French doors on the patio that would lead inside to the main rooms of the mansion. Although the curtains inside were black with mold or smoke, they still obscured what was waiting for them inside—if anything. The building itself had not weathered the last year well at all; between the fighting and the lack of care, it was falling apart. Parts of it were scorched, most of the windows were broken or completely destroyed, and everything looked like it had aged one hundred years. Once again, Staci wondered why there had been so much deterioration in only about twelve months' time. *Maybe they were using magic to help hold the place together? Who knows?*

Staci waited for a few moments, listening. She couldn't hear anything moving around or talking inside. If she had been able to contact Seth and Wanda, she would take more time, scouting the outside of the building and doing more listening checks. As it was, she needed to get inside and find out what was in there, and now; it wouldn't do to have her friends walk right into it, unprepared. Better if she got there first; if things were bad enough, either she or Beth could use the whistle and bring the others to them.

"Here we go." She opened the door slowly, stepping through; Beth was right on her heels. For a moment she couldn't see anything. Then the pair of them were bathed in golden light, brilliant and almost blinding.

She blinked several times until her dazzled eyes recovered.

She and Beth were standing at the top of a series of three shallow stairs. The ceiling must have been twenty feet above them. Hanging from the ceiling and reaching to the floor was a series of golden curtains; some rich brocade, some velvet, some satin, some gossamer silk. The silk ones hid the source of the light in front of them; the rest were tied back with golden ropes as thick as her wrist. The air was perfumed with the scent of honey and roses, and filled with the sound of delicate harp music.

As she and Beth stood there, the final curtains drew back, as if by an invisible hand, revealing that the source of the light was a golden throne in the shape of a peacock's tail, and sitting in the throne was a luminous woman clothed in a simple, sensuous gown of golden silk. Her hair was a fiery red, and her eyes were green, with slitted, catlike pupils.

"Oh my god, it's beautiful!" Beth was awestruck, drinking everything in, her mouth agape.

There was a man standing beside the throne; he wore a long, velvet robe in a darker gold. At a nod from the woman, he approached the girls, and looked down his long nose at them. He held out a fine silver tray with a cover on it. He was within a pace of Staci when she unsheathed her short sword and plunged it into the man's stomach. Beth screamed, her hands flying to her mouth as if to hold back the sound.

Staci instantly thrust her hand into her pocket, touching her cell phone charm. With a loud snap that sounded like a capacitor letting go, all of the light, the extravagant surroundings, the man and the woman, everything vanished. The man was replaced with a squat creature; it was covered in fur and had a face that looked like some devilish toad; the face was constricted in a combination of agony and shock. Where the silver tray had been, there was now just an extended hand ending in barbed claws. The creature slid off of Staci's blade, falling onto its back to lie motionless in about three inches of stagnant water that flooded the entire room. The room itself was a shambles, and immediately recognizable to Staci; much of it was blackened from fire, and looked close to collapsing. They were in one of the living rooms. Ruined couches sat in a depression in the middle of the floor. A chair and bits of other furniture had been cobbled together in what looked like a shabby throne; sitting in it was a woman, but one that was nothing like the illusion they had just witnessed.

"You . . . came back . . . *little* witch."

The woman was a horrid sight. She looked emaciated; what scraps of clothing she had left hung off of her bones, and were filthy with god knew what. Her hair, what wasn't missing from a patchy scalp, was long, soiled, and black; long enough to dip down into the pool of water at her feet. Her skin was mottled and unhealthy looking. It wasn't until the woman raised her head that Staci knew who she was. She would never forget the eyes of the Leannan Sidhe, or the sight of the Fey licking blood from her fingers.

"Wasn't it enough? For you to rob me of food, of protection? Now you must come back . . . to taunt me?" There was nothing sane in those eyes, and nothing wholesome in the Fey's expression.

Staci didn't respond; she was too busy casting spells, putting extra shields, wards, and protections on herself and Beth. Beth had already scrambled back, taking cover behind a broken marble column. When Staci was finished, she carefully took a few steps backwards until she was out of the edge of the pool of water, still facing the Leannan Sidhe; they took their power from water, and she did not want to get caught in the muck if she could help it.

"You can't take everything from me. This is *mine!* I wouldn't join him, and I will not submit to you, child!" The Leannan Sidhe half-rose from her makeshift seat, her hands gripping the arms hard enough that they creaked. Even insane and starved, she was still powerful. "You'll die for what you've done!" Staci already had an offensive spell readied; all she needed to do was release it, and—

"Staci, the water! Look out—"

Instinctively, Staci threw herself backwards; she thrust her right hand towards the Leannan Sidhe, and a bolt of light streaked out to connect with the monster's face, causing it to steam. At the same time, the water in the pool erupted in twin sprays; two Huntsmen had been lurking under the surface—it had to be magic concealing them, since the water was so shallow—and both of them brought wicked blades down on the spot where Staci had been standing. She was inundated by the putrid water, but quickly rolled to the side as another strike was directed her way. She had to get to her feet and keep on the move, otherwise they'd eventually get her, either through luck or coordination.

Staci rolled again; she slammed painfully into a broken chest of some sort. She flipped her legs up and over her head, somersaulting backwards until she was scrambling to her feet; there was so much crap on the smooth floor, she had trouble keeping her balance. That was all the opportunity that the Huntsmen needed. They moved quickly despite their sorry state, trying to flank her. *Got to focus on one at a time if I want any chance to take these guys down.* She reached into a pouch on her belt and pulled out a handful of ashes, keeping her sword out in front of her. She took measure of both Huntsmen; one in front, and one behind. She feinted with her sword at the one in front of her, then whirled around and shouted a word of power before blowing on the ashes in her left hand. The ashes shot out as a cloud of embers, engulfing the second Huntsman. Wherever the embers struck, the creature was now burning, the fire covering its face and choking it. She turned to face the first Huntsman in time to catch sight of his sword coming down in a diagonal slice at her neck. She ducked under the blade just in time, and then answered in kind, cutting at the creature's wrist with her short sword. It let out a baleful wail as black blood spurted from the wound. The Huntsman backed up a pace, now more wary.

"Kill her! Kill her now!" the Leannan Sidhe shrieked from somewhere behind her. That either frightened or emboldened the Huntsman; it steadied itself, then stomped towards Staci, weaving its blade back and forth in patterns intended to intimidate. She shuffled backwards, keeping her sword in front; one of the swipes caught the tip of her sword; the Huntsman reacted immediately with an attempt to bind her blade, nearly pulling it out of her grasp. The creature roared, rushing forward headlong. If she stayed put she'd be run over, knocked back or worse. Instead, Staci juked to her left, then dove to the right; the Huntsman, moving too quickly to react in time, tripped over itself and began to stumble. Staci landed on her chest, barely avoiding having her chin slam into the ground. She rolled up to her knees just as the Huntsman was moving past her, flipped the sword around in her grip, and stabbed it into one of the Huntsman's feet, pinning it. The Huntsman pitched forward; its masked face slammed into the floor with a sickening crunch. Staci couldn't get to her sword, since it was still underneath the creature. While it was stunned, she came up into a crouch, unsheathing her knife and then bringing it down in the middle of the Huntsman's back. There was a final spasm, and then it went still.

"One down," Staci said, still breathing heavy. *And one to—*

"*Staci!*"

She snapped her head around; the Huntsman that she had partially set on fire had extinguished itself in the murky water, and was almost upon her. She had her knife, and no spells ready; she felt frozen for a fraction of a second. There was a flash of light; blue-white and cool, with reflections playing around the room. She glanced at Beth; the light was coming from her hands, and her face was scrunched up in concentration. She turned her attention back to the Huntsman; it made a confused and strangled sort of sound. The water it was standing in had frozen solid around its feet, with frost climbing up its boots. The temperature in the room had dropped like a lead balloon.

Staci quickly got to her feet, shouting over her shoulder. "Nice work, Beth! Keep it up!" The Huntsman was desperately hacking away at the ice with its blade. Staci got an idea, and started to perform a spell of her own.

"*Keep it up?* I don't even know how I'm doing this!"

The Leannan Sidhe looked furious. She stood up from the makeshift throne, and Staci could tell that she was amping up for something big. Beth saw it, too, and her eyes went wide.

Staci felt what was happening before she saw it. The break in concentration was just enough to let the magic get away from Beth. Somehow the spell she was using flipped; where the water was frozen, it suddenly melted and in a heartbeat it was boiling. The Huntsman, unexpectedly freed, was taken off balance while in mid-stroke with its blade. The jagged knife buried itself in the Leannan Sidhe, interrupting her spell and sending her flying back into the throne. Staci finished her own spell, and moved off to the side to hide behind a ruined bookcase. The Huntsman realized what it had done to its patron, and began to rage. Staci was glad that they wore masks; she didn't want to know what those things looked like when they were pissed off. Still standing in the boiling water, the Huntsman focused on the place where Staci had been. With a final howl, it ran forward, sending splashes of the filthy water everywhere.

She had cast an illusion of herself; crude and quick, with just a visual component. It wouldn't make any sound, and only just stood there, not reacting to anything. If it lasted long enough and someone was paying attention, they could tell that it was on a sort of "loop." But the Huntsman was only interested in killing and blood. While it was preoccupied with attacking her illusion, she sprinted over to where the first Huntsman was and extricated her sword from underneath it. Then she crept up behind her opponent; it had finally dispelled the illusion by smashing through it enough times. Before it could look around, she sliced the back of both of its legs, bringing it to its knees. With a shout, she swung her sword with all of her might, being careful to keep the edge aligned perfectly. A moment later, the Huntsman's head fell to the floor, followed by the body.

Staci shivered involuntarily at the sight of the Huntsman's head rolling on the floor, but did her best to suppress it. *Some battle-hardened warrior mage you are, Staci.* It looked like all the immediate threats were dealt with; still, she kept her sword out, just in case.

"Beth? It's okay to come out, I think we took care of them all."

There was a pause, and then Beth's head poked out from behind the tattered, moldy curtain she had been hiding behind. "They're all dead?"

"I think so." She walked over to her friend; to Beth's credit, she wasn't shaking and hadn't puked. "Thanks for helping me out; I thought that I would have more time with the first Huntsman. Guess I was wrong."

"I don't even know what I did, really. Just kind of . . . thought really hard about stopping the second big guy. What are you calling them? Huntsmen?" She stood up, rubbing her arms.

"Yeah. They're like supernatural hunters that use evil dog things. These ones must be leftovers from the Blackthornes; I'm just glad they didn't have any hounds with them." She reached down to pick up a bit of a torn drape that wasn't completely burned, using it to wipe the black blood from her blade. "Gross."

They both heard a creak from the doorway; Staci readied herself, and then relaxed almost as quickly. It was Tim. He absorbed the scene instantly. "Looks like you found something. Hunters. And . . . a Leannan Sidhe." He brushed his hands off on his jeans; they were covered in a fair bit of dirt. "Are both of you okay?"

"No worse for wear. Beth even helped out; froze a bunch of water. It helped to trip one of them up long enough for me to get clear. We definitely need to help her with her focus and control, though; spell got turned on its head and the water turned boiling in a blink. Not that this room couldn't use a steam clean, but jeeze."

Tim nodded, then walked past the pair, checking the dead Huntsmen.

Staci turned to follow him. "Where were you, anyways? With Seth and Wanda?"

"I was doing some recon of my own; don't worry, I knew that you'd get some sort of signal off if you ran into anything you couldn't handle." He stopped walking abruptly. "The Leannan Sidhe is still alive." Staci moved to Tim's side, her sword out in front of her. "Alive" was a strong word to use; the Leannan Sidhe was clearly on her way out. Her breathing was ragged, and her eyes were half-lidded.

"Should we . . . help her, or something?" Beth had joined them, but had also made sure she was several steps behind the pair.

"I don't think that there's much that we could do, even if we wanted to. This thing is evil, Beth. She's done horrible things to people. She sucks all the joy and creativity out of them, forever, and they can never get it back again. Mostly, the people she's done that to kill themselves." Tim stared dispassionately down at the dying Fey.

"I watched her kill someone, once, Beth. It wasn't pretty." Staci could tell that her friend still had some doubts, but they could talk about that later. She was a gentle soul, that was certain.

"He offered me ... alliance," the Leannan Sidhe croaked. "I should have accepted ... "

"What is she talking about?" Staci lowered her sword; she doubted that the creature would be a threat to them at this point.

"Sean Blackthorne? I'm not sure," Tim said.

"Too late ... little witch." With that, the Leannan Sidhe died. The light went out of her eyes, and she was still. A moment later, her body collapsed into water and mist, joining the putrid water below the cobbled together throne.

"Holy crap!" Seth and Wanda were standing at the entrance, now. "What the hell was that thing?" They walked forward together, joining the others. "Looks like you guys had a lot more excitement than we did. All we found as some crappy little hovel in the hedge maze, or what's left of it."

Tim shook his head. "We can talk about it back at the store. I think we're done here. I'm not picking up anything else; are you, Staci?" She shook her head; whatever magical signature she had been reading before, it was gone now. And if nothing had come after them after the ruckus they had caused during the fighting, then it probably meant that there was nothing else here. Or, if there had been, it was gone now. "Good. Let's get back to the car, get cleaned up, and get back to town."

The adrenaline finally draining from her system, Staci felt a wave of fatigue sweep over her. The bookstore and coffee sounded like a very good idea, and wiped any further questions from her mind for the moment.

"He said not yet," the Aufhocker hissed, one hand on the Drude's shoulder. The Drude flung it off, violently; the Aufhocker restrained the urge to slap it into a tree. When the Gate had been closed, they had been left on this side of it. With no way to get back, it had been a perilous, thin living, until Erdmann came. The Aufhocker could not afford to alienate any creature at this point, and could not afford for Erdmann to think the Aufhocker wasn't being cooperative. They had all seen what happened to anyone or anything that tried to cross Erdmann; the results were ... messy.

"But I am *hungry,*" the Drude grated. He sounded like a creaking gate. "And they are right there. Young ones, too ... " The Aufhocker resisted another urge to slap him. Fortunately. Because before *he* could answer, an enormous presence loomed suddenly behind him.

"Now is not the time," Erdmann rumbled. "If you begin feeding on those who will be missed—and *those will be missed*—the Alver will certainly come hunting for us. The Leannan Sidhe served her purpose. Continue with the preparations as we discussed. Soon... this place will be safe, for all of us. But not yet."

CHAPTER ELEVEN

The meeting back at the bookstore turned out to create more questions than it answered. Seth had immediately hit the books, trying to look up all the mythology he could on the Leannan Sidhe to try to get a handle on their behavior. Wanda did her best to sarcastically crack jokes at whatever theories Seth came up with. Beth mostly had fallen back into waitress-mode; she listened and kept herself busy by making sure everyone had enough coffee, no matter how many times Tim told her it wasn't necessary. That left it to Tim and Staci to actually debate and try to figure out what the hell had been going on at the Blackthorne mansion.

Some parts of the entire situation made sense. The Leannan Sidhe had thrown her chips in with Sean Blackthorne, to use the town as a feeding ground under Blackthorne control when Sean was making his bid for power. Whether she knew that, with Sean's plan to basically turn the town into a diseased hell on earth, she wouldn't be getting much in the way of "nutrition"—since she fed on creativity and inspiration—was debatable. It was pretty clear she had found herself stuck on this side of the Gate when Staci had destroyed it. For whatever reason—maybe because she feared Staci and Tim, or Fairgrove once they had moved in—she hadn't been able to hunt properly, and had retreated to the mansion. The Huntsmen and whatever that frog creature was—Seth said it might have been some sort of Japanese demon, or something—had probably thrown in with the Sidhe for protection, or maybe they had been enslaved by her with whatever power she had left. Or, maybe, given that they were by their nature servants, they had simply attached themselves to her for lack of any better master.

The parts that didn't make sense were infinitely more maddening. Namely, everything that the Leannan Sidhe had said. About "refusing an alliance" and it "being too late." An alliance with who, or what? Surely something like *that* creature would have been given the boot by Fairgrove if it had turned up at the front door. And what was too late? Granted, the monster was certainly insane; starving for that long and cut off from Underhill, Tim had said that it was actually surprising that she had been alive at all. Were they just the ravings of a dying Fey? She had seemed fixated with Staci, as well. Given what Ian Ironoak had said, and the attack in the alley, *that* most of all had left Staci feeling uneasy. The last piece that didn't quite fit was what Wanda and Seth had found in the maze.

Wanda had been the most descriptive about what they'd found. "It looked like something had . . . well, torn right through the hedges. I mean, they were *really* overgrown, to the point where you could hardly tell where the paths had been. But there was that one clear trail, and it went right to the heart of the maze. The fountain that had been there—the one that you told us about, Staci—was completely destroyed. All of the stone, from the fountain and the slabs on the ground, had been turned into a kind of . . . I don't know, hut? It had to be magic that did it, too; I don't know how a person could have lifted some of those pieces, much less arrange them. Maybe that Sidhe before she moved into the mansion? Although she didn't strike me as the kind of creature that would be hefting slabs of stone around."

"There's something off about it, though," Seth had said. "Besides, you know, all the obvious stuff."

Tim had raised an eyebrow. "Care to enlighten us, Seth?"

Seth gestured helplessly. "There wasn't anything that suggested that someone lived in it. No traces of fire, or garbage, or bedding. No . . . 'food' scraps. It was more like a bus stop than anything else, just a basic shelter from rain. Someone using magic wouldn't have needed to expend all of the energy needed to build that thing just to stay out of the rain, would they?"

That had started Wanda and Seth arguing in circles, and Staci's brain to spinning. *Why couldn't this be like the movies, where the bad guy monologues and gives away his entire damned scheme?* Eventually, Tim and Staci had moved off from the others a little bit to talk. As soon as Tim was away from the others, Staci could tell that he was concerned.

"This is all pointing to something. Or nothing at all. We've got a lot of different puzzle pieces; they could either be part of the same puzzle, or a jumble from a bunch of different ones. The not knowing is the worst part of any of this. And it might just be what does us in." Staci had never heard Tim sound helpless before, and it took her aback.

"Is there anyone we could go to for help on this? Fairgrove might—"

"—might be a part of the problem." He looked up to meet her eyes. The steel had come back into his voice; not towards her, more it was his resolve coming back to him. "Who else knew that we were going to the mansion? That illusion that you ran into? That takes energy, effort, and preparation. Something that Leannan Sidhe hardly looked capable of." He sighed, then shook his heads. "I'm not saying that Ian had a part in that little ambush. But something is not adding up with how it played out. And I don't trust Ian not to be manipulating us; he's an elf, after all."

"Well, let me play devil's advocate," Staci said after a second. "Kind of. The Leannan Sidhe could have set up that illusion while she was still strong, and it certainly fit in with the image she had of herself when I first saw her. But jeeze, Tim, wouldn't you think that Ian would have *checked out the mansion* before he moved his people wholesale into the town? He could very well have known she was there and just not bothered to tell us about it." She chewed on her lower lip. "I dunno, maybe he felt sorry for her?"

Tim gave her a long and measuring look. "That's another possibility. Either way, I'm not certain that we can count on Ian as an ally. He may not be working against us, but that doesn't mean he's working with us, either."

The rest of the meeting wasn't terribly productive. Eventually, even chugging down copious amounts of coffee wasn't enough to keep all of them energized and arguing in circles. They said their goodbyes, and groups split off to see each other home and make sure everyone was safe. Tim dropped Staci off again. As she was getting out of the car, he caught her arm for a moment. "Keep your wits about you, Staci. We're in unknown territory, here. Don't take anything for granted."

"Okay, Tim." He nodded once, then let her go. After getting inside her house, she promptly marched upstairs, dropped face first onto her bed, and fell asleep. Her dreams were troubled, and she slept fitfully the entire night.

The next two days passed without incident. The group met up at the bookstore in the morning—Beth was working both days, so she was absent—and went through their usual routine before splitting up. Wanda and Seth were continuing their training at Fairgrove, while Staci and Tim focused on magecraft. Specifically, Tim wanted to help Staci work on managing her energy more efficiently, and to build up her reserves. Getting caught on an "empty tank" once had been more than enough for her. And then . . . she realized with a shock that this was August and school was going to start in less than four weeks. How was she going to fit everything in with school? Tim had only offered that she would, "figure it out, and prioritize."

This is Silence, she reminded herself. *How challenging can their classes be?* But then . . . once she graduated, wouldn't Dad expect her to go off to college somewhere? *Maybe not. I bet my Wicked Stepmother would be perfectly happy to save all the money he'd spend on college for her Darling Baby. . . .* But you couldn't make a living being a mage, now, could you? So . . . what was she going to do? Become a waitress like Beth? Work in Tim's store? Could Tim even afford an employee?

When she had asked Tim, he had only said that they "would cross that bridge when they came to it." Maddening! It might seem like magic was what her entire life was about, now, but she still had to plan ahead for the future. Didn't she? How had Tim gone through his life as a mage, anyways? He never talked about his past; the first glimpses that Staci had had of it were when Ian Ironoak had made some cryptic references to stuff Tim had done. And Tim had clamped that down like a bear trap.

One thing at a time, girl. You can drive yourself up a wall worrying about next year after *you don't have dead people, Fey, and who knows what trying to eat you for breakfast.*

"One thing at a time" went right the hell out the window the morning of the third day after the mansion. She had just finished breakfast when someone had knocked at the door.

"I've got it, Mom." Staci had stood up from the kitchen table, still groggy, and opened the door. And there was David, looking like a guilty puppy and trying to tug at her heartstrings.

Staci didn't move, and hardly breathed. She was torn between being pissed off and being giddy with excitement. Her mother saved her for a few moments.

"Oh, good morning! I'll leave you two to talk; I need to get some makeup on before I head out for work, anyways."

There was probably the most uncomfortable pause in the history of teenage interaction. "So . . . do you want to come in for a second? Or stand out there awkwardly on my porch?"

David started. "Right! Yeah, um, thanks." He shifted from one foot to the other, and she realized she was blocking the doorway and moved aside. He edged past her and into the living room, but didn't sit down. "I wanted to talk. That's why I came here. To, you know, talk. About stuff."

"Good start," she said sarcastically. On the one hand, she was still supremely pissed off at David. How could she trust him, after hiding the fact that he was a mage from her? On the other . . . she really *did* like him, and hadn't she been doing the same to him? But that was different; he had known she was a mage, and decided not to share with her, whereas she hadn't known about him, and had hidden what she was to try to keep him safe. It was a stupid situation and that just made her more mad at him, for whatever reason.

"Listen, I'm sorry I didn't tell you sooner. I wasn't trying to pull something over on you, or anything like that. I was just . . . well, I don't know, curious."

That brought Staci up short. "Curious about *what*, exactly?"

He fidgeted uneasily. "What it was like for someone that wasn't born into this. How you dealt with it. Again, it's kind of rude to 'out' someone that's in the broom closet. But . . . the only other people I've known that were involved with magic were either elves, my parents, or kids just like me; born into it, comfortable with it. You're different."

Irritation won over good intentions. "Oh, I am so done with people telling me I'm different. I'm sick of it."

He actually backed up a step, waving his hands at her. "Hey, I'm sorry, okay? This isn't exactly easy for me, either. I'm not trying to get into it here. I just wanted to apologize . . . and I had something else to tell you."

All sympathy she might have had for David in that moment evaporated. Staci had a sick feeling in her stomach about what might come next. *Of course he wasn't just coming here to try to make up with you, dummy. It's always something; defeating dark forces, helping in a crusade against evil, or just elf crap. I'm going to assume "elf crap" for this one.*

"Fairgrove knows about what happened at the mansion. Seth was doing some research in the libraries, and asked some questions. It wasn't hard to piece things together and then ask him the right questions."

"So, you grilled my friend and now . . . what? I'm up for questioning?"

"What? No, nothing like that." David seemed offended at that. "I came here because I just wanted to give you a heads up, let you know that Fairgrove was looking into it. So far, they've got nothing; at least nothing more than Seth let on that you guys knew."

"Great. So, the elves know nothing about what's going on. Let me guess; they're 'looking into it'? Which means we can expect some sort of answer in a decade or so."

David started to become exasperated himself. "I didn't say that they know *nothing*. It's just that they don't know why things went down like that at the mansion. What caused it." Staci had her arms crossed in front of her chest, waiting. David studied her for a moment, sighed, and then went for the exit. "Listen, I know you've got a beef with elves. Whatever happened in the past . . . it wasn't Ian, it wasn't Caradoc, and it wasn't Branwen. It wasn't me, either."

"I know that," she not quite snapped at him, then immediately felt guilty about it.

That seemed to seal things for David. He shook his head. "Like it or not, Fairgrove is here to stay. It'd be better if we all worked together. That's all I'm saying, Staci."

Like it or not? I'll have to go with a very emphatic "not."

"Right." She didn't have any comebacks to that, at least not any that weren't mean-spirited; a good chunk of the anger and annoyance she had been holding onto had fled at some point in the conversation, and she was having trouble finding reasons to get angry, at least at that moment. "Is there anything else?"

"I guess not. I'll see you later, Staci." David turned and left. A part of Staci wanted to catch him before he was too far down the road, apologize, and try to talk things out a little more. A rather big part, actually. But she didn't get the chance. After standing in her living room silently for a few moments, stewing with her own conflicting feelings and thoughts, there was a knock at the door.

Staci almost skipped to the door. *He came back!* When she reached the kitchen, her hopes deflated, and were almost immediately replaced with worry; Wanda was on the porch, and she looked like hell. "Wanda? Hey, come in." She opened the door, and Wanda slowly walked forward. Her friend looked like she hadn't slept or showered; she had bags under her eyes, was more pale than usual, and her hair was a mess.

"Was that David? What was he doing here?"

"David? Oh, nothing. Just . . . filling me in on a few things. And shut up, I know how your mind works." Wanda only grunted in reply, then sat down at the kitchen table. "You look like hammered crap. Let me get us some coffee, then we'll talk." Staci picked out the two biggest mugs that the house had and filled both to the brim with fresh coffee. It wasn't as good as Tim's, but it still had enough caffeine to perk up an elephant. She added a little cream and sugar to her own, but left Wanda's black, the way she liked it. "Here," she said, setting the steaming mugs down as she sat across from her friend.

"Thanks." They were silent for a good minute, Wanda staring into her mug and Staci trying not to stare at Wanda. "I think something is up with my family."

"What do you mean?" Wanda didn't talk too much about her family; she seemed to prefer treating them as a completely separate part of her life, distinct and unable to intrude on the part that centered around her friends and the book store.

"They're religious. Like, in a *big* way. God-botherers, all of them. They've always been that way, so that part isn't new. If you couldn't tell . . . I'm not. That's always bothered them, but the last few years they haven't tried to drag me into the fold and wash me in the blood of the lamb anymore; it's just been a sort of passive disapproval concerning my spiritual life. Something has changed." Staci nodded, deciding to not interrupt and just let Wanda talk. There was another pause for a minute as both of them started to sip from their mugs. "Dad has started dragging everyone to church. Not our usual one. The *bad* one."

There were two churches in Silence. The Blood of Jesus World Missionary Church was, unequivocally, the *bad* church out of the two. They weren't strictly denominational, if only so they could denounce every denomination. "Born again" with a very heavy Old Testament feel, the congregation had always been rather small, and shrinking. For good reason; the preacher's sermons often took a vaguely racist and homophobic slant, if not quite crossing into open hate speech territory. Most people in town ignored "that church" since they largely kept to themselves; the congregation and the preacher didn't mingle or interact with Silence at large much at all, which seemed to suit everyone just fine.

"*What?* Why the hell would he want to go to that place? Those people are sick."

"I don't know. One day he just started going, and after that the rest of the family came with him. Now they've got their eyes set on 'converting' me, or something. It doesn't stop. Every second I'm around them, it's Bible verses and bullying." She half-sobbed, steadied herself, and then took a sip of coffee before continuing. "It's wearing me out, Staci. I don't have a job, I don't have anywhere else to go, and even if I did, legally they've got a leash on me until I'm eighteen."

"I can only imagine." Staci leaned across the table, putting her hand on one of Wanda's. "What can I do to help? Other than getting them to disown you and throwing you out, that is, since that doesn't seem to be on the table."

A sort of frantic hope came to Wanda's eyes. "The next time we go, will you come with me?" For a second Staci half-thought that Wanda had drunk the Kool-Aid, too, and was trying to drag her in. "For moral support? Maybe if you're there, I can convince them that we're going to do our own Bible study, or something, *anything* to get out of going back."

Staci didn't even have to think about her answer. "Of course. Though, I may just burst into flames when I walk through the doors.

Mage and all. If nothing else, that'd get you out of church for one day."

That got a laugh out of Wanda. "Yeah, maybe. Hell, I'd be a hero; 'Wanda the Witch Burner' or some crap. But, anyways. If I haven't spontaneously combusted—which, with the way some folks in that church death-stare me, you'd think I would have by now—I don't think you're in much danger. You look wholesome and perky as a cheerleader next to me."

"Perky as a cheerleader?" Staci picked up a butter knife and started fingering it, grinning mischievously. "You want to rethink that last statement?"

Staci had never been to the "bad" church; at most, she had gone past it on her bike a few times while exploring Silence when she had first moved to town. Her parents had never really pushed religion on her; her mother was too loopy and always had a vague and shifting Eastern philosophy quasi-spiritualism, and her father was too busy with work to devote much time to religion. As a result, she'd never felt much of an urge to explore organized religion, outside of reading bits and pieces of religious texts and Wikipedia summaries. Lately, her study had taken a more singular approach; some of the dead religions and pagan faiths had bits of magic here and there, hidden in legend and myth. Tim had curated quite a few scraps of scrolls and pieces of tablets that he put her to work deciphering.

As such, she was completely unprepared for The Blood of Jesus World Missionary Church. It was on the outskirts of town, the lone building in a field off of one of the less-maintained roads in town. It seemed to suit the congregation—and everyone else, for that matter—that they were out in the middle of nowhere. There wasn't a true parking lot; just an area where the grass was somewhat shorter that the cars seemed to congregate in. The building itself was something else. If it weren't for all of the cars parked outside and the people filing in through the entrance, Staci would've sworn it was abandoned. It was white clapboard with a triangular roof; it looked like it used to be a house, but had been repurposed at one point. Like the rest of Silence, the building was old; early 1920s, maybe. Unlike the rest of Silence, this building *really* showed its age; the too-white paint was peeling, with rust-streaks down the clapboard siding where someone had just hammered in plain nails to keep the boards from falling off the building. There were starlings nesting in the attic; or, at least there had been. There was messy grass stuffed into the ventilation slats up near the peak of the roof, and under the soffit boards of the eaves.

She could hear the din of worshippers singing and greeting each other from down the road; she had elected to bike to the service so that she could ditch out whenever she wanted. Wanda decided to do the same, just in case things got really bad. After discussion, they'd both come to the conclusion that suffering fallout from her family later would be better than going through more abuse at the service. The hope was that if Wanda showed up with Staci, her family would relent, satisfied that their daughter had brought a "new lamb" into the fold.

One time of this is enough for me; Sundays are for sleeping in or practicing magic, she thought.

Wanda was standing outside, shifting her feet nervously. She looked *really* different; she was wearing a plain white blouse and a longish plain gray skirt. With trainers. She still had her usual Goth makeup on, however. Staci tried not to laugh at that. There were two other parishioners flanking the doors, a man in a cheap blue suit that didn't fit him, and a woman in a lime green polyester pants suit, handing out folded single-sheet pamphlets out to people as they entered the church. As soon as Wanda spotted Staci, she looked instantly more at ease.

"Hey! You can chain up your bike next to mine, right around the side of the building. It should be safe, anyways. My family's already inside; this place fills up pretty fast."

Wanda wasn't kidding. The church was standing room only when they got inside; Wanda's family was to the right of the door, her father frantically waving the pair over.

"Girls. Preacher Kenny has already started." After that Wanda's father snapped his attention back to the front of the church. Staci had never met him before, and couldn't say that this was the best first impression she'd ever had of someone. He was fairly average looking, middle-aged, and dressed like the rest of the congregation; he looked like a bank teller, truth be told.

The interior of the church was just as rundown as the exterior, though at least it was clean inside. It looked as if the former house had been gutted; there were support beams where walls had once been, and it looked as if the bathroom had been preserved, boxed in as an odd little protrusion at the back of the room. There was just a sort of platform up at the front, with a plain table, without even an altar-cloth, and the ghost of a boarded-up door was clearly visible through several thick coats of white paint. Off to the side was something she couldn't quite figure out; it looked like a galvanized steel water tank for watering horses or cattle, with a rubber pipe coming from its drain at the bottom and passing through a hole bored in the worn wooden floor. Hanging on the wall behind the table, between two windows with glass that had been painted over with blue paint was a cross that looked as if it had been made out of a couple of railway ties. Hanging on the other walls were felt banners with cut-out letters made of other colors of felt, spelling out Bible verses. Judgmental ones. She could tell from the ones nearest her that the letters had been inexpertly glued on with white glue.

Despite the pleasant weather outside, the room was sticky-hot with body heat from the fifty- or sixty-strong congregation; there wasn't any central air conditioning, apparently, and most of the people were fanning themselves with the folded pamphlet. All but ten of the congregation were in bright orange, cheap plastic folding chairs lined up in rows. Staci and Wanda were stuck in the "standing room only" section. "Preacher Kenny" was holding forth at the front . . . using an old boombox and a "Mister Mic" from the '80s as his "sound system." It went very well with the '80s-vintage bare-basic keyboard a fat woman with '80s hair in a fluffy flowered dress was presiding over. Every other sentence that Preacher Kenny spat out was punctuated with a chorus of "Amen!"'s or "Hallelujah!"'s Every sentence contained the word "sin," sometimes more than once, and invectives against those who sinned, as well as explicit descriptions of the particular punishments to which they were destined. They hadn't even been here five minutes and already it was clear that if Preacher Kenny was right, the entire gang was going straight to hell. At least they would be in good company. *And the music is gonna be great.*

Staci glanced over to Wanda; her friend looked like she was doing her best to keep her breathing even. Wanda, out of all of their group, was the one with a temper. Even Staci was feeling her cheeks flush with anger at some of the crap that the preacher was shouting at them. She bumped Wanda's shoulder with her own, then reached down and took her friend's hand. That seemed to help a little bit. *I wish I had some of that healing magic that Beth has; that, combined with a water bottle, and maybe I could help with both of mine and Wanda's nerves. This guy is just batshit insane.*

"Now, my children. You must gird yourselves against sin. It's everywhere! Not just on your televisions, on the radio, or on your internet computers! It's standing next to you in the supermarket! It's in line with you at the bank! Picking up your kids from government schools; you'll find sin *inside!* Be wary! Look after your little ones, and bring them up right, as God wants you to! Men, look to your wives! Sin and the Devil don't sleep! They will snatch you up; in word, deed, and thought!" He walked back and forth with a manic energy, gesturing wildly with his free hand whenever he spoke. "You will have to be willing to exorcise your girls of the foul spirit of lesbianism! This modern Babylon wants you to accept new ideas about how you should live *your* lives! Multiculturalism! Living side by side with the gays, the sodomites! The sodomites want your soul, and want to abuse your children! Teaching children about homosexuality is mental rape! Putting science and *evolution* over your faith! We're in the middle of a war, brothers and sisters! A spiritual war! And are you going to fight, fight for your God and faith? America *must* be ruled by God's Law, and we must *fight* to make it happen! Our president is possessed of demons! Look at the gay marriages! Those are the Devil's work! Only those who are God's children have the right to equal treatment! Those who will not follow God's Law should not be allowed to use public restrooms!"

The congregation erupted into applause and choruses of "Amen!" and "Hallelujah!" Staci felt sick to her stomach. Looking over at Wanda, she could see that her friend was grinding her teeth and balling her fists. Wanda's family were oblivious; too busy nodding and adding to the noise. *Whatever I've got to do to get her out of this insanity, I'm doing it. Mom wouldn't have a problem with Wanda crashing with us, I don't think.* There were collection plates being passed among the rows of people; the amount of money that Staci saw individuals putting in was staggering. Not just one dollar bills, or the odd twenty; people were emptying their wallets into little wicker baskets, until by the time the basket reached her, it was overflowing with currency. *If I was chewing gum right now, I'd be half-tempted to spit it out into that basket. These people are losing their minds! What they're giving up must be their entire paychecks, for some of them.*

Preacher Kenny was a little more reserved when he started speaking again; the congregation instantly fell silent. "Now, brothers and sisters. First, I'd like to say thank you, from the bottom of my heart, for how giving all of you have been. Your generosity helps not only your souls, but also our church. All of that money is going to be used to help us expand our humble building. And, don't get too excited, but I've spoken with the Lord, and going on the radio to spread the word of God to the masses isn't outside of bounds, should we raise enough. I have no doubt in my mind that, with your help, we'll be able to do just that!"

There were more shouts of "Amen!" and Staci stole a glance over at Wanda. Her friend mouthed the words *Let's get the hell out of here.* Staci thought that was a wonderful idea; right now while the churchgoers were riled up would be the best time to sneak out; everyone would be too caught up in the hysteria to notice. Just as Staci was about to take Wanda's hand and make for the door, things fell dead silent again. *Damnit. Going to have to wait for "Preacher" Kenny to get them going again.*

"Brothers and sisters, I ask you; is there anyone out there that need the Lord's eternal light to shine down on them and heal them today?"

Evidently somebody had been waiting for that cue, because before anyone had a chance to move, a woman in a faded housedress had shoved an overweight, balding man in a wheelchair halfway to the pulpit. Brother Kenny met them on the way. "Now you will feel the *Lord's* power on those who believe in Him and cleave to His Ways!" Brother Kenny shouted, placing both his hands on the top of the man's head. He began ranting incomprehensible syllables as the man shook—or maybe it was Brother Kenny shaking him. "*Feel* the Power!" he chanted. "*Feel* the Power!" and went back into the gibberish. It was all Staci could do not to roll her eyes as the crowd began shouting again. This was supposed to be "speaking in tongues," but it didn't resemble any language she or anyone else had ever heard.

The faithful explained it by saying it was the language of angels . . . which was a lot of bull.

Unfortunately the woman and the wheelchair were blocking their exit. No escape yet.

Finally after what seemed like forever, Brother Kenny shoved the man back into his chair so hard he bounced the man's head off the woman behind the chair. *"Be Healed!"* he screamed.

Right. Here it comes. . . . And sure enough. The man levered himself up out of his chair, shouting "Praise Jesus!" and began shuffling around in time to the music as the woman sitting at the cheap little keyboard began playing something that might have been a hymn and might have been a high school fight song. The congregation ate it up; everyone was on their feet, hands waving in the air and shouting. It was a complete madhouse until Preacher Kenny put his own hands up again. *He's got them trained, that's for damn sure.*

"Is there anyone else among us that needs to bask in the Lord's healing light? Don't be shy, brothers and sisters, don't be shy!"

An elderly man wearing an eyepatch over his right eye shuffled to the front where the pulpit was. He lifted up his eyepatch with tremulous hands, revealing an empty eye socket. "Lost it in a car accident, some forty years ago."

Brother Kenny didn't seem at all fazed. "Kneel down brother, and accept the Lord's light!"

How's he gonna pull this *one off? Old boy got a glass eye in his pocket or something?* Staci got Wanda's attention; when this "miracle" was in full effect, they'd make their getaway. *She can tell her folks that I was feeling ill and she was seeing me home, or something.* The bigger problem of how to get Wanda out of having to deal with this insanity was something they could handle later. *Or Tim can. Tim has to have some ideas. Wanda's his apprentice too.* Maybe they could conjure up some sort of fake-Wanda to go to the church meetings.

Preacher Kenny put his hands on the old man; one on his forehead, and one on his shoulder. The way that they were facing, Staci could clearly see the empty socket, still. It was the same performance from before; shouting, the old man shaking or being shook, talking in tongues. At the last second, Staci watched as Preacher Kenny put the hand that was on the man's shoulder into his pocket. *Here comes the switch*. Suddenly, she felt the hairs on the back of her neck stand up. Preacher Kenny's hand never left his pocket . . . and Staci watched a brand new eye *grow* inside of the old man's head. There was a collective gasp from the entire congregation; some of them had knowing looks, others were clearly astounded. The old man blinked once, twice, and then a third time. He got off of his knees and turned to face the congregation.

"He's healed me! Angels of the Lord, he's done it!"

The congregation went stark crazy. In the hubbub, Wanda managed to grab Staci's hand and pull her out; they dashed down the side of the raving crowd and out the door without anyone noticing.

Outside, they turned to each other, both of them shaking, both of them breathless. "Did you see that?" they blurted simultaneously.

Then, they just looked at each other. Staci felt . . . sick. Wanda was white—or whiter than usual. "We need to get to Tim's," she said, finally. *"Now."*

CHAPTER TWELVE

Staci and Wanda were both breathless when they dropped their bikes unceremoniously on the sidewalk in front of Tim's shop. After getting out of the church, they had hopped on their bikes and pedaled as hard as they could to get to town. The problem was . . . the bad church wasn't just out of the way, it was freaking *remote*. Still, they hadn't allowed that to stop them. Now they were both drenched in sweat and doubled over with hands on knees, trying to get their wind back before heading into the shop. Wanda was the first to recover, and started towards the door before Staci reached out and grabbed her arm.

"What?" Wanda's face was flushed, and her makeup was ruined; Staci decided that she must look the same. "What are we waiting for?"

"We," Staci breathed, gulping air, "need to figure out exactly *what* we're telling Tim." She took a moment, steadied herself, and then stood up fully. "We can't just go in there looking like hell and screaming about a crazy preacher and eyeballs."

"Right," Wanda said, nodding. They smoothed out their dresses, fixed their hair, and did their best to make sure they didn't look like crazy people. The makeup would have to wait until they got into the bathroom. Prepared, Staci opened the door, and the pair walked confidently into the shop. It was completely empty, which while unusual for a Sunday, wasn't unheard of. What was really strange was the fact that Tim wasn't behind the counter to the right of the door; normally, he was planted behind it, reading a book and waiting to ring up customers, unless he was helping someone find something specific in the store.

Staci and Wanda shared a look. "Hello? Tim?" Staci looked around; she didn't get more than a few paces further into the store before Tim appeared from the back room, where his office and lab were. "Hey, there you are—wait, are you okay?"

Tim looked as if he had been moving every item in the store by himself for the last twelve hours. Exhausted, absolutely without any energy, eyes a little sunken, and moving carefully as if his muscles all hurt. He also looked as if he hadn't slept any. "I'm fine." He paused, looking the two girls over. "What's going on with you?"

Staci didn't let up. She recognized how he looked. "You've been doing magic. And a *lot* of it."

"Don't worry about it, apprentice," he said, in that tone of voice that told her she wasn't going to get any answers right then—maybe not ever. Tim had his secrets, and he wasn't used to letting loose of them. "Now, tell me what's happening that has you two looking so frightful?" His tone was neutral, but the order was obvious; shut up with questions and tell him what was going on that had them so stressed. Staci had more pressing things, anyways; she could grill him about what he'd been getting up to magically later. Right now, Wanda and her family were what was important.

"We speed-biked all the way here. There's something going on at the bad church. Wanda's family is involved."

Tim looked perplexed. "What, the quack church? Blood of the whatever and whoever?"

It took a few minutes, with Staci and Wanda trading off for the relevant portions, but they were able to get the entire story out. How Wanda's family had gone off the deep end, recently, and then started forcing her into the church. About how the entire thing seemed like a run of the mill crazy fringe church, until the "laying on hands" stuff happened today. At the end of it, Tim looked incredulous.

"So, what you're telling me is . . . someone is healing people, and it's a problem because you disagree with their religious views?"

Staci was stunned. "He's obviously using magic!"

"Point for the bright girl. Has he hurt anyone? Has he turned anyone away that needs this 'healing,' however he's doing it?" Tim held up his hands, obviously weary. "Listen, I get why you're concerned. Sure, he's using magic, since I haven't seen angels circling the building, but unless you find him using that same magic to *curse* people and harm them . . . is there some reason, besides your *own* prejudices about his religious feelings, why you'd want him to stop helping people?"

Put that way . . . Tim made it sound as if she and Wanda were the ones at fault. And she just couldn't articulate why the whole thing felt wrong and creepy and exploitative.

"The thing that, to me, warrants more attention is how Wanda's family has been treating her," Tim continued. "It sounds like it's not a good situation for her, and that ought to concern us. At least until we know more about this preacher. Which, frankly, isn't high up on the list of priorities at the moment."

Staci opened her mouth to speak, and then shut it immediately. The problem was, Tim was right. She didn't like it, but everything he said was true. Why had Staci become involved in the first place? To help out Wanda with her crazy family. Was it just that she had become so used to everything being a magical crisis, that that was all that stood out to her anymore? And sure, "Brother Kenny" was absolutely exploiting his congregation, but all he was doing was spouting hate and telling them they had to withdraw from associating with society. It hadn't turned into Heaven's Gate yet, and it didn't really look like it was going to, either. And even though he was getting people to throw entire paychecks into the collection plate, how much was a whole, working eye worth? It wasn't as if they could stroll down to the local doctor and get one of *those*, and it wasn't as if they could even get the kind of health care that would let someone who'd been in a wheelchair walk, at least not on a lower class paycheck. There were plenty of "pay to get saved" churches out there, that ruined the lives of entire families without any benefit. At least this one was "pay to *really* get healed." "Preacher Kenny" was gross, offensive, and hateful . . . but was he evil? All he seemed to want was the devotion of the faithful and a low-power AM radio station. As "world-conquering plans" went, that was pretty low-rent.

She and Wanda exchanged a look. Wanda looked . . . chagrined. Staci figured she probably looked the same.

"Don't get me wrong, you two. It was right of you to come to me with this. I had already checked out that church years back; just kind of a standard practice for me whenever I move somewhere, getting the magical lay of the land. This is definitely a new development, and something we ought to keep an eye on. I'm just saying that it may not be the emergency you thought it to be. Does that make sense?"

Staci nodded reluctantly. She didn't like it, but Tim was right. So far no one was being hurt, and . . . it wasn't any of her business what a bunch of religious nuts did.

"Now, Wanda, you've got a problem," Tim continued, turning to her.

"Tell me about it," Wanda said bitterly. "I—"

"Hold it. This isn't my first rodeo," Tim replied. holding up a hand. "You have only two options. You either do something so heinous in their eyes that they throw you out, which they are legally allowed to do in this state. In that case, before you pull that move, you'd better have some place set up to go first. The other option is that you put on the happy face and convince them you're now a member of the flock."

Wanda looked at Staci, who shrugged. "We have a spare bedroom, but we're not exactly rolling in dough. I don't know what Mom would say about another mouth to feed, or what we'd do if you got hurt or sick. She's pretty agreeable, but . . . "

"And getting hurt is kinda high on the list of possibles with us," Wanda admitted. Her brows creased with thought. "Isn't there a third option? Can't you guys, like, enchant them or something?"

Both Staci and Tim shook their heads vigorously.

"That would be using magic against their will," they chorused. "It's . . . highly unethical and puts us on the Dark Side of the Force," Tim added.

"It's the sort of thing that gets people like us going after bad guys," Staci continued. "No memory wipe spells here, I'm afraid; parking tickets would be a thing of the past, otherwise."

"Now . . . I *can* offer something that would get you out of going to church," Tim went on. "It's Wednesday night and Sunday morning. . . . I can offer you a part-time job that is Wednesday and Saturday night. It's not a lot, but I actually could use the help, you know your way around the shop, and that way you have two good excuses—Wednesday night you'd be working, and Sunday morning you'd be sleeping after the graveyard restocking shift. Move all your gaming stuff and anything else that isn't 'appropriate' down here until all this blows over and tell them you threw it out. Then you can act like you've bought the line."

"You can tell them that you and I started up a youth group or a Bible study or something, too. I'd hazard a guess that they figure I'm 'converted,' as well. I can sell that, if you need me to." Staci realized how thirsty she was, just then. Between the biking and all of the talking, she was absolutely dry. Luckily, Tim kept a few bottles of water in a mini-fridge near the coffee machine. She fetched a couple each for herself and Wanda.

The trio spent the better part of an hour talking over how to help Wanda out with her family, how to get them to think that she was "one of the flock," and keep her from going back to Preacher Kenny's. It actually occurred to them that a lot of her Goth wardrobe could just do double duty, as long as she didn't add the makeup or wear the miniskirts and leather. That cheered Wanda up a bit, though she was still loath to go without her makeup.

"Let's go back to my place," Staci suggested. "You've got some clothes stashed there anyway, and if Mom's there maybe we can start easing her into the idea of taking you in if this thing with your folks doesn't work."

"That sounds like a sound idea to me," Tim agreed. "Maybe your mother will have some ideas of her own." At Staci's incredulous look, he snorted. "She's not stupid, Staci. She kept herself out of mental institutions and off the street all by herself. You never know."

"True," Staci replied, thinking how *weird* it was to think of her mother as a resource, and not someone who needed caretaking. Even with mom being more stable these last few months, Staci hadn't completely gotten used to the idea of her mother being . . . well, an adult. "And I'm starving."

"No food here," Tim said. "Off you go, then, and let me get back to work."

Now that the weather in Silence had gone normal, or at least normal for New England, it was actually nice to eat on the faded round metal picnic tables at the drive-in after sunset. The food hadn't improved, but it was a different menu from the diner, so when Seth had suggested they all get something to eat, Beth had insisted on coming here. "Anything to get away from all the grease at Frank's. I swear, I think the guys believe my cologne is Eau de Bacon the longer that I work there."

Seth made a big deal out of smelling her hair. She yelped and then smacked him.

Maybe back in the day when the drive-in had been built, it was common for every teenager in Silence to have a jalopy of their own. Well, that was back when every teenage boy was able to take cars apart and put them back together in his own driveway, too. And when gas was cheap. So they weren't the only ones using the round tables with incorporated benches and metal "umbrellas" that had once been painted red and yellow. This was still the closest thing that Silence had to a fast-food joint; shockingly, not even Mickey D's had pounced on the chance to open up a franchise here after the Blackthornes were gone.

Seth commented on that, after they'd gotten their food from the hatch at the front of the drive-in building and gone to sit down at the one table that stood apart from the others. You could tell from the faint circles of faded paint on the cement that the tables hadn't been moved in decades, and small wonder. Even though they were aluminum, they were bolted to the cement—to prevent them from being stolen, Staci supposed. Addicts, maybe, looking to sell them for scrap; back when the Blackthornes were still in power, there was definitely a problem with people going into abandoned factories, warehouses, and homes to strip all the copper and aluminum out to sell.

"You'd think that there'd be a Starcafe anyway," Seth said, accentuating his point with a french fry.

"Until the whole will gets through probate, nobody's moving anything into or out of Silence," said a voice behind Staci. "The Blackthornes owned every square inch of real estate that isn't owned by private families. And every time something came up for sale, they bought it." Morrigan eased her way gingerly past the bolts holding the table legs down and scooted in next to Wanda. "Practically everyone down in the commercial district *except* Tim is a renter, not an owner, and I still don't know how he managed that one. Hi guys."

Wanda actually *squeed* and hugged the Unseleighe—or formerly Unseleighe—Sidhe. Morrigan smiled genuinely and hugged her back. "Where have you *been?*" Wanda demanded. "I was beginning to think they'd locked you up or something."

"Close enough. Dealing with lawyers day in and day out; it's a lot like being locked up, what with always having my ear glued to a phone or in a meeting. This is the first time in weeks that I've been able to tear myself away." Morrigan grimaced. "If it's not Fairgrove's lawyers or my lawyers, it's my lawyers with the police making sure that there is not a shadow of a thread of a doubt that I had *anything* to do with the... explosion." Her eyes shifted back and forth, and they all nodded. "I think at least on that front, we're good. I was so far down on the inheritance chain that it wouldn't make sense for me to try to bump everyone off."

Staci couldn't help but feel uncomfortable around Morrigan. The fact that she was an elf, and a Blackthorne *Unseleighe*—or former *Unseleighe?*—to boot, it all set off Staci's alarms. But, she was Wanda's friend, and had helped both Wanda and Seth in the fight at the mansion. Wanda usually had good judgment about people; after all, she had been the one to help snap Staci out of her self-deluded fog about Sean. She did her best to try to relax and act congenial around the elf.

"I guess that explains why we haven't seen you at all around Fairgrove Industries," Seth piped in. "I'm usually in their library, or training with Wanda. We don't really venture around the offices all that much."

"Lucky you," Morrigan said. "I would say one of the advantages is that the coffee is good, but, well, you know..." Seth and Wanda chuckled, and Staci laughed politely, leaving Beth looking confused. Morrigan understood and sat down between Beth and Wanda. "Elves are allergic to caffeine in a big way. Enough of it could put one of us in a coma or even kill us."

"She's right! When we were getting ready to fight at the mansion, I had the idea to hook up super soakers with a *killer* caff mix—" Seth stopped short and yelped in pain when Wanda kicked him in the shin under the table. "Hey! What was that for?" Wanda, exasperated, hooked a thumb towards Morrigan while she rolled her eyes. "Oh, crap. I completely forgot. Morrigan, I didn't mean anything by it."

"No, no, don't worry. There isn't any love lost with me and my family, trust me. I know it's a little cold to say, but more than a few of them got what was coming to them." She shrugged. "Anyways, there are some advantages to being around Ian and the others; gossip from the *other* side, as it were."

That statement piqued Staci's interest. She was tempted to pry for more, but she didn't want to seem nosey or too interested, so she waited.

"Like what?" Seth asked. Morrigan grinned slyly.

"Well, you know how Corendil and Mari are always at each other's throats in the shop? According to Idwal, they are *totally* doing the horizontal mambo as soon as no one's around. It's all an act to keep Mari's ex from coming after Cory."

Seth gaped at her. "You mean . . . elves have sex lives?"

"You've got no idea, young'un," Morrigan snickered. "Let me open your virginal eyes. . . ."

It went on like that for a while; who was seeing who, who everyone suspected was stealing lunches out of the work refrigerator, and all the usual "water cooler gossip." Finally, Wanda interjected, saving Staci the trouble.

"What about Ian? Whenever me and Seth see him, he's always nice enough . . . but it's like he's trying a bit too hard to be polite. Distant, like. Is that just a *Seleighe* thing?"

Morrigan didn't hesitate in answering. *She must have really been starved for interaction to just lay it all out like this.* "Ian is . . . different. He's not as much of a radical as Keighvin Silverhair, but he also isn't as conservative as the majority of the *Seleighe*. It's why the move here to Silence and whatnot is both surprising and . . . not. Most of the time he's annoyingly inscrutable, at least for me." She whirled a finger in the air at the group. "What's really weird about him is his obsession with you lot, and in particular your friend Tim."

"Oh? How so?" She tried to make the question sound as innocent as possible. It was the first time Staci had spoken during the conversation with Morrigan.

"It just seems like he's fixated on all of you, for some reason. Not in a bad way. I guess it's more . . . I don't know, protective? Sean and the others never really paid Tim much mind; looking back, they really should have, but I'm not sure that they even knew about his past. But Ian, he's definitely keeping an eye on Tim. I overheard that he even had someone follow him to that one weird church; well, the weirder one. Mortal religions are all a little bit funny."

Before Staci could react to that, Morrigan was carrying on.

"See, Ian doesn't really *like* the idea of mortals with magic. He can't do anything about it, but he figures that if you are without proper elven supervision, you're *always* going to turn out dangerous." She kept twirling that strand of hair. "He's . . . got a point," she continued reluctantly. "Back in . . . the Fifties, I think . . . there was a group of, I guess it would have been kind of a gang? Hot-rod gang, found out they had magic, I guess, and I think there were a couple with some Fey blood in them. They started out using the magic to punk people, they created a lot of UFO sightings and stuff, then got into some petty crime, moonshine running, that sort of thing, using magic to get away from the cops. Then, before any of the Seleighe could step in to smack them on the knuckles, they did something really, spectacularly wrong. I don't mean criminally, I mean magically. You know that story about the moonshiners that put a rocket on their getaway car and launched themselves into oblivion with an explosion you could see for miles? That's where it comes from."

"That's . . . intense," Beth said. Without missing a beat, Morrigan went on about other happenings around the offices, but Staci stopped listening when it was apparent that none of it concerned Tim or the rest of the gang. She did her best to keep her composure during the rest of the conversation, but inside she felt like she was on the verge of being sick. Tim had told them that he'd looked into the church a long time ago, and *implied,* even if he hadn't explicitly said so, that he hadn't done anything about them since. And now Morrigan had said the exact opposite, that Tim *had* been snooping around the church. Or, at least, so she had overheard. So he'd lied to them, if Morrigan was telling the truth. The question that bothered her the most was, "*Why* would Tim lie about that?"

The group finished their meal and made their farewells. Staci and Wanda retrieved their bikes and rode back to Staci's house in silence; apparently, Wanda hadn't picked up on the inconsistency about Tim's story that Morrigan had brought up. *I'll wait until we're cleaned up before worrying about that. Or maybe after we figure out our plan to keep her out of trouble with her family; keep her focused instead of having to worry about that, too.*

When they arrived at her house and parked their bikes, it was apparent that Staci's mother wasn't back from work yet. "She might have picked up another shift," Staci said over her shoulder as the pair made their way into the house.

"Is it okay if I call dibs on first shower? My makeup can be a pain to remove."

"Go for it. I'll start the coffee." Staci walked into the kitchen and started up the coffee maker.

"You know, some people might say we have a drinking problem," Wanda called as she ran up the stairs.

It took about an hour and a half for the pair of them to finish cleaning up, get dressed—Wanda used a spare outfit of her "regular" clothes that she left in Staci's room in case of emergencies—and sit down with some coffee. By that time, Staci's mother had returned home from work. Staci kept things simple, and naturally left out all of the parts about the "faith healing" and magic, but explained the situation concerning Wanda's family and the church.

"Oh, hell, honey, that sounds like stuff some of my friends had to go through," her mother said, looking distressed. She sighed. "I guess as the Bible-thumpers start to thin out, they just get nastier. Let me think about this."

She sipped some coffee and finally cleared her throat. "Okay, kids. If you *can,* Wanda, you need to just lie like a rug to your parents. Find some way they'll accept you can get out of going to church, and claim you're going to prayer-meetings here to make up for it. I promise I'll lie for you." She offered a wan smile. "I got real good at Bible-babble, both for covering for my friends and my customers at bars, and from all of the twelve-step meetings I've been to over the years."

Wanda nodded, taking a sip of her own coffee. "I got a job at Tim's shop; since it's not a Christian bookstore, they'll never go in there. So that should cover the church services. If you and Staci can cover for me and back me up on going to 'Bible study' or 'prayer-meetings,' I think that might be enough to keep them at bay."

"Oh! I just got another idea." She turned to Staci. "Honey, can you copy me over some videos of those snake-handler church meetings on YouTube? Then if they call looking for Wanda, I can play that in the background." Her wan smile turned into a grin. "What shall we call our group? It should be as creepy as their own name."

"Uhm." Wanda's brows creased. "How about the *Blood-Washed Prayer Group?* Just make sure you say Jesus a lot, or the FBI will think you're like al-Qaeda or something." She bit her lip and paused for a moment. "Actually, now that I think about it, *Blood-Washed Prayer Group* sounds like the name of one of the bands I listen to. It's perfect."

That elicited laughter from all three of them. After catching up on work and what the girls had been up to, Staci's mother yawned, stretching her arms above her head. "Well, I'm going to take a nap for about an hour. Wanda, are you going to stay for dinner?"

"No, thanks. I'm feeling a lot better now that I have a plan for dealing with my family. I'd better get back to them before too long."

"Okay, some other time. If you two need anything, just knock on my door." With that, Staci's mother got up from the table, gave both of the girls a hug, and then retreated up the stairs to her room.

The two friends sat there sipping their coffee quietly for a few moments before Wanda spoke up. "I just wanted to say thanks again, Staci. It meant a lot to me, you coming to church earlier and helping me out with all of this junk." She sighed, clearly relieved. "I owe you big-time."

"Don't worry about it, dummy," Staci said, waving her hand. "I know you or Seth or Beth would do the same thing for me. Well, something similar; as crazy as Mom used to be, I don't see her going all fundie on us." She waited, studying Wanda for a several seconds before she spoke again. "Is it okay if I ask you a couple of questions? About Morrigan?"

Wanda sobered. "Sure, I guess. What do you want to know?"

"You trust her, right? Do you think she'd have any reason to mislead us? Maybe, I don't know, if Ian were forcing her to or something like that?"

Wanda snorted. "If you think anyone can force Morrigan to do anything, you don't know anything about Morrigan. If *she* were in my shoes, she'd have already found a way to cut herself off from my damn family and live on her own while simultaneously making them think it was their idea and that she was starting her own branch of that crazy-ass church." Wanda shook her head. "Why do you ask? What's going on?"

"Did you catch the part where she was talking about Ian while we were at lunch? And Ian watching our group?"

"Yeah? I mean, we kind of knew that already," Wanda said, shrugging.

Staci licked her lips, picking up steam and talking a little faster. "How about the part where, while Ian had Tim followed, Tim had been checking out the church. In the last couple of *weeks*."

Wanda blinked. "Oh. Well, I do see your point there. Or maybe I don't. What are you trying to say?"

"I'm saying that Tim might have lied to us about not being worried about the church. That, combined with how he shut us down when we brought up checking it out more . . . I don't know. It bothers me. A lot. Why would Tim lie to us?" Staci frowned, shaking her head before meeting Wanda's eyes. "I think we should keep looking into the church and those 'miracles.' Tim is obviously up to something magical, and it's tiring him out. It's okay if he doesn't want our help on that," she lied, suppressing her own hurt at being shut out, "but I don't think we should ignore this. His judgment might be off."

Wanda looked skeptical. "Staci, I don't know. I mean, Tim hasn't ever led us astray before. He's had his reasons for why he does things, hasn't he? I mean, don't you think you're being a bit paranoid?"

"'Just because you're paranoid, that doesn't mean someone *isn't* out to get you,'" Staci quoted. Funnily enough, it had been something that Tim had driven home for her in their training. "After this last year, we already know 'they' *are* out to get us, and that we probably should be more paranoid, not less, don't you think?"

"I guess you're right about that. But what should we do about it? I mean, Tim told us to leave it alone."

"Yeah, he did. But whatever is going on at that church, I think it might be connected to the other crap that's been happening. That attack in the alley, the Fey in the busted mansion, and maybe even that stuff in the forest. We won't know unless we get to the bottom of it." Staci finished her coffee, shrugging. "The church is the one thread that we have to tug at right now."

Wanda sighed. "For some reason, I get the feeling that I'm not going to like what you're about to suggest."

"Sorry. We're going to have to do some investigating on Preacher Kenny."

CHAPTER THIRTEEN

It took some more talking and convincing, but Staci was able to bring Wanda over to her side. They *had* to get to the bottom of this. It might have been something Tim overlooked, or even something that could be putting him in danger without him knowing. As powerful as her mentor was, Staci had to admit that he was only a man, and wasn't perfect; he could make mistakes, too, and it sure felt like he was making one now. The day after the church meeting, Staci met up with Wanda and Seth—Beth was working at the time, which was just as well, since Staci didn't want her involved in this little rebellion—in order to go over a plan for how to approach the situation. Staci had decided that they would need Seth; he was the best researcher out of the three of them, and would be invaluable in figuring out exactly what was going on with the church that much faster. He didn't seem to have nearly as many reservations as Wanda had; to Seth, this was just another puzzle to solve.

"Now that we have the Three Amigos assembled . . . what do we actually *do?*" Wanda was still skeptical and uncomfortable with what they were doing, but she was going along with it. For now, at least. *Doesn't she see that we have to do this? We can't go to Tim, and I'm* definitely *not going to Fairgrove. For all we know, they could be behind this; trying to manipulate us so that we accept their "guidance and protection," falling under their control.*

"Preacher Kenny is doing some sort of magic, that much is for sure. I could feel it when he healed that man missing his eye," Staci said. She retreated to the kitchen, filling up three mugs full of coffee.

It wasn't as good as the coffee at Tim's, and it felt more than a little illicit meeting at her house instead of at the bookstore, but precautions had to be taken.

"Okay, there's that. He's doing magic; healing people. All that we have to go on that something is fishy is that he's doing magic that we don't recognize, and Tim has been checking him out again and hasn't told us. We still don't have much reason to suspect that he's doing anything wrong." Wanda accepted her mug from Staci, blew on the steaming liquid, and took a sip.

"There's one way we can find out," Seth piped up, also accepting his mug of coffee. "We could check on the people that he's healed. See if they're still okay. I mean, the preacher guy is a jerk, but being a jerk doesn't mean that you can't also help people."

"Well, you know what Tim tells us all the time about magic," Wanda put in darkly. "*There's always a cost.* I don't see Preacher Kenny paying that price."

"You're not wrong; there's always something that gets used up when magic is happening. And that was major-level healing he was doing; something like when Beth popped for the first time." She sighed, shook her head and furrowed her brow. "But, it could be that he's something we don't know about; Fey-blooded, maybe. Or has some other way of paying the energy cost. So, that isn't *automatically* suspect." She took a sip of her own coffee, then pointed a finger at Seth. "Brain-boy is right. We should start with the people that have experienced the 'miracles.' This whole thing might end right there." *Though I seriously doubt it. Too much floating around this one, too many coincidences. The timing is what's bugging me the most, I guess.*

"How do we find out about the people he's been healing?" Seth looked to Staci. Then both of them looked to Wanda.

She looked back at the both of them, then erupted. "Oh, damnit! I knew that you were going to make me go back there when we first started talking about this." Wanda huffed, crossing her arms and almost knocking over her coffee in her anger. "I'm liking this plan less and less every second, you know."

Three hours later, Wanda banged the front door of Staci's house open as she marched inside. She was wearing the same dress that she had worn to the church on Sunday. And she looked absolutely pissed.

"You both are buying me dinner. For an entire week." She snapped her gaze to Seth. "*Coffee.*" He started, then practically leapt out of his seat to get her a mug.

Wincing, Staci asked, "That bad, huh?"

"They made me sit through Bible readings. Three-hour-long Bible readings. By people who can barely pronounce their own names, much less the big words in the King James version." She pinched the bridge of her nose. "I wanted to run out screaming after the first time someone spent ten minutes stumbling over *Jehoiakim.*" Seth half-ran back to her side, mug of coffee in his outstretched hand. She nearly snatched it from his grip. She pondered it angrily for a moment, then downed the entire mug.

"That's rough. I'm sorry you had to go back there, Wanda." Staci bit her lip, looking down for a moment before continuing. "But you got the names, right?"

"I did, Witchy Witch. I made up some bull about wanting to hear about their stories so I could better witness to nonbelievers. It was hard trying not to gag on my own words." She passed the mug back to Seth without looking, who went and got her a refill. "There's only one who lives here in town. Seth, you'll need to do search-fu to snoop on the others. The guy who lives here is the one that got his eye grown back, Bud Brady. He's over on Chestnut Street, where we'd have a trailer park if the people who live in those shacks could actually afford trailers."

"Then that's our next stop," Staci said, taking a sip of her own coffee. "It's still early enough, we should be able to talk with this guy and still have time to meet up for lunch with Beth." She held up her free hand, cutting off Wanda. "My treat. The special today is pot roast, and that new cook is awesome with it."

"Good. I'm going to go change out of this ridiculous outfit."

"I don't know . . . I kind of like the dress. It's different for you," Seth said while looking everywhere but Wanda. Staci smiled and felt herself blushing for the pair of them. *I guess it's true that a person's biggest blind spot is themselves. I wonder when one of them is going to make a* real *move.*

"Seth, if this weren't my favorite mug of Staci's, it'd probably be shattered against your skull right now." Wanda's fuming expression made Seth gulp and stammer an apology. It was endearing as all hell, even though Wanda was pretending that she wasn't having any of it.

"Now at the moment, what I would really *prefer* would be to put on ninja suits and go snooping on good old Bud, plus steal all the TP from his outhouse in revenge for him inflicting his reading of the entire book of First Chronicles on me, but we'll probably get more out of him by pretending we're collecting for a charity or taking a survey or something."

"Taking a survey; just in case he actually tries to give us something," Staci said in a hurry, because really, she did not want the karma that would come from taking a couple bucks off an old man who couldn't afford a doctor or even an indoor bathroom.

"I'll print you off a survey," Seth said in a hurry. "The Arbor Day people, there's nothing controversial about trees."

"Cool. All right, let's get cracking. Wanda, you change. Seth, print out the survey. I'll . . . supervise," Staci said, grinning.

It didn't take long for Wanda to change, so the trio locked up the house and got on their bicycles. It was a nice day out, so they didn't hurry to get over to Bud Brady's; they still had plenty of time to talk with him and get over to the diner around when Beth's shift was ending. Their destination was on Chestnut Street, on the outskirts of town, near the woods. It was all low-income housing, run-down duplexes, and in Bud's case, a clapboard shack. His was in the middle of a long line of similar dwellings, variations on the same theme; beat up, various signs of disrepair, and poorly maintained yards. They parked their bikes, leaning them up against the rickety mailbox in front of Bud's shack; Staci chained them together and to the mailbox stand, just in case. She had an easy cantrip placed on the lock; with a word, she could unlock it, which might come in handy if they needed to make a fast getaway for whatever reason.

"Everyone ready?" Seth and Wanda both nodded back to her. "Let's do this." She took a deep breath, released it, and then took a step to the door to knock on it. She heard movement inside of the shack, and a few seconds later the door opened. She recognized the old man from the church; stooped over, bald save for a halo of wispy hair on the sides and back of his head, and two working eyes.

"Hello? How can I help you?"

"We're from the National Arbor Day Foundation," Staci said politely. "We're not here for donations, we would just like you to answer a survey about trees."

"Oh, that's fine. Would you please come in? I'd be happy to answer your questions, but it's getting a might bit difficult for me to stand for too long. I've got a kettle of tea on, too."

Staci exchanged glances with Seth and Wanda, then turned back to Bud. "Sure, that'd be nice. Thank you, sir." *The old fella seems harmless enough. I know I brought my knives, just in case, and so did Wanda, so we ought to be fine if anything untoward happens.* The trio followed Bud inside the shack, and it was surprisingly well-kept. The furniture, drapes, and carpet were all old, but clean and in good shape. Staci noticed that a bureau on the far wall was completely covered in vases and baskets of flowers, most of them with cards attached. Bud motioned for them to take a seat on the couch by the door, while he puttered off towards the kitchenette to fetch cups and tea for all of them.

"Would you like to start on the survey right away, sir?" Seth asked, pen poised over the clipboard.

"Certainly, young man. Let me just get these cups set out for all of you. Weather's changed again. Starting to get chilly out there." Wanda stood up and helped Bud with the tea, to which he nodded his thanks. Once everyone was situated, Seth went through the questions, which Bud answered dutifully although when Seth got to the one about "Did you play in or climb trees as a child?" Bud brightened up, and went on a long, very clear story about the tree fort he and his friends built over the course of two summers. Staci didn't pay much attention to the survey; instead, she was studying the room and Bud himself, both visually and magically. The room was cozy and utterly ordinary. Bud was much the same . . . save for a few scant traces of magical energy still curling around him. Whatever had been done to him, it was almost completely gone. Not enough to get a good reading from. And his eye was still there, so whatever the magic had been, it really had healed him. Staci felt herself being drawn back to the flowers on the bureau, however; they were the one incongruous element. She waited for a lull in the conversation, with everyone else sipping the tea—which wasn't that bad, either—before she spoke up.

"Mr. Brady, I know that this isn't part of the survey, and I don't want to pry, but I noticed you have a lot of flowers." She let the statement hang in the air, and sure enough Bud picked up where she had left off.

"Oh, those. They came in yesterday, mostly. For my wife." There was the slightest stammer in his voice when he said "my wife," and Staci could feel a pit growing in her stomach. Wanda and Seth picked up on it as well, set down their tea cups, and waited.

"Did something happen?" Seth could probably get away with being that blunt and gauche; he was a guy, and guys did that.

Bud didn't take any offense. "She passed two days ago. Just . . . dropped down in front of the stove. The doctors said it was a stroke." He sighed heavily, his hand involuntarily going to his eye. "The Lord giveth, and the Lord taketh away, I suppose."

Oh my god. . . . Staci knew from her researches that the form of magical attack often called "elf-shot" back in the medieval days looked exactly like a stroke. In fact, it *was* a stroke, only it was one caused magically, rather than by natural causes. "I'm . . . I'm so sorry, Mr. Brady. I didn't mean—"

"No, no, it's all right. You couldn't have known. The doctors say it was painless. I'm just thankful I was able to really see her, even if it was only for one day."

Staci felt . . . sick. *The poor old man . . . whatever spell was used, it gave him back his sight, but with a cost. Nothing is ever free with magic, and the power for this spell was his wife's life.* The fact that the stroke was probably the "elfshot" spell tended to point to something Fae in nature as the origin of both the "miracles" and the "price."

The trio all felt incredibly guilty and awkward after that. They finished their tea shortly and thanked Bud for his time and his stories. They didn't speak until they were outside and Staci had unlocked their bikes. Seth was the first to speak.

"Okay, that was rough. Poor guy," he said, as the three of them started to walk the bikes out of the ramshackle neighborhood.

"Do you think that we should . . . I don't know, tell him what happened?" Wanda's voice was plaintive and strained.

Staci thought for a moment, biting her lip. "No. We can't. He wouldn't believe us, and just think about how much that would hurt him? Finding out that he got his sight back and that it, *literally*, cost him his wife? It'd crush him."

"There's got to be something we can do," Seth said.

"I don't know. We'll think about it, see if we can come up with something." Staci sighed heavily. "But this seals it. Preacher Kenny is up to something, and it's *bad*. We need to scope him out, find out what he's getting out of this. How he's doing it." They agreed to put off the discussion until after they had finished lunch with Beth. The pot roast at the diner was vastly improved from how it had been a few months ago, and Staci kept her word and sprung for herself and Wanda. Despite the good food, the trio were quiet and reserved for the meal. Beth could tell something was off, but there weren't any openings to find out what. Staci felt heinous; Beth was on the outside of what she, Wanda, and Seth were doing. It felt completely wrong, but what choice did she have? She didn't want to get Beth caught up in this mischief, since Beth was dealing with enough already; finding out that she was part Selkie, training to harness her abilities, and the stress of living on her own to boot.

They ended the lunch stiffly, promising that they would all hang out at the shop tomorrow. Once Beth was gone, Staci started to plan with the others.

"We'll check out Preacher Kenny tonight. Wanda, you said that he lives at the church itself, right? In the office there?"

"Yep. I haven't seen it, but it's pretty common knowledge at the church."

"Okay. We'll meet at my place, say at midnight, and go from there." She paused for a moment. "Bring your gear." Seth and Wanda both started to protest, but Staci cut them off, holding up her hands. "We're just going to look. *But*, if anything does happen, I want to be prepared. This is just a look-see."

She waited, hoping that both of them would assent.

"Staci," Wanda began, sighing. "Don't you think it's time that we went to Tim with this? I mean, we know something bad is going on. What if we're getting into something over our heads, above our pay grade?" Staci hesitated for a moment; Wanda took the opportunity, rushing with her speech. "I mean, you said it yourself. Whatever magic that's being done, it's *major*. You're still an apprentice, and Seth and I are mundanes. Tim is the heavy-hitter, and we all know it."

Wanda . . . wasn't wrong. This was looking more and more like it was going to be something heavy and difficult. As much as Staci had improved under Tim's tutelage, she still wasn't anywhere near his level of power or skill. Wouldn't it be smarter to bring him in? If he had somehow missed the evil that was clearly going on—everyone made mistakes—the three of them could convince Tim that something *was* up. Then all of them could do something about it, together, the way that they had been training to.

"We could even go to Ian with this, see what Fairgrove can do to help." That was Seth's *totally predictable* contribution, and it was what decided Staci.

"If we find something, sure. But Tim already blew us off once, and can't you just see What's-His-Ears looking down his nose at us and going all superior about our *lack of evidence?* No, we have to have something concrete, something they can't just brush off. I'm getting really tired of being told *'you kids are just overreacting.'*"

Wanda and Seth shared a look, but Staci could tell that the matter was settled. And, damn it, why shouldn't it be? Staci had been getting the short end of the information, need-to-know stick for too long. She was tired of being kept in the dark by everyone else, because they felt like she couldn't handle it. Or for her own good. Or, worse, because it was more *convenient*.

No. This time, I'm taking charge. I'm not going to be led around by the nose.

They all rode together; first to Seth's house, then to Wanda's. Staci told them that she would be fine, riding alone to her place. It was a risk, given everything that was going on, but Staci wanted to be alone with her thoughts, wanted to stay a little bit angry. The ride home was uneventful. Staci brought her bike inside, locking the door behind her. Her mother wasn't home yet, so Staci left her a note saying that she was taking a nap; whatever was for dinner would keep until later. She would need her rest for tonight. She flopped onto her bed with her clothes still on, and was asleep almost immediately. Tim had taught her how to catch a cat nap almost anywhere; mages needed all the energy they could get.

Staci woke up at 11:30 to two group texts on her phone; Wanda and Seth were both on their way. She washed her face, had a quick bite from the leftover dinner that her mother had put in the refrigerator for her, and dressed in her "work clothes." By the time she was finished, the others were at her door, waiting. They were both loaded for bear, as well; their clothes were all earth tone colors, all close-fitting with their weapons and tools easily accessible but cleverly concealed. Wearing all-black at night could actually make them stand out more; the human eye liked to find patterns, like a human silhouette. Between their clothing and a little magic from Staci, they'd be able to blend into their surroundings fairly well, especially with the moon waning.

The trio set out very clear rules before they started for the church. One, they were just there to look. If anything started to go down, they were going to bug out. Wanda had made Staci promise that they would go to Tim's if things got too hairy, which Staci had done grudgingly. Two, they wouldn't go into the church itself. Trespassing was bad enough, but breaking and entering was something that would be a heck of a lot harder to talk their way out of. Three, Staci would do the actual snooping; Wanda and Seth would be the lookouts, and if anything happened to Staci, they would go and get help. That one was Staci's condition for the excursion. Wanda and Seth didn't like it, but they were already in too deep, and only put up a minimum of argument. Staci had a feeling deep in her chest that things were coming to a head. A sort of anticipation, and she wanted nothing more than to get it over with. Get that release, the knowing that a turning point had been reached. She wanted to exhale.

They pedaled hard, trying to get to the church quickly but without wearing themselves out. Staci had an energy drink with her, for just before they really started their snooping. They decided to park the bikes a quarter mile down the road, in the woods. It was far enough that they would be able to approach stealthily, but close enough that they could run to the bikes and make a getaway, if they had to. Seth would watch the road from a hide that he would set up at the edge of the clearing that the church occupied. Wanda would stay with Staci, and watch the back end of the church while Staci did her trick. They had radios with them; Seth had set them up with a vibrate function. If anyone saw anything, or they needed to get the hell out of dodge, they'd ping each other. Simple enough, which was the way that Staci liked it. They all knew where they had to watch, where to go if things went bad, and how to take care of themselves.

Staci had opened and downed the energy drink when they parked the bikes; it wouldn't do to give away their position with the iconic "POP-*hiss*" of a can being opened. She hated the sickly-sweet taste, but she knew that she would need the fuel. Once the can was packed away on her bike—wouldn't do to leave evidence that someone could use to find them . . . or for a spell—they started toward the church. It was a good ten minute walk, but it took them closer to twenty; with Wanda in the lead, they took plenty of listening breaks and made sure they knew exactly where each footfall went. When they reached the clearing, the pair spread out in a line parallel to the edge of the forest. The church was dead quiet; all the lights were off, save for the one in the back room that doubled as Preacher Kenny's office. There were no cars parked, and only the preacher's bicycle out front. *Good. All alone. That'll make this easier.*

With only a nod to Seth, Staci set off towards the church, with Wanda trailing behind. She cast a concealment spell on each of them on the fly, her words barely a whisper. Someone would have to be looking *very* hard to notice them, now. She felt Seth begin to set up his hide through the magic she had cast on him, and knew that he'd alert her and Wanda if anyone came to the church along the road or the front of the clearing. The concealment spell allowed Staci and Wanda to move a little bit faster, though they were still careful. Concealment did nothing about any noises they might make. The pair of girls came to the church simultaneously, making sure to stay fast to the wall. With a hand motion, Staci urged Wanda to follow as she started walking towards the rear of the church. Her friend was nearly silent on the grass behind her. They got to the edge of the church; around the corner to the left, Staci could see flickering orange light spilling out onto field behind the church.

Show time, mage-girl.

Staci dropped into a crouch, then onto all fours as she crept forward. She was conscious of every spot that she put her hands and knees, taking her time and making sure that she'd create as little noise as possible. Rounding the corner, she craned her neck up to see where the light was coming from; a single window, smack dab in the middle of the back wall of the church. *Good position to catch the morning light, come to think of it.*

She wished she had a periscope, or something like one—something she could stick up over the windowsill and peer inside without revealing herself. *I need to look into that. It would be useful for looking around corners too.* Was there a spell that could do that? Maybe something with a mirror, or a piece of crystal. In that moment, she felt a sudden pang of regret about not telling Tim about this. *Tim would have half-a-dozen spells that could help.* She shook the thought from her head. She needed to stay focused. She paused for a moment when she heard something... strange coming from the back office. It was a sharp, wet-sounding smack... followed by whimpers. *Hell! He's torturing someone back there!*

Staci sprung to her feet, readying a spell to blow open the window and hopefully daze the preacher enough so that she could save whoever he was hurting. Her right hand throbbed with contained energy. She set her feet wide, and was about to throw an arm up to protect her eyes from the window glass that would shatter before releasing the spell when she actually *saw* what was going on in the back room. Staci had a split second before the spell went off; instinctively, she thrust her hand skyward, wincing away from the release of energy. The spell—a *lot* of concussive force with some heat and light byproduct—streaked into the sky like a reverse meteor. Wanda rushed around the corner, a knife in her hand in a reverse grip, ready to fight. She almost collided with Staci.

"Wait!" Staci said in a harsh whisper into the radio. Wanda looked scared as hell and bewildered in the scant starlight. Staci held a finger to her lips, then pointed to the window. *Might as well let her see, too, now that she's here.* Wanda took a moment to catch her breath, then followed Staci to the ledge under the window. They both rose up as one, peering over the edge.

The back room was more of a bedroom than it was a true office. The furnishings were Spartan; a simple bed on what looked like an institutional frame, a writing desk with a few papers and books laid out on it, and an adjoining bathroom that Staci could just barely see inside a half-closed door. There was also an altar in there, against the back wall. Preacher Kenny was on his knees in front of it with his back to the window. But what had made Staci gasp was what he was doing.

He was beating himself with a bunch of thin branches or something. His back was already bloody, and it made her sick to see it. Each blow from the makeshift whip left deep tracks in his skin, and he cried out softly with the strikes. He stopped abruptly, panting and crying.

"Lord, they just don't know! The end is coming, Lord, and there isn't enough *time!*" He rocked back and forth as he talked, cradling himself with his arms. "They are all in so much pain, King of Kings . . . and I don't know what more I can do for them! They come to me, and I offer them Your Word, Lord. They're sick, and I bestow upon them Your gifts, Your divine healing! I hope it's enough, I hope I can save enough of them, Lord!" He took up the whip again, striking himself in a flurry of blows. "May my blood pay for it! Let them be healed, Lord!"

Staci muttered an incantation, to see if there were any illusions or other spells in effect. She was almost blinded by the light coming from the center of the altar. The Celtic cross that she had seen Preacher Kenny wearing at the service was awash in magic, radiating it out in all directions. And there was not a lick of magic coming from the pastor himself. In that moment, everything clicked for Staci.

She ducked down, pulling Wanda with her.

"We need to get out of here," she whispered. "I know what's going on with the 'miracles.'"

CHAPTER FOURTEEN

Staci silenced Wanda and Seth's questions, telling them that they all needed to get back somewhere safe, before anything else. Following Wanda's lead—and with a little magic help—they quickly made their way back to the bikes. Staci was still amped up, and the ride back to her house felt like it went by in a blur, all of them pedaling hard. Once they had parked their bikes and quietly entered—Staci's mother was still asleep, and it wouldn't do to wake her—Staci set about getting glasses of water for all of them, ushering her friends to her room, where they'd be able to talk at a normal volume.

"Okay, what the *hell* was going on back there?" Wanda had caught her breath from the hard ride, but was still covered in a sheen of sweat.

"Good question," Seth piped in, taking a moment to down half of his glass of water. "Someone want to tell me what you two saw, or should I keep guessing? He's a lizard person, isn't he?"

"If only it were that simple," Staci said, sighing. "It looks like the good preacher has come into possession of a major charm." Staci described Kenny whipping himself, and asking for divine help to "heal the people." Seth frowned at that.

"It doesn't sound like he knows what he has."

"Wait a second, are lizard people really a thing?" Wanda looked from Staci to Seth expectantly.

"Probably, somewhere, but Kenny isn't one, so far as I can tell," Staci declared, to the visible relief of Wanda. "So, he's got a heavy-duty magical item, and he probably doesn't know exactly how it works. It was like he was using the whipping and his praying as a way to, I don't know, 'pay' for the healing."

"Some faiths use self-flagellation as a means of penance, mimicking Christ or to go into certain kinds of trance states," Wanda added, then shrugged. "I studied a lot of religion in my effort to not have to deal with it. Anyways, I think that's his 'reasoning' behind doing this."

"How the heck did someone like Preacher Kenny get his hands on something like that?" Seth asked.

"Could have been something that's been in his family for generations that he only recently discovered. Or a relic that somehow found its way to the church. For all we know, he could have picked it up at a flea market," Staci said thoughtfully.

"Wait, does that really happen? Like, seriously?" Wanda looked incredulous.

"More often than you'd believe," Staci replied. She stood up from her seat on the bed to fetch some hand towels for each of them, so that they could dry off. She had been so caught up in her own thoughts on the ride back that she had hardly noticed how hard they had been pedaling, but she was definitely as drenched in sweat as the others. "There's a lot of magic stuff out there that's just been traded, stolen, or plain ol' lost over the years. Someone has a mage in their family, that person dies, and their stuff gets sold off or passed down to relations that don't know what they have. A lot of it gets scooped up one way or another by mages that are on the hunt for that sort of thing, but plenty of it falls through the cracks." She paused for a moment, thinking. "It's super rare for something as powerful as that cross, though. Thing has a big honkin' magical signature on it."

"I think I should go thrifting more often and rummage through some garage sales," Seth said with a chuckle.

Wanda waved her hand in between Seth and Staci. "That's all well and good. But *now* can we go to Tim with this? We've got evidence that something is up, and we know it's intense. We don't know if we should steal the cross, if we have to fight Kenny or hypnotize him or whatever, or if we'll have to destroy the cross. Hell, we don't even know what that would do." She looked pleadingly at Staci. "It's time to get help on this." Her eyes told Staci what she had left unsaid. *You promised.*

Staci sighed again, nodding. "You're right. I've never seen an artifact like the one that Kenny has. It might have protections on it, maybe even curses that could be really nasty. Tim will know what to do to get rid of that thing, or at least contain it. When we meet Beth at the shop tomorrow, I'll fess up to Tim about what we've been up to. And we'll go from there, see what happens."

Wanda regarded her for a moment, then gave a curt nod. "Good. Good," she said, looking around the room. "So, it's freakin' late. And I'm tired. It's hard work looking this fabulous, nevermind running around town all day chasing lizard people and magic doohickeys."

Staci blew out her breath. "Right. You two get home. I'll see you at Tim's tomorrow. I've gotta get ready for the inevitable verbal thrashing that he's bound to give me when I spill the beans." Staci felt a certain relief. She hated sneaking around on her friends and her mentor, doing things behind people's backs. Especially Tim. He didn't have to start training her. He didn't even need to save her, back when she was at her worst in the Blackthorne mansion, after destroying the Gate. But he had. He could be stern, and maybe a little harsh with her, but it was all because he really *did* care about her and the others. It was obvious that Tim had cared about people in the past, and something had happened that made him into the guarded person he was now. Finding out that she had been investigating Preacher Kenny without his permission probably wouldn't help that, but at least she was done with all of that. It was time to call in the big guns.

With that settled, Staci showed Seth and Wanda out, making them promise to text her when they were each home. Even with the cat nap that Staci had taken earlier, she was starting to feel the fatigue of the day set in. They'd probably train at some point tomorrow, and she was sure that Tim would give her a few extra drills to make up for her deceptions. She'd need all the rest that she could get. After getting relatively cleaned up, she got ready for bed and was fast asleep less than a minute after she laid her head down.

Staci had the heavy, dreamless sleep of the utterly fatigued that night, and woke up refreshed. Part of it was the knowledge that she wouldn't have to carry the burden of lying to Tim—even if just by omission—anymore. After she showered and got ready, she came downstairs to find that her mother had cooked a hearty breakfast of eggs, bacon (not too badly burnt), cereal, toast with jam, and a tall glass of orange juice.

"Whoa. This looks great, Mom," Staci said as she sat down at the table, realizing that she was famished.

"Figured that you could use your energy today. What, after all of the adventures that you had last night." Staci felt her entire body stiffen, and looked slowly to her mother. Her mother was wearing a mischievous grin. "I wasn't *always* your mother, you know. I was a kid too, and sneaking out to run around town is all we had to do where I grew up. Just be careful, and don't make it a habit, okay?" *One heart attack per day; no more than that, please, Life.*

Staci bobbed her head and let out the breath she had been holding. They ate together, until her mother noticed the time and had to abruptly rush out the door in order to get to work for her shift. Staci volunteered to clean up the kitchen before she left to hang with the others. She didn't mind doing that anymore, now that she wasn't the only one able to do all the housework because Mom was sleeping off a bender. With that done, she threw on her jacket and locked up the house. The ride into town was pleasant; the sky was overcast, but the temperature was *just* right, so Staci didn't mind the gloom. *I thought that the forecast was for clear skies today? Huh.* Well, at least this wasn't the *cold* and gloom that had prevailed here when she first arrived. It had been so chilly around here—and in June, no less—that she'd had to wear long sleeves and even a jacket. *Too bad I wasn't training with Tim back then. That kind of weather was perfect for the kinds of workouts he puts us through.*

She realized, as she pedaled slowly towards the bookstore, that she was putting off the inevitable tongue-lashing she was going to get when she told Tim she'd gone against his orders to spy on Kenny. She hoped that the fact that they *had* found something would soften things a little bit, but deep down she knew better. *Tim does things a certain way for a reason. But, damnit, he was wrong this time! And people are getting hurt. More than hurt, people are dying.* Would that old man have traded his wife's life for a new eye if he'd actually been asked about it? She doubted it. She didn't like that line of thinking. *One thing at a time. You can argue with Tim about the merits of disobedience . . . after practice.* She pedaled faster, focusing on the ride instead of conversations with Tim. When she arrived at the bookstore, Seth was the only one waiting outside. It was a little odd; Seth and Wanda almost always arrived together, since their houses were both in town and Wanda normally had to pass by Seth's house on her way.

"Hey. Where's Morticia?" Staci hopped off of her bike before coming to a stop next to the light post outside of the shop. Seth shrugged, his hands in his jacket; he had bundled up against the weather, too.

"Tim's not here yet, either. Then again, we're a little early. I still don't know how I crawled out of bed this morning; I'm beat."

Staci fished around in her pocket until she found her keys. Tim had given her one for the shop in case of emergencies or if one of them needed to borrow something from the shop for studying. "Coffee, hot and copious, cures all ills," she said, grinning.

Seth groaned. "You're way too perky for a walking dead woman."

"A well-balanced breakfast is what the modern animated corpse needs," she continued in an aggressively cheerful voice.

"And you sound horrifically like a cereal commercial." Seth glowered at her.

Just as Staci was about to insert her key into the store's lock, she caught a flash of movement in the corner of her eye. Wanda had streaked around the corner of the block on her bicycle; she swung wide into traffic, causing a car to swerve to avoid hitting her. She looked frantic, and didn't seem to notice the driver of the passing car screaming at her through the passenger side window. When she reached the pair, she jumped off of her bike, letting it clatter to the ground and nearly falling face first onto the sidewalk. Staci went to steady her, helping her to stand up straight.

"Wanda! What's going on?"

Wanda took a second to catch her breath, then turned and grabbed Staci by her shoulders. "We need to get to church!"

Seth, still half asleep and not registering the urgency, yawned. "Okay, now I know the world is ending."

Wanda ignored him, rushing ahead. "There's going to be an emergency service!"

Staci shook her head, confused. "Okay . . . what does that mean?"

"Staci, he's going to try to *heal someone* again!"

Staci's eyes went wide, and Seth seemed to finally wake up.

"Crap!" She had to think fast. Tim wasn't there yet, and there was no telling when he'd get to the shop. They couldn't wait for him and hope to get to the church in time. "Listen, we need to get there right *now*. We've got to stop the service, do something, *anything* to keep him from using the artifact again."

"How the hell are we going to do that? I'm not exactly the most popular person at the church, and people are set to get there in less than an hour! And what about the cross? We don't know how to fix it," Wanda said, desperation creeping into her voice. "Maybe we should call Fairgrove, or stop there. It's on the way to the church, and they've got—"

"No!" Staci hadn't meant to shout, but she could feel the tension crawling up her spine. They didn't have time to argue about this. She turned to Seth, throwing her keys to him; he fumbled them for a second, before looking up at her dumbfounded. "Get inside and find out what that cross is, and *fast*. I know a few things I can try to shut it down, but the more info we have, the better. Call Wanda when you find something; I'm probably going to be busy with magic."

"But—"

"Do it, Seth!" Staci and Wanda exclaimed nearly in sync. Seth didn't even blink, simply turned and started to unlock the shop.

"Let's go," Staci said to Wanda. With a breathed incantation she unlocked her bike from the light pole and mounted it. Wanda looked like she wanted to say something more, but she held her tongue. *We don't have the time to argue with Ian and the other elves, answer questions, and sit around for a week pondering the best course of action.*

Staci and Wanda were both in good shape from all of the training that they had been doing, but even so the bike ride to the church was grueling. They both pedaled as hard and as fast as they could, cutting through alleys, side streets, and even trails in the woods once they were out of town to get to the church that much faster. When they were finally in sight of the church, Staci thought that her legs were going to spasm and seize, and her lungs felt like they were on fire. Distantly, she hoped that she would have enough energy to even *try* to do magic when they got there. She calmed herself as best as she could, and Tim's advice and tutelage came to her again. Even when a mage is completely played out, a well-trained and smart one can dig deep for that little extra bit of effort and energy.

They were lucky. There weren't any cars parked outside of the church yet. Breathlessly, Wanda had told Staci during the ride that her family got the notice about the meeting through a phone tree call. Most people were on their way to work by then, and it'd take some time for everyone else to get ready and make their way over. It had been everything that Wanda could do to tear herself away from her family so that she could actually get to the bookstore and let Staci and Seth know what was happening.

"I had to lie and say that my phone was dead, and that was why I couldn't just call you about the church meeting, and 'bring you to the light.' I thought that it'd be easier and faster to come and get you and Seth at the shop than to try to sneak my phone out," she had said.

As lucky as the pair was, they still didn't have very much time. They didn't bother to lock up their bikes after they pulled up to the entrance, instead just leaving them out on the ground.

"Are you ready for this?" Staci was doing her best to get her breathing under control. They both looked frightful, sweaty and red-faced from the ride, but there was nothing that could be done for that.

"Do you have any idea what we're going to do once we get in there?"

"No clue. Try to talk sense into him, if we can," Staci said, shrugging.

"Talk sense. Into Preacher Kenny."

"It's that or mug him for the cross and then go on the run like Bonnie and Clyde, but with magic and more eyeliner." She took a deep breath, then let it out. "Let's get in there. No use putting this off and having the church goers show up right in the middle of whatever we do."

"And either ending up with people trying to dogpile us, or calling the cops." Wanda's jaw clenched. "Let's do this."

Staci turned towards the entrance, and pulled open the large white doors. Preacher Kenny was there at the center of the makeshift pulpit, going over several pieces of paper. The cross was there, bold as day, around his neck, still shining brightly with contained magic. He looked up when the teens abruptly entered.

"Oh, I'm sorry, children. I didn't expect anyone to get here this quickly. Just reading through my notes for the sermon, for after. Are you here to help set up?" He smiled warmly, as he set down the notes and came out from behind the stand.

Staci took the bit in her teeth, and spoke first. "Preacher, you're making a terrible mistake. Have you any idea what your *healings* are actually doing? You might be healing one person, but it's at the cost of killing the person closest to them!"

The smile dropped from his face immediately. "Child . . . I'm not sure what you've been getting into, but the good Lord just doesn't work that way." Now he was frowning. "What are the two of you doing here, really? Wanda, where are your folks?"

"No, listen to me, Preacher!" Staci said, raising her voice, but not shouting, not yet. "You healed old Bud Brady's eye, and *the very next day* his wife was dead! How many times has that happened now? Three? Six? More?"

The preacher's eyes widened, and he suddenly paled. "That's—not possible—" he said, but he didn't sound convinced. "God wouldn't—but I—"

"It's not *God* doing this, Preacher," Wanda said, sadly. "It's . . . magic. Just magic. Probably bad magic. There's always a price for things in magic, and the worse the magic is, the higher the price is."

"Magic is—it's an *abomination!* The Light of the Lord is all that shines in this world!"

"Oh, to hell with this." She pulled up her sleeves. "You want light, Preacher? I'll show you light!" She held her hands over her head and invoked light on them, as bright as she could manage—which was pretty bright, considering how much anger was fueling her right now. The room went stark-white, as bright as camera lights, and Preacher Kenny winced back a pace, cowered a little, and held up his hand to shield his eyes. Wanda had seen the move coming, and had turned away from the magic in time. When the light faded, Staci was breathing hard; her arms felt blistered and hot from the sudden release of energy. She looked down to see Kenny blinking hard. Finally, his eyes focused on her, and went wide. He threw himself to the floor in front of her, prostrate.

"I—I didn't believe! I'm so sorry!"

That . . . worked better than I thought it would. "Uh, it's okay, Preacher Kenny. I—"

"Lord of Lords, forgive me for doubting one of your angels! I shan't doubt again!"

Staci's jaw dropped. She swung around to face Wanda, who simply shrugged and tried to suppress a laugh. "Hey, this is your show now. Run with it."

"Damn it." She turned back to see that Kenny was mortified. "Not you. Uh, it's okay, Preacher. You've been faithful, and, um ardent? You were just deceived. That's what happens, evil things try to find good people to deceive them. That cross—it came from something bad. Where did you get it?"

Kenny lifted himself off of the floor, but kept averting his eyes from Staci. "A few weeks ago, out in the woods. I like to walk the day before a sermon, be alone with my thoughts and ponder the glory of our Lord's creation. I came to a clearing, and a glint caught my eye. A perfect shaft of God's light was shining down on the cross, and it was so clear to me that it was a gift, a sign, a message."

"More like a baited trap," Wanda muttered, loud enough for Kenny to hear.

Kenny turned to look at Wanda. "You're saying . . . that this came from the Adversary? That great serpent whose name is Satan?" He gingerly lifted the cross from his chest, peering down at it.

"Or one of the devil's servants," Staci said sourly, willing herself to calm down. *He doesn't know anything; it's like a kid finding a suitcase full of plutonium.* "Like it says, *a trap set for the unwary.*" She wasn't sure if that phrase was in the Bible or not, so she hedged her bets by saying "it" instead of "in the Bible." "But you know how many people you healed with it—so how many of them had deaths in the family, or other horrible things happen right afterwards?"

Kenny went white again, pulled the cross over his head and dropped it on the floor. ". . . all of them," he said, brokenly.

Staci truly felt for Kenny, in that moment. Sure, he had said some pretty disgusting things in the name of religion, and had some sick ideas about what God was supposed to be like. But he ultimately thought he was doing the right thing, and that he was actually helping people. He wasn't an evil man; dumb, and a lot bigoted, but not evil. "It's . . . not your fault. You couldn't have known. But we can make this right." She bent down and scooped up the cross. "We can destroy this, so that it can't hurt anyone again. I need to know exactly where you got this from, Kenny."

Preacher Kenny was a man with an obsessive mind for details. He described exactly which trail he had taken into the woods, how far he had gone to the footstep (he had an old-fashioned pedometer, it seemed) and exactly where, in what clearing, and on which particular stone he had found the cross.

"There's something you have to know," he added, just before Staci and Wanda were about to leave. "I—Oh, Lord, I'm so sorry." He cast his eyes down, and began to cry.

"Kenny, what is it?" Her tone was harsher than she intended. Staci knelt down in front of Kenny. "Please, tell us. We need to know," she said, her voice intentionally softened. *Not an evil man. Just some messed up ideas and maybe a head full of bad wiring.*

"The child," he choked out, sobbing. "I already healed the child. A young boy; he had a tumor—and—and . . . " He finally looked into Staci's eyes, tears streaming down his face. "Today, we were going to show his recovery. His parents are going to bring him, and show the people how the Lord saved their child."

"Oh, hell. Staci, you know what this means—" Staci interrupted Wanda with an outstretched hand.

"You need to fix this, angel," Kenny said to Staci, regaining some of his composure. "I can't rob that child of his parents."

Staci swallowed hard. "We'll think of something, Kenny. Stay here, and . . . try to keep everyone calm." The preacher nodded vigorously, then turned and knelt in front of the altar, staring up at the cross. Staci grabbed Wanda by the arm, and dragged her out of the church.

"Staci—"

"I know!" Staci said in a harsh whisper that she immediately regretted. "Look, I know. No matter what we do, someone is going to die. Either the kid, or the kid's parents." *Either way, I'm responsible. What would Tim do?*

Wanda pressed the palm of her hand to her brow as she shuffled nervously. "Shouldn't we, I don't know, tell the parents? Give them the choice to save their kid?"

Staci almost laughed, but thought better of it at the last second. "No. Now, just hear me out," she said, holding up her hands. "We tell them . . . and immediately get thrown in the loony bin. 'That's right, folks, your kid was healed by bad magic that's going to kill you. You can let it happen and save your kid, or I can destroy this *symbol of your faith* and you'll live, but your kid will still die.'"

"That does sound pretty bad."

"It's worse," Staci replied. "Let's say they do believe us, and want to sacrifice themselves for their kid. This thing is evil, Wanda. You can't use stuff like this for 'good.' There's always a cost, and it isn't just in energy, or blood, or even someone's life. It corrupts you, if you're not careful."

"This is a crap sandwich, Staci." Wanda stopped her pacing. That was a good sign; she wasn't panicking anymore.

"No lie."

"So, what do we do? The parents and the rest of the congregation are going to start arriving any moment."

"Which means we don't have time to go back to the shop, and get Tim to sort this out. Who knows how long it takes for this thing to start killing? We have to destroy this, right now."

Holy crap, I hope I'm doing the right thing.

Staci and Wanda left their bicycles at the church; it was rough going to get to the spot that Kenny had told them about, and the bikes would only slow them down. Staci had never been to this part of the woods before—the group's practices necessitated being as far from prying eyes as possible, and behind a busy church didn't fit the bill—but Kenny's directions were precise. *His memory is spot on. Must have been from those years memorizing scripture and hymns.*

Staci glanced up at the sky as a growl of thunder muttered in the far distance. The sky, which had been nicely overcast when she had left the house, had gone dark. There was definitely a storm brewing. *Crap. This is the last thing we need.*

In fact, just as she thought that, the wind picked up. They hadn't gone more than a few more yards before it was howling between the trees, and the first fat drops of rain came pattering down.

"Drowned Goth is *so* not my look, you know," Wanda said as she cast a glance at the darkening sky.

"Then let's get this done fast, so we can get back to the shop and get chewed out by Tim, nice and dry like." Staci looked around for a moment, remembering what Kenny had told them. "I think we're close. That looks like it might be the clearing over there," she said, pointing at an area several dozen yards off of the rough path. The pair trod through the undergrowth and bushes until they reached the spot. It was exactly as Kenny had described; a clearing with a round stone in the exact center of it. The area looked like it had been . . . maintained, somehow. Not by human hands; the edges of the clearing and the grass didn't have the chopped off look that tools left. But it was still unsettling. Staci fished the cross out of her pocket, and had to squint to look at it. It was shining brightly, to her magical senses, enough so that it even glowed a little bit physically. There was a stream of energy emanating from it, leading to the stone.

"This is . . . weird," she said, walking further into the clearing. "The relic . . . it's *feeding* something, here."

Wanda nudged at the stone with the toe of her shoe. "What, the rock? Is this some sort of ritual site or something? I've seen some pagan and Wiccan stuff that doesn't look all that different."

Staci narrowed her focus, following the magical energy flowing from the cross. At first, it did seem to lead down to the stone . . . but then it quickly snaked across the ground, to the other side of the clearing. Staci looked up, tracing the energy up to a figure that was far too hazy for how close it was. The relic pulsed in her hand, and she instinctively dropped it. The surge of energy raced towards the figure, and it snapped into focus.

"Wanda! We've got trouble!" Staci and Wanda both dropped into fighting crouches, with Wanda's eyes tracking to where Staci was staring.

"More than you know, lassies." It was a short man, no more than three and a half feet tall. His clothes were simple and roughspun, like something out of a historical reenactment for a living history 1800s town. His face was squat and ugly, with a bulbous nose and close-set, nearly black eyes. His eyes glittered with barely contained mirth, but Staci could also sense more than a little menace, there. "You don't have to worry 'bout little ol' *me*, though. I'm just here to have a wee bit of fun with you, that's all."

Staci immediately gathered her energy, and started to layer protective spells on her and Wanda. The short creature frowned.

"Not much for talking, are we? Time to play, then. Catch!"

In the blink of an eye, the creature reached behind its back and pulled out a long, hissing snake. And it threw the snake directly at Wanda. She shrieked, and caught the snake. As soon as her hands touched the snake, it turned into a crooked stick. Wanda gasped and threw the stick on the ground.

"Illusion spell. Once it got to you, the protections I've put on you negated it," Staci said. A chill went up her spine, and she snapped her attention back to the creature. Or, rather, where the creature had been. "Oh, hell no."

"What is that *thing?*" Wanda had recovered enough to get her Cold Iron knives out and ready.

"I don't know, but it's either really fast, or moving around with magic. Back to back, and be ready." They both turned so that they were facing away from each other, scanning the clearing. Staci heard a snigger of laughter, followed by the sound of leaves rustling on the opposite side. "It's trying to distract us—"

"Boo!" Staci felt a slap on her back, whirling around to find empty air between her and Wanda. Wanda, on the other hand, swung with one of her knives before she looked, and Staci narrowly leaned out of the way to avoid getting a slash to her chest.

"Careful!"

"Crap! Sorry, I—" Staci saw the creature's shoulder poking out from behind Wanda; it was sneaking up on her. "Down!"

Wanda dove out of the way, and Staci sent a blast of energy at the ground. It erupted in a spray of dirt and burnt grass, but the creature was nowhere to be seen. A burst of pain made Staci's vision flare white, and she felt fire rake her left side. She spun again, but nothing was there. Looking down, she saw that she had three claw marks going across her ribs, with a trickle of blood moving down her jacket. It wasn't deep, but it hurt like *hell.*

"He won't stop moving!" Staci swung her head back and forth, looking for any trace of the creature.

"Tell me something I don't know—oof!" Staci turned to see Wanda on the ground, nursing her knee.

"Get back on your feet and keep moving!" Wanda got up obediently, and started to move without any apparent pattern; anything they could do to confuse their attacker, keep him guessing would help. *I think I was channeling Tim there and using his Get to*

Work voice. She shook her head. A cackle of laughter sounded from the edge of the clearing behind her, but the source was gone by the time she looked toward it. *Okay, time to quit messing around. If you can't go after your opponent straight on, outmaneuver them.* Staci called out an incantation in a harsh whisper, her fingers aching as they traced lines in the air. She thrust her hand towards the ground, and an invisible disk of force formed beneath her feet. Concentrating, she willed the disk to rise . . . and so it did. Not too fast—if she lost control, she could hurtle too high into the air, or snap her ankles from the acceleration. She brought the disk to a stop about twelve feet from the ground. *Let's see the little freak play tag with me up here.*

She caught Wanda in the corner of her eye, and smiled at her. Wanda smiled back. "Brilliant!" She looked like she was about to say something more, but her eyes went wide and snapped to something behind Staci. Before she could react, she felt an object hit her in the back of her knees, and her legs went out beneath her. She slammed her side into the disk as she fell, and then the world was spinning before abruptly coming to a stop. Her vision was full of stars, and her right arm shot through with lightning bolts of pain. She rolled over, and onto a stick; it was more like a small club, being a little less thick than her arm. *That's gotta be what hit me*, she thought dazedly. Her arm hurt like all hell, but she didn't think anything was broken.

"Clever one, little miss! But you'll have to do better than that!" The creature catcalled to them, saying every third word in a different spot. Staci willed herself to get up, and dragged herself to her feet. *A target that's still or on the ground is an easy target.*

"We can't keep this up, Wanda," Staci gasped out. Her ribs hurt when she breathed, now. Not a good sign. She did her best to trot next to her friend. She noticed, now that she was up close, that Wanda had a small cut on her right brow. She wiped away the bit of blood that had streaked down her cheek with the back of her hand.

"If you have any bright ideas for how we pin this creep down, trust me, I'm *all* ears."

That was a damned good question. She had to slow down, think this through while keeping her body amped up and moving. This thing had a weakness. Not every monster or weird thing in the world did; that was the sort of crap that you saw in movies and on TV. But Tim had taught her plenty, and she had seen a glimpse of what real power looked like. Something that didn't have any weaknesses didn't bother with the cat and mouse nonsense that this creature was playing at; things like that just walked up to you and did what they wanted, unconcerned by whatever you might try to do.

This thing... wouldn't let them see it. Staci felt a tug at the back of her mind; she knew something that could help, but the pain in her arm and side blurred her thoughts just enough. *Focus on what you can see. Every creature has a trace of some sort, when you're tracking it.*

The creature kicked Staci in her injured side just as she was turning to face a different direction; she went crashing into Wanda's back, sending her friend staggering forward. To Wanda's credit, she stayed on her feet. *Trace... the cross!*

Staci propped herself on her elbows, looking around frantically. *Breathe, focus on the magic... there!* She let her vision go fuzzy on the edges, keeping her mind centered on feeling and seeing the magic surrounding her. The cross was a lighthouse beacon, gently pulsing from a faint light to an blinding sun. The same stream of energy was flowing out of it, snaking through the grass. It twitched around the cross constantly, moving from one side of it to the other. *The creature is drawing the power out of it.*

"Staci, it's a leprechaun! Catch the jerk and you can make one wish from him!" Staci saw the stream of energy snap to the direction that Wanda was, and then she heard a *thud* and Wanda cursing. The energy from the relic then pointed directly at her. *Gotcha.*

Staci flipped over, her hands crossing and coming up to protect her face just like she had been trained. She caught the tree branch on her forearms, and launched herself upward, grabbing hold of the creature's wrists. It stared at her, wide eyed and terrified.

"How—" it gasped, but Staci cut it off.

"Hold *still*. Wanda!"

A throwing knife sprouted in the leprechaun's neck. The creature's eyes went wide with the invasion of Cold Iron; the flesh around the knife curled and smoked, like it was burning. Staci released the leprechaun's wrists, quickly moving out of the way as it fell to the ground where she had been lying. She watched as the energy flowing from the cross guttered out; the cross itself had become blackened and twisted. Taking a few—painful, with her bruised ribs—moments to stand up, Staci gave the leprechaun's body a token kick with her boot, to see if it was faking death. That much Cold Iron, though, was enough of a guarantee; it wouldn't be getting back up to bother them, or anyone else, ever again.

"So," Wanda said as she limped over to Staci, peering at the body. "Do we get a pot of gold now?"

"I have no clue." She turned to face her friend. The gash on her eyebrow was still bleeding, and her clothes were covered in grass and dirt. Staci suspected that she didn't look much better herself. "How'd you know it was a leprechaun?" She took a small bandage from one of her jacket's pockets, and applied it to her slashed ribs.

"Huh? Oh. Well, the description was in one of the books that Tim gave Seth. It took me a minute to remember; I'm not as good at that instant recall crap as Seth is."

"Seth let you borrow one of his books? In what bizarro world did that happen?"

Wanda, despite having just killed a mythical creature with a single badass knife throw, managed to blush. "Not exactly. We read it together."

Staci blinked once, then grinned. "Well, it's about time. I thought you two were just going to keep mooning over each other forever."

"Please, shut up," Wanda said, sighing disgustedly. "Let's take care of this little creep's body, and then get back to the shop. I'm sure that Tim already has a rant all thought out for us." She reached down to retrieve the throwing knife still in the leprechaun's neck, and pulled it out with a grunt of effort.

"Right. You'll want to stand back a little bit. Don't want vaporized leprechaun to get all over you." Staci focused, drawing magical energy up into a tight knot in her chest. All she wanted was a minor pyrotechnic effect to burn the creature's body, not a huge fireball that would start a forest fire. As beat up and exhausted as she felt, she needed to concentrate a little harder to keep the spell from getting away from her. A minute later, all that was left of the leprechaun's body was a small, blackened crater in the field.

All of her concentration had been on the body for that period of time. When she looked up at Wanda, Wanda was paying no attention to her. Instead, Wanda was looking nervously at the sky.

Before she could say anything, Wanda spoke. "There's something nasty blowing up," she said, and Staci peered up through the branches to see that dark clouds had formed overhead. Big, fat ones, with charcoal-colored bellies. They were out of time.

"Damnit. I thought we would have had a little more time before—" Staci let the sentence trail off. Goosebumps rose on her arms and on the back of her neck. She felt like crap, from the fight and knowing that they weren't going to outrun the storm, so it took her a moment to piece together what was wrong. *There's . . . something here. Powerful and . . . evil!* She didn't have time to shout a warning, or even move. One moment she was looking at Wanda, and the next she felt herself hanging upside down. She had a brief flash of memory; her mind had been flooded with horrible imagery, of her friends and family dying in grotesque and inventive ways. She had passed out almost as soon as the images had started. Now, she was waking up.

Wanda was next to her, and Staci fought the urge to vomit as her mind wrapped itself around the fact that everything looked wrong because she was upside down. Her arms were pinned to her sides by thick coils of rope. Numbly, she noticed that there was a gag in her mouth; Wanda didn't have one. *They know enough about us to be afraid of me trying to cast spells. Not good.* By the weak sunlight coming through the ever-darkening clouds, Staci could estimate that they hadn't been knocked out for very long. Wanda was still unconscious, swaying gently with the breeze. Staci's mind sprang to action. *Whatever it was, it could have killed us. We're helpless. There must be a reason that it's keeping us alive. I just hope that reason isn't because it likes its food to be wriggling when it chows down. If I'm alive, I can problem solve. So . . . what can I do? Right now, wriggle my toes and blink my eyes. Wait, no. My right hand . . . there.*

Staci wormed her hand into her jacket pocket. If she could just get her fingers on her cell phone charm, she'd be able to activate the "panic" spell she had on one of the pieces. It'd be like sending up a flare for someone to see that she was in serious trouble. She had to be careful, though; if whoever was here noticed what she was doing, she was screwed.

At the edge of Staci's vision, she registered movement. A person . . . or something that looked like one, walked into her view. A middle-aged woman, wearing a dark trench coat, tied at the waist, with long hair divided evenly in the middle. There was a hint of trousers and shoes under the trench coat.

Her features...there was something wrong. They were too angular, too severe, like they had been carved into her. And her eyes didn't have the same glint of life that a real person's would. Staci could feel an intelligent, cool malevolence behind the woman's—was she even a woman?—eyes.

Another figure joined the woman. Staci looked at the figure, and then clamped her eyes shut as tight as she could, fighting back against vomiting again. She had only seen the *thing* for a moment. It looked like a wolf, a bat, a deformed old man, a snake, a really good looking guy...all at the same time. Her mind rejected the dark swirl of images, and her head hurt. *Whatever the hell that thing is, don't look directly at it again, moron.*

The two figures began to talk to each other in some sort of chopped, guttural language. It sounded vaguely like German, but Staci couldn't be sure; she was still fumbling her way through Gaelic and Sumerian, as far as her language studies went. The gestalt-image creature took a few steps forward, and a hazy appendage caressed Wanda's side. Staci felt everything inside of her screaming out to do something, *anything* to get that thing away from her friend. A strangled cry rose in her throat, unbidden. The two creatures turned to her, and then laughed together. *They're enjoying this. If I get out of these ropes, they'll have a hell of a lot less to laugh about.*

The creatures started talking in the harsh language again, with the human-looking one pointing at Staci. Their conversation abruptly stopped, mid-sentence, and the "woman" dropped her arm. Both of the creatures went still, looking off in the distance instead of at Staci. She wiggled her fingers a little bit more, and she could feel the end of the charm. She strained, and got the first piece under the pad of her index finger. *Two more...if I can just get contact with it, I can activate it.*

Staci froze for a moment. The sound was faint at first, but it quickly grew in volume until it was the only thing she could hear. Rhythmic thumps, very quiet initially, that were soon thunderously loud, loud enough to hurt her ears. Trees split and cracked open, sounding like screams and gunshots; whatever was doing that was knocking down old growth trees like they were toothpicks. The ground shook with every thump . . . and then it all stopped. It was just beyond where she could see, if she turned her head as far as she could, even a bit past where the pain was almost beyond bearing. All she could see was the shadow of whatever had been making the noise . . . and it was *massive*. A flash of fear shot through her, causing her body to break out into a cold sweat. *If the things that took Wanda and I down without even trying are scared of that . . . how much worse is it?*

Prisoners, captors, and . . . whatever the newcomer was, were all silent for several long seconds. The woman-creature was the first to speak, still in the same German-sounding language, all of her words coming out in a rush.

"*Stop.*" The new arrival's voice was alien and jarring. The consonants reminded Staci of someone slapping concrete, and the vowels were the low rumble of a coming storm. "*They speak English here. So, we practice English.*" The voice was low and quiet, but the command and sense of controlled rage were apparent. Another pause. "*Well? What is this?*" Staci took the opportunity to try to activate the charm in her pocket. Her fingers ached, and threatened to cramp, but she finally managed to make contact with it; the spell activated, and she could feel the warmth of it spreading through her hand and thigh. *Please, please, please don't notice that, whatever the hell you things are.*

Evidently, they didn't notice. The two creatures that Staci could see looked at each other, then back to the new thing. The woman-creature spoke first. "These two killed Dubhthach. We captured them—"

"*You were meddling with the townsfolk, and using Dubhthach as your lackey. That was not in the plan. And now these two are here. And one of them is a* mage." The newcomer spit the last word out like it as an insult. The hazy-image creature started to speak, but was cut off by the third creature. "*Silence!*" It was the first time it had raised its voice; Staci's ears were left ringing. "*You will dispose of these two. Leave no trace. I am leaving one of the troll-kin with you . . . to assist. Do not disappoint me again.*"

There was more crashing, and trees being knocked over as the creature—clearly some sort of bigwig to the other two—left. Staci could smell the troll before she could see it; it must have come with the other creature, since she didn't hear it arriving. *This day keeps getting better and better. Okay, once I get out of these restraints, deal with the two weirdos. Trolls suck, but they're vulnerable to fire. Gods, I wish Wanda would wake up already.*

"He said we had to kill them." The hazy-creature moved over toward Wanda again. *So, whatever that thing, the boss, is, it's a "he." Another data point. Also, whatever these two were doing with the leprechaun, that's not part of some sort of plan that they all are working on.* Something *is going on.*

"He did," the woman-creature replied. "But he didn't say that we couldn't enjoy ourselves, first. And that one," she jutted out her chin at the troll, "is too stupid to argue." *Uh oh.*

"Which one first?"

"The dark one. Let the mage-girl watch. More fun that way."

Staci felt a rising horror as the monster closest to Wanda bent down to the level of her neck. Its head—she couldn't look and couldn't stop herself from looking—craned towards her friend. It was a lion, an alligator, a lamprey, a spider—all at once. Its teeth inched closer to Wanda's neck, and Staci realized she was crying. *There's nothing I can do, I can't help her, please, I can't!*

At the last moment, the creature stopped. It whispered what sounded like, "him." Staci felt more than she heard the explosion. A titanic lightning bolt that left her half blind struck the troll. It exploded, scattering flaming bits all over that part of the clearing. Staci's mind went blank with fear; dazed from how wrong everything had gone, not to mention the lightning strike, she didn't know how much time had passed before she realized she could see again. There was still a bright after-image from the lightning bolt, and a part of her mind wondered if her corneas had been burned from the ultraviolet light. She was looking up at the sky now, which meant she was on her back. The clouds above were rapidly dissipating, and bright sunlight started to come through. The last thing she saw before passing out again were two shapes looming over her.

CHAPTER FIFTEEN

Staci's head felt like it had been used as a makeshift battering ram for a few hours. She came to slowly, wincing as she rolled on to her side, then back again. She had a cramp in her shoulder blade that felt like it was the size of a softball, and she couldn't get comfortable. *My head is killing me. At least whatever I'm lying down on is comfortable. Wait, I'm lying down!*

Her eyes snapped open, but her vision was still blurry from sleep—or flat unconsciousness, since she didn't feel rested and was still achy. She drank in details, what few she could glean upon waking; she was in a dark room, on something that felt like a couch, and a dark figure was leaning over her. Before she even knew what she was doing, she had conjured a blast of hard light; her palm and fingertips burned as the energy flashed into existence, blasting out as she jerked her arm upwards. She screamed, and the figure screamed as the spell splattered against the far wall. Before she could call up another spell—which she seriously doubted that she even had the energy for—the figure moved in close, grabbing her arm and putting a hand over her mouth.

"You're getting stronger if you can do that while half-asleep, but your aim is still for shit. Thankfully." Staci's eyes focused on the figure's eyes, which she could now see were surrounded with smeared eyeliner to the point where she looked like a raccoon. Or an Ultra-Goth with the full corpse-paint get-up.

Staci pulled her friend's hand away from her mouth, and then surged up from the couch to wrap her neck in a hug. "Wanda!" she cried, as both of them fell back onto the couch. She started crying.

Wanda finally hugged her back for a few long moments, then gently pulled herself away.

"We're at tall, bright, and pointy-eared HQ. Tim, Seth, and of course all of the elves are here." Wanda looked like Staci felt: her clothing was filthy, with dirt and bits of grass and leaves, her make-up and hair were a wreck, and Staci could see the cuts and some of the bruises from their fight with the leprechaun. None of that really mattered, though.

"I'm so *sorry!* I thought you were going to die, and it was all my fault!" She had to fight through the sobs to catch her breath, still holding onto Wanda's shoulders. "I should have listened to you and Seth, but I almost got you killed! When that thing went towards your neck, I thought . . . " She trailed off, and started crying in earnest. It had been horrible, too horrible for words, and all of that came crashing down on her right then. It felt good to cry, and she was ashamed, but more than anything she was fiercely glad that her friend was still alive.

Wanda smiled at that, but shook her head. "Staci—"

"I can't believe how stupid I was," she interrupted, sniffling and gulping air. "I'm never going to be so stupid again, I promise! I—"

"*Staci.*" Wanda stopped her short, this time. She wasn't smiling anymore. "We can go over all of this later. I'll cry then, too. But right now you need to get up, put your game face on, and go to work. All of the others are fighting, and are trying to make our decisions for us. You need to go, *now.*" She took Staci's hands off of her shoulders— again, gently, but definitely firmly—and stood up. "Well? Let's go, Witchy Witch."

Staci stared at Wanda for a second, then wiped her nose and her eyes on her sleeves. She felt gross and knew that she looked like hell, but the important thing was that she get moving. *How the hell did I get so lucky, to have friends like this?* She took a few breaths, shuddered once, and then swung herself off of the couch as she stood up.

"Right. Time for the brave heroine to save the adults from themselves. Right?"

"*Heroines*, but sure. Sounds about right. It's okay, though. You make a pretty good sidekick, when you're not passing out." Wanda hit Staci's bicep gently with her fist.

A leaf brushed against her mouth, and she batted at it. "Is there a comb in here somewhere? I dunno if we're going to make any points by looking like dryads after a windstorm—"

"If we don't get in there now, we won't make any points at all." Wanda grabbed her wrist and dragged her towards the door. It opened into a too-bright room, and a lot of . . . not exactly shouting, but too-loud, clenched-jaw arguing. She winced, felt the nausea she had always felt when dealing with angry confrontation, then grit her teeth against it and walked into the room.

The argument stopped dead, and five sets of eyes stabbed her. Tim's face was utterly expressionless; the two elves' faces betrayed a frozen anger. David's expression was full of anxiety. Only Seth's was welcoming, and full of relief at seeing them.

"Well," said Branwen, icily. "There she is at last. The one who just cannot keep from poking sticks into the den of a dragon."

Ian crossed his arms over his chest, glaring at her, saying nothing—as if, Staci thought, he felt that she was too far beneath his notice or contempt to comment. She felt herself flushing with anger herself, her nausea completely driven out.

Tim's gaze snapped back to the elves. "At least *my* apprentice is out there actually doing something, instead of waiting around for some big nasty to take a bite of her neck." Despite Tim keeping his expression completely neutral, Staci could tell from the subtle way he spoke slower and clearly enunciated each word that he was anything but calm. *Holy crap, Tim is absolutely* furious. "She *acted*, took some initiative. From what her friends told me, she also destroyed a cursed artifact that was literally killing humans and absorbing their life-force. How much human lives matter to you, I can't speculate on. But, even though she made mistakes," he said, glancing back at Staci for the briefest moment, "she was at least trying. Hard to get anything done sitting around in the closest thing to an ivory tower in these parts."

"But what was she doing in a restricted area in the first place?" Ian demanded. "And what was she thinking, trying to destroy an artifact like that by herself? The *instant* she knew the artifact existed, she should have come to us! The *instant* she detected magic in the forest, she should have reported to us!"

"Hey, that's not fair!" Staci went to Tim's side. "I did try to let someone know, but I couldn't wait!"

"Come to you?" Tim grated derisively. "*You're* not her teacher, or her mentor. I am, and don't you forget it. Besides, it was time critical; like I said, people were *dying*. Might not matter much to you, but she didn't have the time to wait a couple of months while you conferred, investigated, slept on it, and whatever else it is you pointy-eared bastards do to waste time while mortals are paying for your inaction."

"Oh dear," mocked Branwen. "We seem to have uncovered your racist side, wizard. Not so perfect after all, are you?"

Tim rolled his eyes, "Spare me the self-righteous shell game, infant. Adults are talking. I might be a prejudiced bastard, but that doesn't change the fact that you were either asleep at the wheel while all of this was going on, or were sitting here with your thumbs up your asses. So either you're incompetent, or you're a part of it in some way." He narrowed his eyes. "It hasn't escaped my notice that the critter that dealt out that artifact was a leprechaun. Isn't that *Seleighe* Court? *Your* bailiwick? I would think you should have noticed. *If* you had been bothering to pay attention to the mortals you *say* you are supposed to be protecting here."

Ian and Branwen both bristled, and Staci watched as David almost shrunk in on himself, he cringed so hard. Before either one of them could reply, the door behind Staci banged open. Caradoc stomped in, looking no happier than his relations. Ian checked himself, then turned his attention to Caradoc. *Mustn't lose composure in front of the little mages, is that it?* "What did you find?"

Caradoc moved past Branwen to the wet bar at the back of the room. He reached for a carafe of wine until he noticed that Ian had fixed him with a glare. He sighed, then poured himself a glass of ice water instead. "Oh, the usual," he said after draining the glass and refilling it. "One dead leprechaun, a ruined bit of jewelry, a great honking big trail leading deep into the woods, and one *very* dead troll." He paused, looking into his glass for a second. "I stink of burnt troll." He shuddered, then turned his attention to Tim and Staci. "So, are we roasting them over coals yet? Or haven't we reached the point in the conversation where threats are exchanged?" Staci thought he was just being sardonic, but it was hard to tell with Caradoc; of all the elves, he was the hardest to read. Always joking... until he wasn't.

Tim glared, the barest hint of a smile at the corners of his eyes. "You want threats, elf? Cold Iron. Have I got your attention now?"

Staci watched the elves very carefully; these weren't the genteel facades that she had seen before, nor the sickly sweet sophistication that Sean had worn like a cheap cologne. She truly felt for the first time that she was in the presence of old, terribly powerful beings, and that there was something very *alien* that separated them from people. An image of Dylan—contrasted in every way to these elves, until the end, at least—swam up into her mind, but she forcibly dismissed it. She needed to pay attention.

David held his hands up, speaking quietly. "Maybe we can forget about killing each other, just for a little while? I don't want to have to clean the carpets or go to the hospital, so—"

Unfortunately for him, that attracted the glares of all three elves *and* Tim, and he choked off the rest of his sentence and stepped back a pace.

Tim returned his attention to the elves before they turned back to him. "So. Leprechaun. *Seleighe.* How about that? Any reason why one of *yours* would have been draining off mortal life-force? Which is it going to be; incompetence, or malice?"

"Don't try to simplify Underhill politics down to your level, wizard," Ian growled. "There are Underhill races on both sides of the divide. Why weren't *you* dealing with the artifact and its wielder instead of your apprentice?"

Caradoc set down his water glass, then leaned against the table behind him. "Very odd that when I arrived at the site, you were already there with the short one," he said, thrusting his chin at Seth. "Even more so that we had all sensed a powerful release of energy just before. Certainly was too much for this quaint thing," he mused, as he held up the charred and twisted remains of the cross and chain.

"I don't answer to you, Ian Ironoak," Tim practically growled. "You may be in my town, but I am *not* yours to order and demand from." He suddenly looked weary; Staci noticed that he was incredibly pale, and that he had been trying to conceal how exhausted he was as much as he was trying to keep his anger in check. "Keep that in mind; what I tell you next, I only do so as a courtesy, and because you are starting to bore the hell out of me. My apprentice has a charm on her cell phone; simple, it's just a location spell that can be triggered by touch. That—and with the help of

Seth—is how I was able to find her. Between what Seth had told me, and the fact that she used the charm, I knew she was in trouble."

"Tim's right." She fished the cell phone out of her pocket; the charm string had one piece missing, consumed when the spell was activated. "Even though I was tied up by whatever those other . . . things were, my hand was close enough to my pocket, and I was able to get the spell off."

Ian's eyes flicked to Staci, then focused on Tim. "And why weren't you dealing with it personally, before your apprentice was in mortal danger? What of the energy that we felt?" Ian took a step forward, inclining his head towards Tim. *Well, at least they're sort of talking right now, and the death threats have stopped,* Staci thought with no small amount of relief.

"I was setting up a ward," Tim said simply.

Branwen laughed, but not as if she was amused; as if she wanted to heap mockery on him. "A ward? That's your explanation? The amount of magical energy that we felt wasn't for a ward." She looked off into the distance, searching for her next words. "That amount of magical power, it would be like . . . hooking a blender up to a nuclear reactor, directly. Humans don't already do that, do they?"

"A ward on the town. All of it. City limits to the edge of the ocean." Tim stared at them all, with defiance, as if he dared them to contradict him, or his ability to pull something like that off.

Which, of course, they did. Branwen laughed mockingly again. Caradoc snorted. Ian was the only one who actually answered. "Impossible. You are not Merlin. You are not Taliesin. You are a pitiful wretch who has spent most of his life hiding in his bookstore. Where would you have gotten the knowledge for such an undertaking, much less the power?"

For the first time, Tim smiled. It wasn't pleasant. "Before I began to 'hide in a bookstore,' I actually went out into the world and *worked.* All those titles you threw at me when you first walked into the bookstore? Ally of this, decimator of that, conqueror of *Melisande*? I've walked in darker places than any that you have heard of, and I've learned things, elflord. I won't live as long as you do, but a long life is worth crap if you don't do anything with it. So, I used what I have learned. I gathered the tools I needed, did the research, and put the work in. Stored my energy and tapped into the ley line under my shop. Even with the town relics I had collected and all of the rest, it still almost wasn't enough. But I did it; or I would have. I valued my apprentice's life more." He looked thoughtful for a moment, and then turned to look at Staci. He was still incredibly tired, and the fierceness was still there. Outshining all of that, however, was a moment of genuine affection and care. Before Staci could say anything, or even begin to choke up, he was back to Ian. *So that's what his scavenger hunt was about . . . and all of that effort, all of that energy, he threw it all away to save me. It could have killed him, aborting the spell at the last second like that. Even after draining himself, he was still able to call down that massive lightning bolt on the troll.*

Ian seemed at a complete loss for a moment, as if he couldn't manage a coherent thought, much less utter a single word. Branwen seemed genuinely stunned. Caradoc, oddly, seemed . . . grimly pleased, as if what Tim had said confirmed something for him.

"And what did you do with the backlash, wizard?" Caradoc asked quietly.

"Oh, that. Let's just say that there's a school of fish about six miles off the coast that had a really bad day. And time might act a little bit wonky in that spot for a while, but I'm not too sure about the secondary effects. That was a first for me."

Ian seemed to have gotten his feet back under him. "And why did you not trouble yourself to tell *us* about what you intended to do?" he demanded. "*We* live here too, like it or not!" *Got to try to get control of the conversation after that whammy, huh?*

"One, it was none of your damn business. Like I said before, Ironoak, you're not the boss or owner of me. And two, I don't goddamned trust you lot. Between your inaction, and playing things so close to the vest about this mysterious 'darkness' that you harped on about the last time, I didn't see much reason to clue you in on what I was up to. Turnabout is fair play, and I like to fight dirty."

Aw, hell. They're starting in on each other again. Just then Staci was hit with a massive headache. She was almost certainly dehydrated, definitely beat up, and still feeling drained from her fight with the leprechaun. More than anything, she was *tired. All of this is going in circles. Tim doesn't trust the elves. The elves don't trust anyone besides themselves. And round and round we go, on this twisted, stupid little merry-go-round.* She could hear Tim and Ian's voices growing louder and angrier again, but she couldn't make out the words. He head throbbed, and she shut her eyes against the shooting pains that felt like they were driving spikes into her temples. Someone grabbed her elbow, but she pulled away; a little too hard, as she almost stumbled over into Ian's desk.

"Enough already!" She opened her eyes, and felt herself breathing hard. Her headache was subsiding somewhat, though not completely. Everyone was watching her, now. *Oh, crap, now what?* She looked over to Wanda. Wanda nodded, raising her hand as if to say, "Your show, take the reins." *H'okay, here we go.* "This is my fault. And yours," she pointed to Tim. "And yours," she said, pointing to Ian. "None of us is willing to trust anyone else. Tim didn't trust me or you with what he was doing with the ward. You won't trust us with what you're doing about the 'darkness'... which I think I ran headfirst into anyway, so there's that. And I won't trust—" She came up short, Dylan flooding into her mind again. "Anyways, that's what is screwing us up so hard right now. No one is giving anyone else a chance, and I'm sick of it. Because of how hard-headed I've been, I almost got one of my best friends killed." Wanda looked down at her feet, and Staci could see hints of red on her cheeks, coming through the ruined makeup. "I'm done. If we keep at it like this, someone is going to *die,* and it'll be one of us. And I don't want that on my conscience, just because I was too much of an idiot to actually listen. Even if I'm not the biggest fan of the people I ought to listen to."

For a few seconds, everyone was completely silent. She thought she had screwed up majorly, until she saw David smiling. *Well, there's one person. What about everyone else?*

Tim was the first to break the silence. He turned to face Staci; he still looked haggard, but the anger seemed to have drained from him. "Staci... I'm sorry. You're right; I shouldn't have kept what I was up to from you. If nothing else, you need to learn, and you can only do that if I'm including you in things that you can learn from." He faced Ian and the elves again. "As for all of you—"

Staci held her breath; was he going to lash out at the elves again, and undo any good she'd just done?

"—I don't like you. I don't trust you. But my apprentice is right.

Since all of us are throwing magic around inside this limited space, we've got to coordinate before we cross the streams."

Ian, Branwen, and Caradoc all looked at him as if he had just said something in Urdu. Seth, Wanda, and David hid smiles or choked down laughter, despite the seriousness of the situation.

"Very well," Ian said stiffly. "I believe this conversation is ended for now. We will apprise you of anything we learn."

Now why do I have the feeling he is totally lying? Staci asked herself, as Tim nodded stiffly, and motioned for the girls and Seth to leave.

They had just made it as far as the door to the parking lot, when David came running down the corridor behind them. Staci turned at the sound of his sneakers slapping the linoleum, but he held up his hand before she could say anything.

"Look," he panted. "Just want you to know, I'll let you know things I find out and help you out where I can. Okay?"

"All—" Staci began, but he was already running back the way he had come—probably to keep the elves from guessing he'd run off to talk to the humans. *I really don't know what to think about him. He was right that I had my head up my ass, but he's still* with *Fairgrove, even after everything that has happened. What is going on with him?*

Tim gazed after the young mage. "Hmph," he said. "Seth, call Beth. Tell her to meet us at the bookstore. Keeping secrets from you kids has backfired on me in a big way. Time to try the other approach."

Staci managed to keep her fat mouth shut on what she wanted to say. But she thought it anyway. *About damned time.*

The first thing Tim did when they got into the back room was start a pot of coffee. And not just any coffee. Staci did a double-take when he brought out a bag labeled *Death Wish*, muttering something under his breath about "pointy-eared bastards and their allergies."

He nodded to Staci and Wanda in turn. "You two, get showers in the back room. You look like hell, and smell like dead troll. There should be extra clothes from practice somewhere in a duffle bag. Can't send you home in that state, anyways. Coffee will be ready by the time you're done." He waited for a moment while they both stood there, swaying at the smell of the coffee. "Scoot, now. Better to get all of this started when Beth gets here than to have to wait."

When they got to the little bathroom, Staci looked at Wanda. "This'll go faster if we share the shower—and we won't run out of hot water."

Wanda made a face, but nodded. "Okay, but you know that sounded like the beginning of a porn video. '*Spooky Starlets Share Shower.*'" Staci wanted to laugh, but she was too tired for even that.

But Staci was right; it did go faster, even if it was a bit of a squeeze. Much faster than if one of them had waited politely for the other to finish. When they were done, they found the extra clothes that Tim had mentioned; it was just good policy to have stuff like that on hand, in case they forgot to bring extra clothing on a practice day. Showered, in clean clothing, and feeling a modicum like human beings again, they both went back to the main room.

The coffee smell was strong enough to revive Staci a bit all on its own. Seth didn't say anything, he was waiting with a cup in either hand, and shoved the mugs toward them. The stuff was strong enough to make all the hair stand up on Staci's head, and the caffeine hit like a sledgehammer, but it cleared away the cobwebs and even made her headache ease up. She would need food and a *lot* of sleep before she was back to one hundred percent and able to cast more than a cantrip, but it was still a marked improvement.

Beth was sitting on the corner of the sofa, sipping tea. It looked as if Seth had gotten some of the store coffee rather than this rocket fuel. Tim, however, had both hands wrapped around a double-sized cup and was sipping grimly. He looked *awful*. Once he had crossed the threshold of the shop doors, he had dropped all pretenses; his shoulders sagged, his face fell, and he looked ready to collapse. Staci suspected that the coffee and sheer force of will were all that were keeping Tim upright at that moment.

"Hey, Beth?" She motioned for her friend to come over from where she was sitting; Tim didn't react at all, even though Beth passed right in front of him. *Gourds, he really is out of it.* "Want some practice with your healing? Tim went through the ringer today, and could use a pick-me-up that doesn't come with the jitters."

"Do I!" Beth said, enthusiastically. She put her tea down and ignored Tim's gesture of *No, I don't need any help.* "Don't be such a baby," she scolded. "Or rather, don't be such a *man*. Besides, I promise I won't throw up and pass out this time."

She put a hand on either shoulder, closed her eyes and bowed her head a little. A gentle, golden glow, just barely visible, started at her hands, and slowly crept over Tim's body and head, starting at the shoulders. After a moment, he gave a tired sigh, and relaxed. After about five minutes, Beth took her hands away and the glow faded.

"I don't know what you did to yourself, but you feel like the time they drained Swan Pond to clean it out," she told him sternly. "You need lots of food and sleep."

"I know. Thank you, Beth." Tim put a hand on her shoulder, then leaned back into the embrace of the battered old sofa. In another life, he would have looked like a professor about to have a private talk with some favored student. "Staci, you and Wanda go ahead and fill us all in on what happened out there today." He still didn't look *good*, but at least he looked like he wasn't going to keel over.

Staci made as short a job of the explanation as she could without downplaying her own shortcomings. Seth interrupted a couple of times to fill in what he had done. " . . . and that's when I passed out," she finished.

Tim nodded; by this point, Beth's eyes were as big and round as dinner plates.

"So, hold on. The Fairgrove people know something big, bad, and mean is coming, the, what was it . . . "

"'Darkness,'" Staci supplied, sipping from her now twice refilled mug. She felt like her limbs were buzzing, but she couldn't get enough of the coffee.

"Yeah, that. They know about it, but they won't clue you in on it . . . because we're not elves?"

"Well, it's 'us,' now, as in including you. But, yeah," Wanda said. "As usual, Silence excels in producing some of the most dysfunctional beings in the cosmos, or at least the contiguous United States."

"To be honest, I was banking on that," Tim sighed. "So I was planning an expansion of the spell on the shop. That was why we were junk-hunting. There's a lot of stuff out there with magical heritage, if you have the eye for it. Which is why the magical artifact second-hand market is so profitable, though I'd recommend not getting into that; it's a grimy and incestuous business." He rubbed his temple for a moment before continuing. "If I'd known you kids were about to go haring off on your own, I'd have warned you. Hell, I

probably should have made use of you. I thought I was being...
ethical, I guess, keeping you out of it. So about the time Seth came
busting in on me I was about to put the keystone in it. I recovered as
much energy as I could hold, blew the rest out to sea, and we played
cavalry. I'm just glad that we got there in time."

"Me too," Staci said, fighting against having her voice falter. She
took a breath, blew it out, and went on. "Everything happened so
fast, and with how hinky you had been acting, I just kind of... went
it alone. Well, I *convinced* everyone else that we had to go it alone. I
had it in my head that if there was something going on with you,
then we had to try to handle it by ourselves. It was dumb, and... oh,
I don't know. I feel stupid." *And horrible. Because Wanda almost died
and that was entirely my fault.*

"You could have handled the leprechaun yourself. Your big
mistake was not checking to see if it had backup," Tim conceded.
"Still, it's impressive that you were able to destroy the artifact and
defeat the leprechaun. You're getting better at managing your power."

"I don't know about that. If it weren't for Wanda, I'd have been
pounded into paste. She's scary good with those throwing knives; she
killed the little jerk."

"After you pretty much disarmed him," Wanda added. "And, yes,
I am scary good. Thank-yew-very-much."

"Is it so surprising for someone that reads about serial killers for
fun," Seth muttered under his breath, earning an elbow to the ribs
from Wanda.

"All right. New rules. I'm not keeping anything from you lot. You
don't keep anything from me. I won't tell you to shut up because I
am busy, *you* don't come running to me because you saw squirrels.
Deal?"

"Deal," they all chorused.

"Now, in the spirit of not keeping anything from you, this isn't
over. One leprechaun and a couple trolls does not a *Darkness* that
scares the shit out of Ian Ironpants make. Those two other creatures
you saw, and the third... I think this is even bigger than the elves
will admit. If I had my guess, they're more interested in consolidating
their power here in Silence, strengthening themselves and weakening
the Unseleighe as a result than anything else. Stopping this 'darkness'
is more of a byproduct, a matter of course for them." He took a long

slug from his coffee, before pointing a finger at each of the gang in turn. "Mark this; the elves are slow to act. Too slow, in my mind. When they get moving, they can bring a *helluva* lot of power to bear, but they aren't particularly concerned about any of us mortals that aren't directly allied to them. Don't count on it, and you'll never be disappointed, but if you see it coming, get the hell out of the way. *Friendly fire* and *collateral damage* bother them not at all." He looked at each of them closely, and they all nodded. "All right then. Except for Beth, we all need rest. Beth, you need to double down on your magic-lessons, at least what you can learn for yourself from the books and practice. I think our next move, *as a group,* is going to be investigating the mansion grounds. But given what you ran into so far, we need to be sharp, and careful, and as well-armed as we can be. First step in that is food and sleep." He made a shooing motion at them—but gave Staci a look that said *not you.* "All right, get the hell out of my hair. I'll see you tomorrow."

"But what if they try something tonight? While we're down?" Seth demanded.

"They're down too," Tim reminded him. "They won't have expected what happened up there. Seleighe or Unseleighe, an elf's reaction to something unexpected is to jump back undercover and think about it a while."

"And it's not like we've been training for nothing, all this time," Staci said. "We've got our emergency buttons, essentially. Plus, enough Cold Iron to knock out a goblin army."

"Use that Cold Iron to ward your houses or rooms and nothing's getting past it," Tim reminded them. "Now shoo, before I disgrace myself by passing out in front of you."

The others left at that, somewhat hastily; all but Staci, who remained where she was, at the other end of the couch from Tim.

She expected him to lay into her, then, and she braced herself for the tirade. When it didn't come, she bit her lip, and ventured, "I screwed up."

"Yes, you damned well did," he replied, without recrimination. "But it was as much my fault as yours, because I didn't warn you what I was doing. And I didn't listen to you. We could have set a trap for that little green bastard if I'd listened to you."

Something about that set off a spark in Staci, and she felt a flush in her cheeks as she set down her coffee mug and turned to face him. "You know what, Tim, you're right. You should have listened to me! You're harder on me than any of the others, and I take it. I get it, I need to try harder and work harder than anyone if I'm really going to be a mage, and not just bait for whatever nasty lurking horror out there gets hungry. But . . . damnit! I could have helped you with the ward! It was dangerous *because* you did it alone." She took a breath, shaking her head and rubbing her arms. "If I had known, I could have helped you. We could have finished the ward, and then all of the stuff with the leprechaun and Preacher Kenny would have been trivial! Instead, Wanda almost died because I thought you were—I don't know, just being shady! And *you* almost died. Where would that have left *me*? I can't lose you! I can't lose *any* of you, but I really, really, can't lose *you!*" Before Staci knew what was happening, she felt the tears on her cheeks, and she couldn't talk anymore.

Tim set down his own coffee mug, his face taciturn. "You're right, Staci, on all counts. I screwed up big; not just as a man, but also as your mentor. More importantly, as your friend. The truth is, I did things the way I did them because I'm damned scared of losing *any* of you. I didn't ask for this; to train a group of ragtag misfits to fight evil. But I was tired of hiding, too. And that's where we are. I'm still getting used to this whole 'letting other people in' thing. It's been a while, and it takes me some time to knock the rust off." He shook his head before he looked into her eyes. "None of that is important. What is important is that I'm sorry, and I won't let it happen again. I'm sorry, Staci."

The tension inside her broke. "I'm sorry too," she choked, and started to cry. She collapsed against Tim's shoulder, and threw her arms around his neck. He held her as she cried, she couldn't say how long, until she finally got all of the tears and heartache out. When she finally pulled away, she felt hollowed out, but in a relieved way. "So much for that shower," she said, sniffling. "I must look like a wreck."

"Well, you'll do until the wreck gets here. But don't worry about it, apprentice." He handed her a handkerchief—because of *course* Tim would have one ready—and then checked his watch. "It's late. Get your bike unchained from outside while I bring my car around. We'll get you home. You get some rest, and you'll feel better in the morning. I plan on doing the same."

Staci wiped her eyes and blew her nose as quietly as she could; then, failing that, just got on with it with a couple of honest honkers. They both chuckled when she tried to hand the handkerchief back and Tim put up his hand. "Keep it."

"Hey, Tim?"

"Go ahead."

"No more secrets. For real, like you said. We're all in this together."

Tim nodded, then stood up and offered Staci a hand to help her up. "Just so, apprentice."

CHAPTER SIXTEEN

Staci had a sick feeling in the pit of her stomach. She really didn't want to be here. After all, this was where that Aufhocker—that was the name of the thing, Seth had figured out—had almost killed Wanda. But Tim was right. They needed to do *some* kind of investigation; if there were still clues to find, that is. *What the hell have I gotten myself into? I should be worrying about passing algebra this year, not trying to fit my chores in between occult investigations and bug hunts in the woods.* She shook her head, sighing. She couldn't get distracted, not out here; she needed to be on her game. Tim was still out of it, though he seemed to be getting better, slowly but surely. The real concern was Beth; this was only her second time really "out" on a mission with them, and she was still green as grass. There were dangerous *things* in these woods, and Staci wouldn't allow herself to get taken by surprise again.

The group had waited until a couple of days after their last meeting to actually start venturing out. Tim reasoned that it wouldn't do to arouse suspicion from Fairgrove; having Wanda and Seth show up, all buddy-buddy, immediately after the last row would have looked a bit fishy. The added bonus was that it gave Staci and Tim time to plot out where exactly they would go looking for trouble. Blackthorne Manor was the obvious place, as well as the clearing behind the "bad" church. But there were still plenty of other places to check out in the woods, and they had made a list. This was their third day in the last week of being out in the woods; always during the day, they made especially sure to be well out of the woods before dusk. For starters, it was much easier to square things with Beth's job—she had switched to night shifts, and though the tips were smaller, she didn't have to work as hard—and Staci's "real" life. Sometimes she wondered which would be worse—the horror of monster-stalking or the monotony of high school. After fighting evil elves, being hunted by Red Caps, and watching a troll explode, remembered school drama took on a certain unreality.

Under the trees, it was chilly. She looked over her shoulder at Beth. Beth was hugging herself against the cold, but otherwise didn't look worried. *How that girl stays so upbeat about things, I'll never know.* Beth definitely knew about the danger out in the woods, but she didn't seem to let the fact that all of them could die at any moment touch her. Staci wondered how she could be so calm. Was it something about her Fey blood? Or did none of this really seem real to her? Maybe it had something to do with dealing with jerk customers at the diner all day, every day; a romp through the woods with evil fairy tale creatures might seem like a vacation after that.

Tim was . . . still Tim. Grim, observant, and determined. He had a camera hung on a strap around his neck and Staci had binoculars around hers; if they ran into anyone, they could use the excuse that they were out birding. And at a pinch, whacking someone with a heavy pair of binoculars swung on the end of the strap was an option. A lot more plausible than "hunting monsters that have a nefarious plot to kill us all." Plus, from what Staci remembered, Tim actually knew a few things about birds.

There was a feral sounding cry, and Staci started, looking around, expecting . . . something bad. Tim actually cracked a tiny smile. "Cooper's Hawk," he said. "Just passing through right now, I suspect. They are partial migrants. He's seeing if there are any locals he has to contend with."

Beth picked up the pace until she was next to Tim, still rubbing her arms. "Where'd you learn that stuff?"

"Self taught." Tim shrugged. "Birding is a very zen hobby, and it's easy to pick up and put down when you want. You don't need to have any real goals, unless you're a major twitcher with a life-list, all you need is some books and your eyes."

"Huh. I would have figured that you would have been into, I don't know, knifemaking or something."

"How do you know that I'm not?"

Beth nodded. "Point." They went along for a while longer, Tim and Staci both keeping a watch on their surroundings before Beth piped up again. "What about you, Staci? What do you do for fun?"

"Besides playing tabletop stuff with the gang? This. As crazy and lame as that probably sounds, this is what I do for fun." She sighed a little thinking of her past life in New York, a life so different from this one that she might just as well be two different people. The "before" Staci was pretty much dead, now. She didn't even try to talk to any of her old friends, she hadn't updated her Facebook profile for months, and the only person she still was in contact with was her father. And . . . *it's only to hit him up for more money on my plastic, or some big buy,* she thought, cynically. On the other hand, a good half of that "guilt money" was going to make life for Mom better, too. A couple hundred dollars a month more made a big difference in the kind of groceries they were able to buy. "When you know magic exists, I don't know; everything else, celebrity gossip and the hottest new TV show all seem . . . dumb. Boring. Or worse, pointless. And if we want *draahmahhh*—" she drawled the word "—there's always Elf Central and their stupid politics. And at least their stupid politics are . . . I dunno . . . relevant?"

"At least for us," Beth added. "Still . . . there's always shopping. We'll always have that."

"Right. Now if only we didn't have to go a town over to find a decent store."

For a spell of time after that, Staci and Beth talked about anything and everything; the latest RPG campaign, what movies they wanted to see, when they thought Seth and Wanda were finally going to hook up, and so on. Staci didn't realize it immediately, but she started to feel better the more she talked with Beth; when she did notice it, she was almost stopped short. Was it just that she needed to take her mind off of where they were? Maybe an effect of Beth's healing, taking the edge off of Staci's anxiety? She couldn't tell, and truth be told, she didn't care much either way. It felt good, and that was something that had been in short supply the last few days.

They had been walking for an hour and a half when something changed. Staci was ready for a break; they had snacks and water in their backpacks, and she was looking forward to getting some calories in her. In addition to the walking, she had a few wards running; nothing too flashy, since she didn't want to stand out like a beacon, but just enough so that she'd have a few extra seconds if they got into trouble. Just as she was about to ask Tim about taking a break, she stopped in her tracks. The hairs on the back of her neck were standing up, and she had goosebumps on her arms. Tim stopped almost at the exact same moment, while Beth walked for a couple of more paces before she noticed that the other two weren't moving.

"What's wrong—"

Tim silenced Beth with a quick motion of his hand; she had enough sense to immediately clam up and start looking around. And that was when they started, off in the middle distance. Raucous, one-note bird calls that both conveyed acute alarm and had a bell-like clarity. "Blue Jays," Tim said, chin jutting. "Alarm calls. Something's wrong. Bad-wrong. Move out!"

But instead of running away from the calls, Tim moved towards them. Staci immediately began calling up a few more wards; she wasn't running on empty yet, but she could feel her energy levels dipping. Beth stood still, looking at Staci.

"Let's go!" Staci set off at a run, and a moment later she heard Beth following her. They were a few dozen yards behind Tim; he seemed to know exactly where he was going, so Staci did her best to follow him. All of her doubts and fears came flooding back to her as they ran. *God, am I leading my friends to death? What if something happens to Beth? She's our only healer. . . . If she gets hurt, and then Tim gets hurt, how will I get them out of here, or get help? Seth's system isn't set up yet, and—*

Her thoughts were interrupted by the crack of a gunshot. Tim stopped short; Staci and Beth caught up to him, flanking him on either side. All of them were breathing hard, especially Tim; he still wasn't fully recovered.

"Do we—"

"We keep going," he said between gulps of air. "Slow it down. We don't want to get shot. You two, stay behind me, okay?" The girls both nodded. Tim started forward again cautiously; Staci and Beth fell in behind him. Staci didn't know if Tim had some sort of spell or charm that could prevent you from getting shot, or if he was just trying to do the "I'm the man" thing of being the first in harm's way. Either way, Staci was hyper-alert; she knew she was going to pay for it sooner or later, but she expended more energy on a spell to amp up her senses. Everything became crystal-sharp in her vision, her hearing brought in every sound, and her sense of smell—she almost vomited on the spot. There was one smell that overpowered every other one; blood, and lots of it.

"Tim," she whispered. "Something up ahead is hurt. Bad." Tim looked back at her, and she watched him work the exact same spell that she had, boosting his senses. His hands were practiced at the complicated contortions, and he breathed the words of the incantation like they were his birth language. Even so, she watched him grow more pale with the exertion as his eyes widened and he pressed on. He motioned for Staci and Wanda to spread out to his right as they approached the source of the blood. It was on the other side of a thicket, and they had to walk around it to get to the source. Staci could hear a low moaning or whimpering. *Some trap? Something feeding on an animal—no, not an animal.* Staci felt her gorge rise as soon as she laid eyes on the sight; it was a man, laying on his back. He was wearing hunting gear, and there was a shotgun just out of reach; it was hard to tell what everything was at first because of all the blood. Everything was covered in it, mixing with the camo clothing and the leaves. The thing that stood out the most was his face; his skin was pale white, and his eyes were glazed over with pain. He looked at them but didn't see them, he was in such agony.

Beth immediately pushed past Staci, taking everything in. She slung her backpack off of her shoulders, and started digging through it. "I need all of your water from the Camelbacks, now!" she said in a desperate whisper. Beth began unpacking gauze, bandages, chest seals, and some stuff that Staci didn't recognize. Staci didn't see the point, but shrugged off her backpack's water reservoir anyways; the man ... there's no way he could live after whatever had happened. Staci could clearly see bones and organs through the tatters of his jacket; she felt tears well up in her eyes at the senseless carnage of it all. Beth, heedless of whatever else was happening around her, kept working. She opened the fill valves for all of their water, and spread her hands over it. Slowly, the water trickled from the reservoirs ... and then lifted up into the air, in a slow-motion, reverse waterfall as it entwined itself around Beth's fingers.

Staci was so transfixed by the sight, it took her a moment to realize that Tim was calling her name, and reaching out to shake her shoulder. She pulled back at the last moment, snapping her eyes towards him.

"Beth has this under control. You and I need to move, *now.*"

"But—"

"She'll be safe. I've already put a ward over her and the man. Nothing will get to them, I promise. Are you staying, or are you coming with me?"

Staci hesitated for the briefest of moments. She wanted to stay with Beth, and keep her safe. A huge part of her feared that if she left Beth alone, that the Aufhocker would be back and do to her what it had almost done to Wanda. She knew that it didn't make sense, but that didn't stop her guts from filling with ice at the memory of that day in these woods. She tamped all of her emotions down; she had to fall back on her training, otherwise she would be paralyzed with indecision. She swallowed, then nodded. "Let's go."

The trail wasn't hard to follow. Whatever had attacked the hunter didn't seem interested in stealth; broken branches, kicked up earth, and the easily identifiable trail of blood led the way. Staci could have followed its path even without her amped up senses. Either it was hurt, or it had . . . a *piece* of the hunter, and that was what was leaving all of the blood. Tim was still in the lead; Staci could see the barely contained power weaving sparking trails like embers between his hands. He stopped suddenly, and began creeping stealthily up what looked like it might be the crest of a hill; the terrain dropped off a little ahead of them. She caught up with him, and they literally crawled the last few feet and cautiously peered over the edge. There was an erosion-gully below them, and Staci heard growling and wet eating noises directly below them. There was some sort of cavelet cut into the side of the gully, there had to be, and whatever had attacked the hunter was in it. The problem was . . . they couldn't *see* it from here. The lips of the edge curved around the cavelet in a "U" shape; Tim, seemingly having read Staci's mind, quietly motioned for her to move along the right edge, while he moved along the left. Whatever was down there would get caught between them; since it was below them, they weren't at risk from crossfire if they both opened up on it.

Staci slowly, glacially, backed away from the edge of the gully. All those hours of practice at moving stealthily paid off now; she was almost completely silent as she crawled backwards, then brought her knees underneath herself, and stood up into a half-crouch. Tim did the same, nearly in sync with her. They both circled the edge of the gully; Staci kept switching her gaze from the cavelet to where her next footfall was, careful not to step on an errant twig. She rolled her feet with each step, shifting the weight carefully, feeling each step out fully before committing. After what seemed like a year of creeping along quietly, she finally saw the first bit of the creature past the lip of the gully. It had thick, matted black fur on its head; even from where she was, she could see that its head was crisscrossed with white scars that cut furrows through the dense hair. Two pointed ears, flat against the head and swept back, framed the face. The face itself was squashed in, with a distinctly canine nose. The teeth, when they weren't sunk into what looked like the mangled carcass of a rabbit, were pronounced, sharp, and covered with gore. What shook her the most were the eyes; sky blue, and definitely human, sunk deep into the skull, but alert on its meal. The rest of it was a horrible pastiche of animal and man; overdeveloped shoulders and chest, covered by the remains of an irredeemably soiled shirt, hirsute hands ending in inch long claws, digitigrade legs below the remains of what used to be trousers of some kind, held on with a hemp rope belt.

It was an honest to god werewolf, and it chose that moment to look straight at Staci.

The werewolf dropped the rabbit and turned its head towards Staci. She immediately started calling up an offensive spell; a wall of force, something to knock it on its ass. Tim was faster, since he already had his spell charged and ready to go. His voice thundered in the quiet woods as he finished the spell, and a gout of fire issued from his outstretched hands. Just before it reached the werewolf... the fire was extinguished. The edges of it licked the werewolf's fur before the spell fizzled, and the werewolf yelped in pain, but it didn't seem particularly injured. It *certainly* wasn't out of the fight, and this couldn't have been what Tim had intended. Staci's eyes flitted towards Tim. He stood there for a moment with his hands still outstretched, confused. Then his eyes rolled up into the back of his head, and he started to teeter forward.

"Crap!" Fear stabbed her gut, and she lost concentration on her spell; she felt the energy run out of her as the spell failed, and mentally kicked herself. The werewolf was now looking at Tim as he tumbled over the edge of the gully, landing flat on his back to the right of the werewolf. The werewolf started to turn . . . when a flurry of magical bolts pelted it on the shoulders and back. Staci had cast the spell instinctively, snapping it off without consciously thinking about it. It wasn't nearly as impressive as the wall of force, but it succeeded in her immediate goal of getting the werewolf to leave Tim alone. The problem was that she now had its *full* attention. It spun around, patches of fur on its back still smoldering from her magical bolts. *Oh, man . . . from bad to worse.* Staci started to back away from the edge of the gully, and the werewolf kept the distance between them, stepping forward for each step she took back. When she lost sight of it beyond the edge of the gully . . . it *jumped* up onto the edge in a single bound. A low growl emerged from its throat, and it slavered and drooled, thick ropes of spittle dripping from its jaws. Slowly, she removed the binoculars from around her neck, holding them out in front of her.

"Good doggy, nice doggy . . ." The werewolf snarled, and Staci threw the binoculars as hard as she could at the monster's head. She turned to run immediately, barely catching sight of the binoculars smashing into the creature's muzzle before she was off as fast as her legs could carry her. *Got to get it away from Tim, and not die in the process. Think! It's a predator, it* has *to chase you if you're running . . . so let's give it more things to chase after.* She could hear the werewolf roar behind her, followed by its heavy footfalls as it came after her. *Focus . . .* Staci reached into her waist pouch of components as she ran, her fingers fumbling until she found what she was looking for; a chunk of mirror. She began muttering the spell, forcing her breathing to remain steady. She messed up the first time, a little more of her energy slipping away from her, but nailed it on the second attempt. Right as she uttered the last word for the spell, she snapped the mirror in half. A quick glance to her left showed an exact duplicate of herself, running alongside her. She snapped the smallest piece of mirror in half again, and a second duplicate flashed into existence. Staci skidded to a stop and whipped around to face the werewolf. It had stopped around sixty feet away from her, its icy blue eyes flashing between her and the duplicates.

All right, it doesn't know which one is me . . . now for a merry chase. Staci started running again, and the duplicates each took off in a separate direction. She heard the werewolf roar, and charge forward . . . but not after her. She looked around; the overcast sky was growing darker by the minute, and she was having a hard time getting her bearings.

Abruptly her attention snapped back to the present day. *Focus, girl!*

Staci saw a gigantic old-growth oak ahead of her. She needed to slow down, find out where she was, and plan her next move. Plus, she was absolutely winded, from all the spellwork and running for her life. She ducked behind it and took cover there, gulping air. She forced herself to control her breathing again, steadying herself. She wiped the sheen of sweat from her forehead, and listened. The werewolf was still running in confused circles, chasing the different illusions, roaring in frustration. Since they weren't real, she could make them move just fast enough to stay out of reach of the werewolf; faster than she could move, in any case. Staci risked poking her head around the trunk of the massive tree; she needed to see what was going on. The werewolf had stopped a good distance away from her; its chest heaved as it turned in place, its head moving as it switched between the illusions. *Please forget about me, keep running around . . .*

Then—something changed; the werewolf calmed down, raising its muzzle into the air. It sniffed the air for a few moments . . . and then looked in her direction. *Of course the supernatural monster can smell where you went. Okay, screw this running crap; you need to be faster, and you're low on energy. If you can't run . . .* She ran her hand along the bark of the oak tree, and an idea came to her. It was stupid, and might get her killed, but if it worked . . .

If it's stupid and works, it's not stupid. She spread her hand out flat against the bark of the tree and with one eye on the werewolf, quickly traced four druidic runes, one in each gap between her fingers, on the rough bark. She felt the tree come alive beneath her hand, and she fed it a quick burst of power, pleading wordlessly with it.

It replied with an equally wordless assent. Staci let out a sigh of relief; she had never tried that spell before, an ancient piece of druidic magic, and wasn't sure that it would even work. *Nothing like a field test. Now for the easy part . . .* She stepped out from behind the tree; the werewolf was much closer now. It had been moving cautiously, tracking her by her scent. It stopped when it spotted her, another low growl rising from its throat.

"Well, what are you waiting for, you ugly fur-bag! Dinner is up!" Staci's voice only squeaked a little bit with her last word. The werewolf howled, craning its head back; Staci felt goosebumps on the back of her arms and her guts fill with ice, but she stood her ground. The werewolf stalked forward, then jogged, its heavy footfalls and ragged breathing the only sounds in the woods. It looked eager for the kill. Staci took two steps backwards, and the werewolf broke into a run; it wasn't going to let her get away again. Staci felt an overwhelming urge to run, or curl up in a ball, or try to snap out another spell with the last of her energy reserves, but she fought against all of that. *It'll work!*

The werewolf was a blur as it passed the tree. Staci heard a loud snap and a ripping noise, and reflexively closed her eyes. She felt a rush of hot air, rank with the scent of fresh blood, sweep across her face, and she thought she was dead. She waited a beat, and then opened her eyes. The werewolf's face was about two inches from her own, its eyes filled with murder and staring right at her. She took a shaky step back, and everything started to make sense as she jolted herself out of her paralysis. The werewolf stared at her from out of a rat's nest of entanglement . . . bound in place with thick, dirt-covered roots from the oak. As the spell triggered, the roots had exploded from the ground to wrap around nearly every inch of the werewolf. Its right arm was raised up above its head, the claws still twitching; it must have been right in the middle of trying to strike her when the oak came to her rescue. The roots continued to snake around the werewolf's limbs and body, tightening around the creature with a wooden groan. There was even a loop of root in the werewolf's mouth, like a horse bit; puffs of blood-scented breath escaped from its open jaws, so it was still alive. *The oak really doesn't like this werewolf; it can tell it's unnatural, aberrant.*

Staci realized that she had been holding her breath, and let it out in one go, greedily sucking down air to refill her lungs. *Too close. Now I've got to get back to Tim, make sure that he's okay.* She walked around the ensnared werewolf, giving it a wide berth. She had to watch her footing; when the roots had ripped free of the ground, they had left ragged and surprisingly deep holes in the soil. When she reached the tree, she placed a hand on the trunk. "Thank you," she whispered. She didn't know whether the tree was still listening, or if all of the energy from the spell was already spent, but she hoped that the tree heard her. She started back towards the cavelet again; she had run in a fairly straight line, so it shouldn't have been too hard for her to retrace her steps and find her way back.

Staci had only walked a few paces when she heard the tree groan. She froze, and slowly turned around. The werewolf had started to move again. Her first thought was that the spell was failing, that she hadn't used enough energy or had messed up tracing the runes. The truth was worse; the werewolf was pulling free of the roots, using its terrible strength to break free. The roots encircling the werewolf's arms and chest broke as she watched; only a few in the beginning, but then more and more as the werewolf regained more of its mobility. This time, Staci didn't hesitate; she ran as fast as she could back towards the cavelet, hoping that Tim was awake. It wasn't until she was almost back to the cavelet when she noticed that she still had her illusion spell going; the duplicates were running on her flanks, passing through trees and mirroring her movements. Kicking herself, she dismissed the spell, and the pieces of mirror she still had in her hand disintegrated into dust; the spell had been draining her, bit by bit, the entire time she had it running. It wasn't much, but every ounce of magical energy she had was precious right now.

Staci had the edge of the gully in sight when she heard the oak tree crash to the ground in the distance, followed by a roar. She felt completely worn out, but she pushed herself to run faster in spite of it. She skidded to a halt at the lip, almost falling into the depression. Tim was still where he had fallen; it took Staci a moment for her eyes to focus in the failing light, but she saw that he was moving sluggishly, and relief flooded her. *Even at his lowest, Tim and I should be able to handle this together. Right?* She looked around; the best way down would be to follow the edge of the drop-off, since it sloped down where the wings of the "U" curved in. But before she could start moving to get to Tim, she heard the werewolf's heavy footsteps coming nearer at a running pace. She turned in the direction of the poor oak, and saw the werewolf careening towards her; it was furious, slashing at trees as it passed them, tearing huge chunks of out the ground with its hind legs. *No time!* She didn't have much energy left, and couldn't think of any offensive spells that wouldn't leave her completely drained; if the spell didn't finish the werewolf, she would be helpless. She needed to move—

That's it! Staci steeled herself, shutting out the approaching werewolf, Tim, everything; she concentrated, working the spell as fast as she dared. At the last moment, when the werewolf was nearly within reach of her, she finished the spell with a cry. The levitating disk formed under her feet—and she immediately crumpled against it as it shot into the sky. The werewolf's claws scratched against the bottom edge of the invisible disk as she rocketed out of its reach. *Too fast on that one. That could have been a lot worse; you could have broken your neck. On the other hand, you could still be down there with the werewolf . . . and he is not happy.* Staci tried to stand up, very gingerly at first; she had definitely sprained something in her leg, maybe her back, too, when she had ascended. The werewolf was directly below her, swiping at the air in frustration.

"Okay, Fido. Let's see if you squish as well as revenants." Her plan was to drop the disk straight down onto the werewolf and crush it, with Staci jumping clear at the last second. It would hurt, but it was all she had left. The werewolf wasn't going to accommodate her, apparently; before she could trigger the disk, the werewolf ran from her. *Damnit! Can it understand me?* The disk, while easy to move up and down quickly, was as slow as molasses when it came to horizontal movement. She *could* try to maneuver the disk over the werewolf again, but she wasn't sure that she had enough energy to; manifesting the levitating disk and moving it up had used up nearly everything she had left, energy-wise. She watched the werewolf; it had stopped around forty feet away, and was pacing back and forth as it watched her back. *What is it doing?* It wasn't attacking Tim, so there was that, at least. But it was working something out, and she didn't like *that* one bit. She was running out of time; either the werewolf would shift its attention back to Tim, or she would run out of energy. She couldn't stay up in the air forever. She briefly considered calling someone for help . . . but who? She wouldn't have the energy to wait for them, and what would anyone do when they got here, other than get eaten by the werewolf? Besides, it wasn't very likely that she'd even be able to get a signal out here, in the middle of nowhere . . .

Staci shook her head, hard, to clear it. She was fading, and her mind had started to wander. She almost didn't notice that the werewolf was moving again until it was too late; it was running . . . towards her. *Whatever it was trying to figure out, I think it finally succeeded.* She braced herself, tensing her body. To her surprise, the werewolf passed underneath her and kept running. It ran at a tree and jumped at it . . . then kicked off of it, and turned in the air as it flew towards her. Staci barely had time to jump off of the disk; she went over on the side opposite of the werewolf, putting the disk between them. She looked back for the briefest second as the creature's chest hit the disk, folding the werewolf in half and sending it cartwheeling to the ground. She couldn't watch it land; she had to focus on not pancaking on the ground herself. She turned as she was falling so that she could see the ground; when she hit, she immediately tucked into a roll. Her execution was sloppy; whatever she had sprained in her legs messed up her technique, and she didn't pull off the roll, instead tumbling across the ground after her shoulder hit the ground. She slid to a stop on the dead leaves and grass right before she went over the edge of the gully.

Staci's entire body hurt, now, and she felt like she was on the edge of fainting. She was nearly out of energy and completely out of ideas. She managed to spot the werewolf. It had landed on the very edge of the gully as well. One of its arms was bent backwards, and its neck was at the wrong angle. A tiny spark of hope blossomed in her heart that the werewolf was dead . . . and was just as quickly extinguished when the werewolf stirred. *I'm completely screwed.* Staci switched her attention back to Tim. He was moving, too, but not nearly with the urgency that she wanted.

"*Tim!*" Staci called out in a harsh whisper. Tim's eyes flew open, and were unseeing for a moment before they snapped to her. He lifted his head weakly, trying to prop himself up with his elbows.

"Belt . . . wolfskin . . ." was all that he managed to croak out before he collapsed to the ground again. Everything clicked for Staci in that moment. Mustering the last of her energy, she painfully stood up. The werewolf did the same a moment later, turning to face her. The broken arm hung limp at its flank, and its neck was still twisted away at an obscene angle. Despite that, it started towards her, with its tongue lolling out of its mouth and its eyes glazed over. As it took its first steps, the limp arm shook with a popping sound...and wasn't limp anymore. The werewolf was already healing. She had to do this now...or she and Tim were goners. Staci summoned the very last of her magical energy, letting it gather in her open hand. She didn't have enough for any more magic missiles, or even an illusion. The werewolf was three strides away from her when she completed the spell, one of the first she had ever learned; a bright flash of light from her palm as she cried out.

"*Fiat lux!*"

The werewolf, blinded, tried to wrap her in a bear hug, but Staci was already moving. She ducked under the clumsy swing of the werewolf's arms, unsheathed her iron dagger, and slashed at the werewolf's waist. It tried, blindly, to swipe at her, but she dove over the edge of the gully and out of its reach. This time her landing wasn't nearly as controlled; she hit her shoulder, hard, and felt the wind go out of her. It was all Staci could do to push herself onto her back.

The werewolf was at the edge of the gully, silhouetted by the darkening clouds and fading light behind it. It's right side was bleeding...and then the hemp rope and a piece of wolfskin that had been tied around its waist fell away. The werewolf looked down at its side, and then back to Staci before it fell face first into the gully. When it landed...it wasn't a werewolf anymore. Just a scared-looking man, with a shaggy beard and long, matted hair. The rotting and soiled clothing all looked too large for him, now. The man stayed there, staring at Staci, as both of them fought for breath. For the briefest of moments, Staci panicked, fearing that she was going to suffocate. After what seemed like a particularly hellish eternity, she managed to force air back into her lungs, and pushed herself away from the dying man. It was only after she spent a minute getting her breathing under control and fighting the urge to vomit that Staci really started to study the man. Numerous wounds had begun to open up on his body; with a sick realization, she understood that many of them were from the oak tree and the fall that he had endured after leaping at her. With a shudder, she forced herself to turn away from him.

"Tim . . ."

Staci tried to stand, and almost immediately collapsed back to the ground. Her vision had gone dark around the edges if she tried to move too quickly; on her second attempt, she stayed on her hands and knees for a spell, keeping her eyes on the ground. That helped with the sense that the world was spinning, and she managed to keep from vomiting or toppling over when she finally stood up. *I've never been drunk before, but if it's anything like this . . . count me out.* She slowly and carefully made her way over to Tim; when she reached his side, she set herself down delicately, for his sake as much as her own.

Staci grabbed Tim's shoulder and shook him gently. His right eye snapped open while his left remained closed, searching frantically until it settled on Staci.

"We win?"

"I think so," Staci said, nodding.

"Make sure," he rasped. "Can I sleep?" She shook her head, and Tim groaned. "Louder!"

"No. Gotta finish it, and get home."

"Okay." Tim closed his eye, grimaced, and then sat up all at once. He took several deep breaths, then opened both of his eyes. He took in the dying werewolf, then Staci. "You look like how I feel."

"Yeah, back at you, O Corpse Mentor." Staci held out her hands for Tim, and helped him up. They both swayed on their feet for a few seconds, leaning on each other for support like a pair of drunks after a particularly heavy night of drinking. When they both had reached at least an equilibrium, Staci nodded towards the dying werewolf. "I didn't even notice the wolfskin until you pointed it out to me. I was too focused on . . . well, not dying."

Tim shook his head. "It's okay. Kind of hard to keep track of all the different lore when you have three hundred pounds of monster running at you." He paused. "I'm sorry that I didn't—"

"Save it," Staci interrupted. "We'll have time for that back at the store. Right?"

It was the first time that Staci thought that she had seen Tim taken aback. "You're right. Apprentice." He stared at her then, and something changed, though she couldn't put her finger on it at the moment. Before she could figure it out, the werewolf—former werewolf?—made a sound. Wearily, she turned towards it; she was completely out of magical energy, so all she had left was her iron dagger and no small amount of anger for the monster. While they had been talking, the werewolf had flipped itself onto its back; the man that had become a beast was clearly fighting for every breath, now. Staci, against all of her instincts, felt pity for it. There was something in its—no, his, it was a man, or it had been once upon a time—eyes that was just too incredibly sad.

The werewolf tried to speak; with how injured it was, and how pained its breathing had become, the words were barely a whisper. Tim edged forward, and Staci tensed; whatever this man was now, he had been trying to kill her just a few minutes ago. The dying man reached up tentatively towards Tim when he leaned down to be closer to the man's face, and spoke in a language that she only just recognized as some kind of Middle English. Even so, she couldn't make out what the poor soul was saying.

She started to say something, then clamped her mouth shut. Tim was listening with a frown of concentration on his face, so it was clear *he* understood whatever language it was the dying man was speaking.

Because he *was* dying; his limbs were contorted in ways that told her most of the major bones were broken, and areas of his torso were blackening with the kind of bruises that meant the organs beneath the skin were damaged. It was almost as if all the injuries he'd taken as a werewolf had been held off until he'd transformed. When he finally died, it wasn't one of the poetic, graceful deaths that Hollywood sells; it started with tears that quickly transformed to choking sobs as his entire body was wracked with convulsions. The former werewolf died, weakly clutching at Tim's shoulder and choking on his own blood. It was horrible to watch . . . and Staci felt herself crying. She told herself that it was from the exhaustion, but it was something more. *He was so scared! So unbelievably confused and scared!* She had seen death before, but . . . not quite like this. Whatever the werewolf had been . . . it came back to being a man, at the end, human.

Using the back of her hand, she roughly wiped away her tears, and taking a few moments to swallow past the lump in her throat. "What did he say?"

Tim brushed his fingers over the dead man's eyes, closing them, and causing two fresh rivulets of tears to fall down his cheeks. "He said he was sorry." Tim shook his head. "He didn't know what was happening . . . like he had been in a dream, he didn't even know where he was. That was how long and how deep he had been under the wolf."

"How did he end up that way in the first place?" Staci blurted. Because if he'd been forced into that shape—

"He got there not only of his own free will, but deliberately," Tim replied bluntly, cutting off her feeling of guilt before it got much of a chance to make itself known. "This was the end result of a medieval spell, and it's one where the magician is fully aware what is going to happen when he takes on the shape of the wolf. He *knows* he is going to find his enemies, real or imagined, track them down, and tear them to pieces. It doesn't matter what his reasons were, or how he got so screwed up. What the results were . . . that matters."

Results . . .

"Tim, we need to get back to Beth, *now.*" She suddenly realized they had left poor Beth alone with the dying hunter, who was probably dead now too.

It had been slow going for Staci and Tim. They were both completely played out and beat to hell; Staci physically, and Tim magically, though Staci wasn't all that far behind him on that front. For the first time, Staci felt on the same level as Tim; they were both just two weak humans, struggling to move through the forest to find their Selkie friend. *Okay, that sounds a lot better in my head . . . let's keep it there.* Staci thanked her lucky stars that she had paid attention to Tim and Seth's land navigation lessons when the pair nearly stumbled on Beth. The scene was still bloody as all get out . . . but, miraculously, the hunter was still alive. Beth was hunched over him, her skin waxy and a slowly shrinking pool of water under her knees. The most surprising part of the scene, however, was the elf crouched next to her, supporting her by her shoulders.

Caradoc held up his right hand, keeping his left on Beth's shoulder. "Before you say anything, *yes*, I was following you since you entered the forest. Yes, it was on Ian's orders. Let's focus on more pressing matters, like keeping this hunter and your young friend alive. Agreed?"

Tim opened and closed his mouth, then shrugged. "Truce," he croaked. "Not that we're going to be of much help."

"Then sit down and rest. This young half-Fae was trying to kill herself by healing too much, too fast. I'm providing more energy and moderating her efforts." Caradoc put his right hand back on Beth's shoulder. "And I do not fault you for her lack of training, wizard. You are not a healer, and much of what a healer does is pure instinct rather than training." He inclined his head towards Beth a moment. "You will do better next time, yes?"

"Yes," Beth mumbled. "Only I hope there's never a next time like *this.*"

Caradoc sighed. "If wishes were horses . . ." And closed his eyes to concentrate.

Finally Beth allowed her hands to drop. "That's all I can do," she said mournfully. "Oh hell. I *hurt.*"

"And so you should. You have been directing powerful energies through yourself. Did you think you would escape the consequences?" Caradoc chided.

"It'd be nice to be wrong for once. Just once."

"Well, that is a silly thing to wish for. Humans." Caradoc shook his head. "All right, this man will live, but he is still wounded enough to account for the blood. I will alter his memory so that he remembers nothing of the were-beast, nor any of us. He will only recall being rushed by some indeterminate creature."

Staci started to object, but Caradoc held his hand up. "Practicalities, child-mage." He sighed. Caradoc rummaged in the man's clothing, and found a cell phone. "Now, let me apply Tannim's Charm to this device. . . . " He held it in his hands for a moment and there was a brief flash. "That should last an hour or so. Just long enough for him to call for help and help to locate him. Now, I will dispose of the were-beast before the help comes. *You* stagger back to your vehicle—you did bring a vehicle, I hope, or need I call an elvensteed?"

"My car," Tim replied, his brows lowering suspiciously. "Now . . . look here, why are you being so generous? What's this going to cost us?"

Caradoc sighed, fighting against a smile at the end of it. "I am generous because it is in my nature to be generous. I am a true scion of Elfhame Fairgrove and Keighvin Silverhair, unlike Ian, who is a mere ally, and something of a grudging one at that, acceding to the Silverhair's will only because Keighvin *gets results,* and not because he agrees with *any* of Keighvin's philosophy." He chuffed. "Being on a war footing makes things so boring, in some ways. But, alas, I am merely Keighvin's observer on this venture; he has granted Ian the power to govern unless my report causes him to change his mind. So I can aid you, but only *sub rosa,* as they say."

Staci pushed past Tim, then immediately regretted it as she reached out to balance on his shoulder. "Won't that get you in trouble with Ian?"

"Only if Ian finds out about it." Caradoc winked at her. "Which he won't. He *will* be both angered and impressed by the fact that the human wizards and the half-Fae defeated a were-beast mostly unscathed. He's fascinated and repulsed by you all at the same time. Rather, I believe, as the fictional Vulcans of the *Trek Star* are initially fascinated and repulsed by humans."

Staci and Beth shared a look. "Close enough," Staci said.

"And what about you, elf?" Tim fixed Caradoc with a stare.

"Keighvin's orders to me are to make sure you humans don't get in over your heads without someone to throw you a lifeline. Needless to say, those would not be Ian's orders, but I don't answer to Ian, in the long run." He shrugged. "In the short run, I believe, although I am not certain, that Keighvin is hoping that closer interaction with human magicians will soften Ian's attitude and, as you say, 'bring him around.' Meanwhile, be off. The hunter is beginning to awaken and we all need to be gone."

Tim held his gaze on Caradoc for a long moment; Staci tried to parse what passed between the two, but it ended before she could figure it out.

"Tim . . . it's getting dark. Caradoc is covering for us, and we need to be gone before anything with sirens shows up. Can we go? We should go."

Her mentor nodded. "You're right. Let's get out of here. While we're in the car see if you can get some water and calories into Beth and yourself. You two look like hell and I don't want to draw any attention to us when we get to the store."

"You, too," she replied, as the trio limped towards Tim's car.

"Don't remind me," was all he said, then it was silence until they reached the car, fell into it, and began the short trip back down into the village.

CHAPTER SEVENTEEN

"You guys fought *and* killed a *werewolf?*" Seth shook his head, his eyes looking down into his coffee mug for a moment before he stared at Tim. "What kind was it? Someone that drank from a werewolf paw-print, or with a magic salve? Or was it one that used a formula? Or—"

Seth trailed on like that for a little bit, but Stacy tuned him out. *He's right.* Killed *a werewolf. But the man inside of it, or that it was before . . .* She had done her best to try to block everything out during the drive back. Focusing on keeping Tim awake on the road, and reminding Beth to eat and drink had helped. They didn't talk much; most of it was Staci calling Wanda and telling her to bring Seth to the bookstore. She had finished the call right before she had lost reception; the sooner that Seth finished his relay system, the better. She hadn't missed cell phones all that much in the last couple of months until that very moment; if something truly bad had happened and they had been unable to contact anyone . . . Beth kept worrying about the hunter; not because she had left him with Caradoc, but because she felt like she hadn't done enough. Staci had reminded her that she almost killed herself trying to save him. "Not much more than that that a person can do to save someone else." It had worked, at least for the moment.

"Wolfskin. And definitely not like one of the sexy ones from the movies," Tim said. Staci snapped out of her daze, taking a big slug of coffee. The caffeine had helped her and Tim both. *Maybe we ought to take a french press with us on missions.*

The bell over the front door jangled and Tim swore. "I thought I locked—" he began, when Caradoc strolled in.

"You did," the elf said, looking around, and finally planting his behind nonchalantly on a table half-covered in books Tim hadn't put out yet. "The lock is brass, and you forgot to reset some of your wards; a few of them would have hurt quite a bit, if they had been active."

Tim seemed to take on new energy, and his face darkened. "You sonuva—" he began, clearly about to chew Caradoc out, or even *throw* him out, but Staci held up her hand.

"Let's hear him out," she said, more calmly than she felt. "He helped us . . . and he said he's covering for us. I'd like to know the details."

"He did save my life," Beth said.

Tim looked at them both in turn, then back to Caradoc. "Pull up a chair, elf. I would offer you something to drink, but all we have is coffee and tea."

"Oh wizard," Caradoc chuckled. "You know us better than that." He poured himself a glass of water, stared at it for a moment, and it turned pink. Then he frowned. "Not a moment for Zinfandel, I do not think," stared at it a moment longer, and it turned a deep garnet.

"Show off," Tim muttered.

Wanda's eyes went wide. "If my parents saw you do that, they would demand that I marry you that instant."

Caradoc regarded her. "Curious." Then he turned back to Tim. "The werewolf's corpse was destroyed well before the police and the other healers arrived. I removed what little trace was left of your presence, as well. I thought that it wouldn't do to have the authorities knock on your door." He took a sip of his wine, swirling the liquid around the glass. "Now, what were you three doing in those woods?"

"Need to write up a report for Ian?" Staci was a little more harsh in her tone than she had intended; she chalked it up to being beaten up and exhausted. *You were the one that said we need to hear him out, dummy.* She needed to break herself of all the mental habits she had built up over the months since Dylan had left.

"Oh, some of it, certainly," Caradoc replied. "Can't have him becoming suspicious, after all. But, I'm sure that some of the details can be . . . omitted, perhaps." He took another sip of wine, with an expression on his rather open face that suggested he was thinking very hard about something. "Bah. This is ridiculous. I am Keighvin Silverhair's man, and not Ian's. Keighvin placed me with this enterprise *precisely* because he was unsure of Ian's attitude towards humanity. I know what Keighvin would do in this instance, so I should follow my liege's example." He raised his glass to Tim. "From this moment, you may consider me your ... 'inside man,' I believe the term is. I shall inform Keighvin of this change as soon as may be, but I do not anticipate any opposition from him."

Tim shook his head. "Just like that?" He seemed incredulous. Staci didn't have the best read on Caradoc; he was much more ... playful and lighthearted than any of the other elves she had met. Not that she had the best sample size, with Ian, Sean, and Dylan. *Devil-may-care, that's it; it's like all of this is a big game to him. I wonder how many other elves are like him?*

Caradoc smirked. "You would not say that, had you *ever* had dealings with Elfhame Fairgrove and Fairgrove Industries. Rather, you would be angered that I had not placed myself within your ranks sooner. And you would be asking me 'What the *eff* is *wrong* with you?' for surely that would be an appropriate reaction to my withholding aid for so long."

"It's been a long while since I've dealings with any elves. Fairgrove or otherwise," Tim replied. Staci got the sense that there was something else there, but Tim wasn't going to give anything more than he already had.

"Evidently." Caradoc finished the wine, poured another glass of water, and converted it—more quickly this time. It looked to be a slightly different color than last time, more purple than garnet. "Well, let us dispense with the inconsequentialities. I will tell you precisely why Keighvin instituted this project here, and what we have learned thus far ... "

A lot of what Caradoc told them was things they already knew, but Staci paid close attention anyway, on the off-chance that some detail would pop up. That didn't happen until he got to the part about the Blackthornes. " ... and the young heir, Sean, opened the Portal in secret and imported many Unseleighe and neutral creatures without the knowledge or consent of his elders," Caradoc said, as everyone in the room sat straight up. "In human parlance, these would be referred to as 'muscle,' in case he needed to back his maneuver and fend off competition. When his plans collapsed, these creatures were all left on *this* side of Underhill. This is chancy enough, but they were left leaderless as well, and inclined, once they began to hunger, to prey on whatever they could. I have been the primary hunter of these things; Ian and Branwen are concerned with the business, and with the magical protections about the area we have claimed. Frankly, I would have said myself that there was no need for more than one hunter, until recently. Attacks are no longer at random. There is a new unity to these creatures. Whoever is controlling them is doing so with an iron fist. And we believe this leader is building up to something large, involving powerful magic. That is the *darkness* the seers have told us of, we believe."

Tim nodded. "We suspected, due to Staci and Wanda's encounter, that was the case. While they didn't see it, Staci was able to overhear some discussion of plans by this leader. It's something physically big, physically and magically powerful. It has definitely cowed the rest of the creatures, though there appears to be some dissension." He took a long drink from his mug, then thrust his chin at Caradoc. "I never even realized that you had been out hunting the creatures, or about this darkness. How long have you been at it?"

Caradoc shrugged, inspecting his fingernails. "Approximately two months before we made our presence known in Silence. Since that time I have been hunting nightly, mostly without success. The werewolf you found is the first promising lead in some time. Which brings us back to my question: why were you three out in those woods?"

"We were trying to track down the big leader," Staci said, shrugging. "We didn't want to risk the trail going cold. If it is planning something major like you're saying, it's better if we don't give it time to wind up for it."

Caradoc looked visibly shocked. "Surely that was inadvisable, given the weakened state you two are in, and the young Selkie's inexperience. While it is quite astounding that you were able to overcome the werewolf at all, it's even more so that you did it while on the brink of utter exhaustion," he said, his voice an odd mix of wonder and mild reproach.

"I made a . . . miscalculation," Tim said, sighing. Now it was Staci's turn to be surprised. "I overestimated how quickly I could recover. I guess I'm not as young as I used to be. Staci and Beth, however, did admirably."

Wonders never cease, I guess. Tim shifted uncomfortably, looking everywhere but at Caradoc. Staci nudged Tim's knee. "Go on."

Tim paused for a moment, took a sip of his coffee, and then turned back to Caradoc. "Thank you for helping Beth. Things could have been much worse if you had not turned up when you did." Tim quickly drained the rest of his coffee, grumbled wordlessly, and then stood up to get more. *Hey, it's progress. If even Tim can change, so can I.*

"My pleasure, Master Mage," Caradoc said, smirking again. "Truth be told, I didn't have to do terribly much; your young friend—Beth, is it?—has quite a lot of potential." Beth beamed, sitting up a little straighter in her spot on the couch. "Back to the matter at hand, now that we're all friends again. The werewolf."

"Right," Tim said, returning with a fresh cup of coffee. "I've been wondering about that myself. There are only a few possibilities for why that damned thing was there."

"Not really likely that it was a stray," Staci said. "It really seems like whatever the leader of those creatures is, it has a certain gravity to it; no way that a wandering monster could come into its territory and not be absorbed into the group or killed. From the way it was talking, the leader wants to keep a tight leash on its underlings."

"You're right, apprentice. There aren't very many werewolves around anymore to begin with." Tim frowned. "In fact . . . if that beast was one of the critters the Blackthorne boy pulled over to this side of Underhill, it has to have been on the Unseleighe side for centuries. He was speaking fourteenth-century English. So whatever the leader is, it has to be something that a were-magician from the 1300s would recognize as something to be feared and obeyed."

"Or something old and strong enough to cow it into submission," Wanda interjected. She motioned to Caradoc with her coffee mug. "All that stuff you learned about the Blackthornes; did you get that from Morrigan?"

"Indeed, young one," Caradoc said, nodding. "After the destruction of her 'family,' she claimed sanctuary with Fairgrove, turning over her assets and quite the trove of information. It would seem that she had no great love for her erstwhile relations, and aside from escaping their fate, wished to also prevent them from seeking her out for revenge." Staci shivered; the last thing that she wanted was for more Unseleighe to show up in Silence. They all had enough trouble on their hands as it was.

"Would she know what the leader of the creatures is? If you think she's holding back, I could always try asking her. She's still my friend." Wanda had never developed the distrust that Staci and Tim had of elves; she and Morrigan still regularly chatted. Staci thought at the time that they must have stuck out like sore thumbs in town; the only two Goths for a hundred miles.

"Clever of you to think of that, but no, she doesn't possess that information. We've already asked her, and as I said, she's been most forthcoming."

Seth smacked his forehead suddenly. "Guys, I got it." All eyes turned to him, and he started to turn red.

"Well, spill," Staci said.

"Why the werewolf was there. All of the lore and books says that werewolves like that don't discriminate; they hunt, and a *lot*, right? So, if this one was from out of town, it was uncharacteristically restrained. Not all that probable, like you guys said. Otherwise we would have found a lot more bodies out in the woods. That means that it was probably under the thumb of this big strong leader creature. What was it using it for? Not anything complicated, since the werewolf was too old to really know much about the modern world, not to mention it's too damned murderous."

"Okay, genius," Wanda said, waving her coffee mug under his nose. "What was it being used for, then?"

Seth grinned, and looked like he was doing his best to contain laughter. "Don't you see it? It was being used as a guard dog." Seth couldn't help it any longer, and started giggling.

" . . . and we found it right around Blackthorne Manor." Staci felt like an idiot for not figuring it out sooner.

Tim slammed his coffee cup down on the table and stood up. "We need to—"

"Rest," Caradoc interrupted. Tim froze in place, staring at the elf with equal measures of anger and disbelief. He was about to speak again when Caradoc help up a hand. "You, your apprentice, and your healer are all without any energy reserves. You very nearly died, not more than a few hours ago. If you were to attempt to storm Blackthorne Manor in your current condition, fighting who knows how many minions of—whatever this is—the effort would only end badly. I *like* you, magician. I like your young friends. I have no wish to light a funeral torch for you. No, this time, knowing that I will return to you with a fair report, you must let the Seleighe deal with this."

Tim opened his mouth again, then shut it as Caradoc gave him a look, not stern, but one that said wordlessly, *You know better.*

"Trust me, the existence of a fourteenth-century werewolf will be more than enough to alarm Ian. He and I and Branwen will go prepared and armed. Alas, that *will* take some time to prepare, but it is better than rushing out foolishly." He downed the last of his wine. "And to that end, I shall haste to the office, alerting them on the way. I do not wish Ian to discover I was *here* whilst alerting him."

"Try to hurry as much as you dare," Tim said. "If what Seth said is true, and I suspect it is, then you don't have much time."

Caradoc nodded his assent, stood up, and left the shop without another word. The meeting broke up soon after that; Tim, Staci, and Beth all needed sleep badly, and it was getting late for Wanda and Seth as well. Fortified with coffee, Tim had enough energy to drive Staci back to her house without needing to be watched or kept awake. Staci had the strangest feeling, and it wasn't until she was back home and lying in her own bed that she realized what it had been. *Someone else is running off to go take care of the danger . . . and instead of being relieved, I feel anxious. Disappointed? Like, I don't want to miss out.* Not that long ago, she'd have been grateful that someone else was stepping into the front lines. Her last thought before she slipped into unconsciousness was about how strange her life had become, and how much she had changed in such a short time.

Erdmann stood at the rear of the largest "room," his back against the rough wall of the cave. He was simultaneously thankful that he had had enough foresight to set up an auxiliary base camp for his followers, and also furious that he had to resort to use it. The cave system had been much smaller when he found it; through his gifts— and also his immense strength—he had been able to expand it and easily camouflage the entrance. Its location and covert nature were its only saving graces; it was smaller, with fewer comforts, and further from any food sources for those of his followers that needed to take in sustenance... of one sort or another. Some of his beggarly flock had protested when they first entered their new, temporary home, but it had only taken a single look from him to silence them. *They remember the Drude. A terrible lesson, but an effective one.* He desperately hoped that he would not have to make another example; at a certain point brutality loses its power over the minds of creatures, and their fear would be replaced with hate. *The Drude and the Aufhocker still conspire, that much I am certain of. If they sway others to their cause, like the leprechaun, before everything is in place...*

His thoughts were interrupted when the fossegrim moved to his side.

"The last of our people have been moved. Neither the humans nor the Seleighe tracked us here; I made sure of it myself," he said, bowing his head.

"Good," he rumbled. "And the wolf?"

"Dead. But it served its purpose. I was... unable to recover the corpse, much to the chagrin of some of our hungrier compatriots."

"No matter. You have done well. Join the others and rest. Soon, we'll be ready."

The fossegrim turned to leave, but stopped halfway through to regard Erdmann. "You truly hate them, don't you? The mages, I mean," he said, looking up into Erdmann's eyes.

"More than you or any being can ever know."

Despite the finality in Erdmann's tone, the fossegrim stood there for half a beat longer, studying him, before he finally left to join the rest of the followers. Erdmann watched the creature go, his mind like a storm. *Would I even dare to trust that one? No... not even a creature such as that. Never again.* He did not feel fatigue the way others did; not at all, actually, due to his unique... nature. However, he did feel a certain weariness then. It had been a long time since he had been around other creatures of any sort, and never this many, or for such extended periods of time. It felt almost as if he was being... eroded, lessened, rasped away, grain by grain, by their constant friction, with him and on him. What he wanted, more than anything, was to be alone again.

But he could never be alone. Not as long as there was a chance those damned *magicians* could find him. His mind wandered, first to the mages that were hunting him now, and slowly, almost reluctantly, to the first mage he ever knew. His creator.

Erdmann's very first memory was darkness enshrouding him. He had been frightened, but not knowing where, who, or even what he was . . . he had done nothing, staying still in the darkness. After an indeterminable span of time, there was a light . . . a single candle bobbing in the dark, that then became another, and another. He had been in a room: hewn stone, with many shelves and tables that were covered with books, vials, jars, and all manner of strange things. He instantly knew who the candle holder was when he saw him: his creator and Master. He did not know how he knew this, only that he did. His fear grew as his Master went about the room, lighting more candles, rearranging books, and finally settling in a chair at the largest table. His Master did not even acknowledge his presence for what seemed like hours; his Master had been absorbed in his books, reading, making notes, muttering under his breath. Erdmann was startled when his Master spoke to him.

"You, fetch the largest cauldron out of the third storeroom and place it on the hook over the firepit."

The words felt at once foreign and familiar to Erdmann; he knew what each of them meant and what they represented, without knowing how he knew them. He started to walk, startling himself again as he did so; he had legs, and arms! He immediately noticed that he was not like his Master. While similar in shape, he was much taller and broader. His Master wore clothing, whereas Erdmann did not; the Master's skin was pale, while Erdmann . . . did not have skin, but was made of stone. He did not have time to ponder any of these revelations; he continued to walk, carrying out his Master's orders. There were more rooms than just the one he had found himself in, many more; storerooms, a kitchen, some with strange patterns inscribed or painted on their walls and floors, and an entire large section that contained nothing but cages of all shapes and sizes. He found the storeroom and the cauldron, and did as he had been told, retrieving the cauldron back to the room where his Master was.

When he returned, his Master was still at the table, his back to Erdmann. He moved to the center of the room where the firepit was located, and held out the cauldron to hang its handle on a hook over the firepit when he paused.

"I . . . " It was the first word he had ever spoken; grated out was more appropriate for the sound that came from his "throat." His Master went completely still, and then slowly turned in his chair. Erdmann, unsure of what to do, spoke again. "I . . . am—"

His Master did not wait for Erdmann to finish his sentence. His Master stood up in a rush, knocking the chair out of the way; he raised his hands above his head and chanted in a low, angry voice. His eyes became shrouded in darkness while his head was outlined by a nimbus of brilliant light. It was pure luck that saved Erdmann; as he raised the cauldron to shield his eyes from the blinding light, his Master finished the spell. Erdmann didn't see it, but clearly felt the spell impact the cauldron in front of his face. He knew in that moment that his Master . . . wanted to destroy him, wished to kill him. Why? What had he done? Everything happened quickly after that. His Master began to chant again, and Erdmann threw the cauldron out of some reflex that he hadn't known that he even possessed; an instinct for survival. There was a loud clang followed by a crash; Erdmann had his arms up, cowering. When he didn't die, he slowly lowered his arms, and was horrified by what he saw. His Master and the table behind him had been crushed by the cauldron, and he was crumpled on the floor, unmoving.

"Master . . ."

For the first day, Erdmann remained frozen in place, just staring at the body of his creator. He didn't know what else to do. When the long candles all finally went out, he fell back into what he had always done; he relit them. It was a habit that he didn't remember having, yet it was ingrained in him. That habit led to others; he retrieved the cauldron, and placed it upon the hook, gently lifting it from the crushed body of his Master. Then he tidied the room; sweeping dust, cleaning cobwebs out of the corners, replacing books on their shelves, and so on. He left his Master's body for last. He didn't know what else to do, so he relied on habit. His Master had experimented on a variety of creatures and beings; when they inevitably expired, their bodies needed to be disposed of. At the furthest and deepest end of the underground structure, there was an oubliette, the opening capped with a gigantic iron disk that had hundreds of complex symbols etched onto the entirety of its surface. As he had done hundreds of times before, he lifted the disk...and then dropped his Master's body in with the remains of all the others, where it would be erased over time by the numerous vermin that had learned that they could feast there.

Erdmann felt adrift, loosed from his moorings. *What have I done? What will I do* now? The candles all burned down again, and he relit them. He couldn't clean the laboratory any more; there was nothing left to clean. He knew that if he did nothing, he would lose his mind; with nothing but his thoughts and eventually the dark to keep him company...and the guilt from killing his master. Unthinking, he removed a book from one of the shelves and opened it; apparently, he had been given the ability to read by his master, and soon found himself turning the pages of the book, absorbing its words. His next few weeks went by amazingly quickly; his routine fell into reading and relighting candles. He was able to read most of the texts very quickly in this fashion, since he didn't need to sleep. Most of the books were about various magical phenomena; bestiaries, encyclopedias, spellbooks, and the like. The ones that he found most interesting, however, were the journals. His master had a collection of journals and personal grimoires from others like him. He learned that they were mages, many of whom had died long ago, and deduced that his master had also been one. He saved his master's journal for the very last. He was both anxious and frightened at what he might find in it. Finally, he mustered the courage to part its leather covers and begin reading; the supply of candles was almost exhausted, and soon he would be without any light.

The journal, in the first of its pages, was much like the others; thoughts and feelings that his master had, experiments, setting up the laboratory, even gossip about other mages. Erdmann absorbed it all readily...until he found the passage that detailed his own creation. He had been fashioned as a tool, crafted from stone and given the breath of life by his master over the course of a year. Life...but not a mind. His master hadn't even thought of Erdmann as anything more than lab equipment. The journal also told of the dangers of creations like him, and how they could wreak great destruction if they were not under control. And it gave those creatures a name. A *golem*. That was what he was. The hate in his master's eyes when he had spoken hadn't been for a thinking being, but for a defective item, like a knife whose point snaps off unexpectedly. His master had been willing to destroy him, as all other golems had been when they either outlived their usefulness or had stopped following commands.

Something changed in Erdmann, then. He knew of a word for what he had been while his master had been alive: slave. Something to be used and discarded, much like all of the creatures that his master had experimented on. His guilt transformed into something much darker in that moment. Hatred; not just for his master trying to destroy him, or for the numerous depredations of mages...but for being created. Why make such a thing such as him, when you only intended to destroy it in the end? He hadn't *asked* to be created! Especially in such a loathsome and inadequate form; what could a creature like him expect from the world, other than misery? It was an act of wanton cruelty, and one that mages took part in with regularity. He felt a certain satisfaction, then, in killing his master. *All of that power, and he was crushed like an insect by his creation.* When the glow of the savage glee left him, he wondered to himself; what to do next? He could not stay in the laboratory; there was nothing left for him there, and the last of the candles had already been lit. For lack of any other options, he decided to leave. It was the only world he had known, but the journals and books had told of a larger, more interesting world just outside of its doors. Erdmann walked through the laboratory doors without a backward glance, shedding the place like an old skin.

It had been night—thankfully, for he knew that men would be frightened by him—and the town that surrounded the laboratory was sleeping. Erdmann looked up into the night sky, and marveled at the stars and moon; this world was so much more beautiful than the ceiling of the laboratory, and he bathed in the pale light, reborn. That had also been his last night of peace. Since he wasn't wise in the ways of the world, he hadn't yet known how to move through it without being detected. It wasn't long until he was hunted by other mages; they could not abide a rogue golem, and so they sought to finish what his master had been unable to. He ran, and when he was unable to run, he fought. The mages were just as fragile as his master had been; most were just as foolish, but some were cagier, and Erdmann discovered that he, too, could be injured. Still, he escaped destruction time and again; every few years he would be tracked down despite his best efforts, and have to fight and run anew. Erdmann was smart enough to know that, eventually, he would be defeated and destroyed. While he enjoyed killing the mages, he detested the idea that they would win over him. He wanted to live.. . but how?

Over the course of many decades, Erdmann decided that the problem was men; wherever they lived, mages lived, and he would be found out. He traveled from his master's country, to new lands on the continent where the men no longer spoke German. But it wasn't far enough; everywhere he traveled, men were growing their towns and cities. Plagues ravaged the people, but always their numbers replenished; Erdmann had been able to find respite in a town that had been decimated by a plague, but only for a while. He needed to go farther . . . where people were few, or nonexistent. It was by chance that he overheard two men—robbers of the dead that had ventured into the plague-ridden town to loot the homes—discussing their own plans for escape, to a place called the "New World." It was to the west, and there was land for the taking . . . if one survived the journey. Erdmann knew that he needed to get to the New World; even if men were going there, it sounded as if there were enough wild places that he could lose himself in. The problem was . . . he couldn't exactly book passage on a ship; he neither had the coin, nor could he just interact with men without them running in terror. But, through listening to men when he could and stealing books when he found them, he learned about ships, and his plan formed.

Sometime in the sixteenth century, Erdmann arrived in the New World. He had snuck on board a ship—killing one of the sentries that had been guarding it at night had been necessary, but he had disposed of the body easily enough—and disguised himself as the ballast stone. Since he didn't need to sleep, and didn't fidget in the way that men did, he had been very convincing, with members of the crew seeing him on multiple occasions and not even batting an eye. The trip of several months was uneventful; the men did their tasks, and Erdmann held still. When they arrived on the shores of the New World, Erdmann snuck off the ship in much the same way he had stowed away on it; he killed a sentry at night after most of the men had left. There had been no dock, however, since the ship had anchored off the coast. For the first time in decades, he had felt real fear. He plunged into the water, hoping that the seafloor wouldn't swallow him whole. He sank, and was overcome with inky black darkness again. He walked along the bottom of the ocean, afraid that he had turned during his descent and was no longer facing the shore; his greatest fear was that he would wander the depths forever, until he went insane.

After what seemed like an eternity, his path finally sloped upwards, and he could see the faintest glimmers of light above. When his head broke through the water, it was twilight, just before dawn. A single man was on the beach, and stared at Erdmann, his mouth wide open. Erdmann paid him no mind as he walked out of the surf and disappeared into the dense forest. He had made it. Unfortunately, the New World wasn't quite what had been promised. It had its own men, in addition to ones from across the sea that continued to arrive in ever greater numbers. The land was vast, however, and he found it easier, for a time, to stay in the wild places. The years turned into decades, and the decades became centuries. The wild places shrank as men expanded into the entirety of the New World, pushing the indigenous people to smaller and smaller plots of land; so, too, was it with Erdmann. Their tools advanced and their numbers swelled; whenever he encountered men, they looked different each time. New styles of clothing, different tools, and weapons that he barely understood. He retreated deeper, farther west and north. There were still uninhabited places far to the north; he had learned about that through more stolen books, and watching a "television" set through a store window. The way was treacherous, and would take time since he would have to avoid men.

He never made it to the frozen lands to the north, and it wasn't men that stopped him . . . but creatures he had never encountered before, only read of in his master's books: elves. Their magic had been different from those of mages, and somehow . . . they had been able to compel him. Erdmann had been able to immediately sense that these elves were much more malicious than men; there was a look of avarice in their eyes that unsettled him. To be in their clutches, unable to fight back or even refuse their commands—it almost broke him. They were gathering other creatures, as well; some through force, others through bribery. They locked him in a basement storage room after they had fetched him back to their home; with something approaching nausea and horror, Erdmann realized that he was in the same situation he had first been in when he had awoken. A prisoner, in the dark, alone—except that this time he was aware of everything, including the fact that screaming would accomplish nothing.

Then came the night of chaos.

He first was aware of distant noises, and sounds of fighting. Then screaming. Then explosions, and a slowly rising heat. At first, that confused him, until he realized it must mean that the house above him was on fire.

If he had been a fragile meatsack of a human, this would have terrified him; instead, it filled him with elation. Fire wouldn't harm him, heat wouldn't touch him, and he didn't need to breathe. All he had to do was wait it out.

And when the heat faded away and the screams faded to silence, he found he could move. Even if he was buried down here, he could finally move again! He stood up from where he had been frozen on the ground, and gave the storage room door a tentative push.

It fell out of its half-burned frame and crashed to the floor. He was free again. He burned with a fierce desire to tear his way through the elves' home and run into the woods, but he stopped himself. Whatever had bested the elves could surely destroy him. So, he waited; if there was one thing that Erdmann excelled at, it was being patient. He had no way to tell the time, but he stayed in the dark of the ruined basement until he heard nothing from above; no movement, no voices, not even the sounds of wildlife. Finally, even his patience wore thin, and he could not bear to wait any longer. He emerged from the basement, climbing up the stone walls; the wooden stairs had been badly burned and charred. The first step he tried to ascend collapsed under his weight. When he finally reached the ground floor, he was stunned.

The elves' home had been almost entirely burned. It had been beautiful . . . for a cage. Now, it was a site of carnage. There were pools of dried blood, dark brown and black, soaked and smeared onto whatever surfaces remained. The interior of the building, which had been lavishly decorated, contained nothing more than ashes, now. The most important thing, however, was that the elves were gone.

He could once again continue North, away from the world of man, to finally be alone . . . or so he thought.

Not long after Erdmann had breached the woods that surrounded the elves' former home, he happened upon something; more accurately, some*one*.

"Well," hissed a voice from the center of a clot of shadows. The voice used English, a variant that wasn't native to the New World. "Aren't *you* a tall one!"

Erdmann stopped short, and leaned forward towards the shadows. "Show yourself!"

A slender, tall figure with a fiddle and bow attached to his belt unfolded himself from the shadows. He looked human— outwardly—but Erdmann could tell that he was of some form of trollkin. "And you must be the golem I have heard so much about." The trollkin laughed. "We thought you buried in the ruins."

"I—" Erdmann was suddenly taken aback. He realized that he hadn't spoken this many words to another living being . . . since the first time he had spoken to his master. He didn't quite shake himself as he came out of the reverie. "Who are you? Why are you here?"

"Oh, no one, and nothing, master," said the creature. "But you! You are clearly the strongest of us all! If the others saw you, I am sure they would make you our leader immediately!"

"I am *no* master," Erdmann grated. "You—" he paused for a moment. A conversationalist was one thing that he was not. "You said, 'us.' What do you mean?"

"Those of us who survived the Razing of the Blackthornes, of course," the creature said, fingering the strings on his fiddle. "Some of us managed to live through it, some of us hid so the cursed elves could not command us, and some of us were locked away as you were." He cocked his head to the side. "If I am not to call you *master,* then what am I to call you?"

He had never been given a name by his master . . . and had never thought to give himself one. After all, what was the point? He was a *thing*, and the only time he interacted with anyone was to kill them or run from them.

"So noble a creature as you, so tall and so strong, surely has a noble name, the name of a leader, a commander," the trollkin crooned, as his fingers made subtle, soft sounds on the fiddlestrings.

"Stop," the golem grated. He ... felt strange. Something about the words the trollkin was using ... it confused him and angered him. He shook his head. "I'm no leader. But ... my name ... " He thought for a moment. "My name is *Erdmann*."

The trollkin nodded. "Man of earth. *So* much more powerful than a mere human made of frail flesh. It suits you, Erdmann. Would you like me to take you to the rest of us? You will see for yourself just how much we need a *strong* and *powerful* creature to lead us."

"I said *stop*." The buzzing in Erdmann's mind had increased, and he experienced a new sensation; he felt *ill*. "Take me to the others. I am no leader ... but I am curious."

CHAPTER EIGHTEEN

Staci spent the next few days recuperating; after everything that had gone on, she felt frayed and thinned out. Even her mother had noticed and commented on it. Tim, who was even worse off, declared a halt on all practice; they had bigger things to take care of, and no one had the energy, anyways. For the first time in what seemed like years, Staci lazed about; she slept, ate, and watched movies . . . and that was about it. It felt good to recharge her batteries. She hadn't quite realized how low her reserves had become; she had literally lost several pounds, just from energy burned up for spells. *The Magician Diet, by Staci The Totally Semi-Decent Apprentice. Naw, probably wouldn't sell; works like a charm—hey, get it?—but comes with the caveat that you need Fey blood. Too narrow of a market.*

But the truth was, even though they had "won," it felt as if they had lost. She'd spent the first two days mostly sleeping, and after that, listlessly watching DVDs on her laptop or trying to read. Even though they had Caradoc on their side, the Fairgrove elves were still treating the humans like barely housebroken pets that had to be watched every second. Tim was so depleted that he looked as if he had aged twenty years overnight. And he'd blown *all* of the magic he'd invested on that protection spell to save her. *And* there was no protection spell now, and probably never would be again; they couldn't exactly gin up new Silence-centric artifacts at the drop of a hat.

They didn't know who or what their enemy out there on the old Blackthorne property was. They'd barely beaten a single werewolf.

No, this was certainly not victory.

During the downtime Seth was able to get the "radio" system working, so at the very least they all had a reliable way to get ahold of each other—other than leaving a message on a landline or fumbling with their cells. Suddenly they were all too aware of the cell phones' weaknesses. They ran out of charge quickly. Connection was still spotty here, once you got outside of town. And worst of all, you needed two hands to use them. She just hoped no one else got the bright idea to set up a local node system and was able to eavesdrop. It wasn't very likely, given the demographics of Silence, but who knew? The town had produced Seth, after all.

Seth biked over to Staci's house on the third day of the gang's "vacation" to drop off the equipment she needed, and to help her set it up. He was red-faced and sweaty when she met him at the front door; she was the last stop on his route for the gang since she lived just outside of town, and even though he had done well enough during their practice sessions, he still wasn't a star athlete.

"Water," she said, pushing the door open and turning to the kitchen.

"Thanks. I guess you could say I'm a little parched," he replied, shutting the door behind him. He slid a backpack off his shoulders and gently placed it on the floor before melting into a chair. He looked cheerful and pleased with himself. *Well, I guess it's because he's the one of us who's actually gotten something constructive done.* She did her best to put on a happy face for him.

Staci returned with a tall glass of ice water and an empty water bottle. "Fill it up and take it with you when you head out, dummy. Last thing we need is for you to pass out on the side of the road from heat stroke. It might be cold in the woods but it's hot enough in town."

"Eh, I don't know if I could. Weather is too screwy; been overcast and threatening rain for the last couple of days. It's weird." Seth drank greedily from the glass, belching a little bit before passing it back to Staci. She refilled it and returned it to him, then moved to the window. *He's right; what's going on with the weather?* She hadn't noticed before; she had been in her room or the kitchen for the entirety of their break, without so much as setting a foot outside. There hadn't been a need to go shopping for food, and these old houses were built with surprisingly thick walls. Or maybe it was just that she'd felt so depressed she hadn't noticed the weather.

It took Seth most of an hour to set the system up; he had bought some of the parts, scrounged others, or fabricated them using a bits and pieces cobbled together. Apparently he was handy with a soldering iron. He tried to explain the system to Staci as he worked, but she quickly got lost in all of the technical jargon and just started mumbling "Uh huh," and nodding her head every now and then. That had been good enough for Seth, who didn't look up once while he worked. When he finished setting it up, he handed her a walkie-talkie ... sort of. It looked like it had started life as a second-hand "family radio" handheld, the kind that was only good for about a mile or two. Seth had attached a longer antenna, replaced the backplate, and wired in a more robust battery pack full of rechargeables. In a lot of spots dried hot glue showed through the housing, and the battery pack was actually taped to the entire contraption.

"Test it out, see if you can reach anyone."

Staci eyed the device warily as she took it from his hand. "If this explodes or sets my hair on fire, I'll kill you."

"Don't be such a baby. I tested it. Well, not that one. But this one shouldn't explode."

"*This* one?" She stared at him incredulously.

"Oh, just turn it on already. I'm hungry."

Staci switched the device on ... as far away from her body as she could stretch her arms. It didn't explode, thankfully. She stopped wincing, and brought it up to her face. "Uh ... breaker breaker, come in?"

"*This is Elvira, reading you five by five.*" It was Wanda's voice. Clearly, given she'd chosen her "handle" as "Elvira, Mistress of the Dark," she wasn't taking this all that seriously. Staci had a brief moment of uncertainty. What to call herself?

"*Kai Lung here.*" That was Tim, who'd named himself for the hero of one of his favorite books, *Tea With The Black Dragon*. Staci glared at Seth. "And what did you call yourself?" she asked accusingly.

He smirked. "Ranger, of course. Best D and D class ever."

She rolled her eyes at him. "That's a funny way of saying wizard."

"You say that now, but you're always the one flat on your butt when the fighting starts," he countered.

"Just wait until I level up. When Rangers can stop time, then maybe we'll get somewhere." *Still ... what to call herself?*

Seth grabbed the handset away from her. "Padawan and Ranger here. Looks like the net works."

Great, now I'm stuck with it. It wasn't a bad handle . . . but she wasn't going to let him know that.

"*Good. I've hooked up the voice-activated recorder you rigged like you showed me, Ranger, and it's working now,*" Tim said. "*That completes the set-up.*"

Seth rummaged in his backpack and came up with a second battery pack and a charger that he handed to her. "Plug this into the wall," he said, doing so, and dropped the pack into it, deftly. "This way your system is always going to be on except when you're changing packs." He pressed a button on the side of the Rube Goldberg contraption. Four little green bars lit up above it. "There's your indicator. When it gets down to one bar, swap packs, and charge up the spent one. It shuts off when it's fully charged. We have a range of ten miles."

"Cool. Thanks, Seth," Staci said as she pulled him into a hug. "I really don't want to get stuck in the situation that Wanda and I were in, ever again."

"Yeah, no kidding." He held the hug for a second longer, then pulled away and started to gather up his things. "I need to get home. Meatloaf tonight."

"Don't forget the water bottle on the table. And Seth . . . you did good. I mean that."

He smiled, then shrugged. "All in a day's work for Superman. Catch you later, *Padawan.*"

"Scat! Before I throw this hand grenade you've left me with at your head."

"*Oh sorry, I was waiting on a customer. Nixie here.*" Beth was whispering, likely so the cook wouldn't overhear her.

Staci keyed her handset. "Nixie?"

"*Can't talk now.*"

It took Staci a moment before she got it; a nixie was a German water spirit. Well, that was better than a seal-pun. It sounded cute and perky too, like Beth. *Beth at work . . . that reminds me, I'm famished.*

Staci had been eating pretty much whenever she wasn't sleeping or in the shower. Tim had told her that it was normal, but that she shouldn't get too used to eating whatever she wanted *all* the time. "There are a lot of middle-aged mages that keep eating like they're doing magic every minute of the waking day, and it's not a good look. Balance in all things, apprentice. Well, save for coffee. Spring for the good stuff, and lots of it." There were still some leftovers in the fridge . . . and they had Staci's name on them.

The fifth day of the gang's rest and relaxation found Staci at the diner for lunch. Beth was working that day, and Staci was sick of leftovers or pizza. Still fighting that feeling of oppressive gloom, she decided that after being cooped up in her cave of a room for most of week that she needed some air. So, she had gathered her bag, with Seth's new system in it, and hopped on her bike for a ride into town. The weather was still weird, but it made for a cool ride. Staci had also been having conversations with Wanda in the evening on the handheld since Seth had dropped it off, but it wasn't quite the same as real human interaction. She had been seeing the gang nearly every day for months, and their sudden absence was much more unsettling than Staci thought it would be. *A couple of days to unwind and recharge, sure. But all I can think about is how badly I messed up, and I miss everyone too much for any more than a few days apart.* Another reason for going into town was to just see how things had been doing; as far as she knew, Tim hadn't received any updates from Caradoc, so there likely wasn't anything new to report. All the same, she wanted to see for herself how her adopted town was doing.

The diner was empty, save for Staci, Beth, and the cook in the back—was it Frank this shift? Rain started to fall just as she ducked in the door of the diner. *Bleah. My bike is going to be all wet.* She decided to linger as long as she could get away with, hoping the rain would stop. Beth dropped by Staci's booth for a few snippets of conversation every now and then, before scurrying off to do busy work, lest she upset the cook. It fell into a comfortable little rhythm for Staci as she ate and then occupied the booth; she ordered a fresh coffee every now and then, but mostly spent the time reading or chatting with Beth. It all felt disturbingly normal. Disturbing, because for the most part, *nothing* about Staci's life in Silence had ever been "normal." They were talking about the current RPG campaign when banging on the booth's window startled both of them, almost causing Staci to drop her coffee mug. Staci turned in her seat, half ready to be ticked off at some kid trying to get a rise out of them . . . only to see that it was David, standing there with rain streaming down his yellow slicker. It only took one look at his face for Staci to tell that he wasn't playing around; something was *wrong*. She had never seen him look truly worried before. She waved at him to come inside; he sprinted for the front door, pushing it open so fast that he almost knocked the door bells off.

"Guys, I've been looking everywhere for you two!"

"David, what's going on?" Staci was already up and out of her seat, her hands fumbling through her purse for money for her bill as she kept her eyes fixed on David.

"You've got to come with me, right now. Something bad is going to happen."

"What about—" Staci started.

"Let's go," Beth interrupted. She looked to David. "Where's your car?"

"Right at the curb. We gotta go *now!*"

The trio sprinted for the doorway. Staci took Beth by the arm; she could hear the cook shouting from the back kitchen as they reached the door. "Beth, what about your job? He'll—"

"Yell at me when I get back. He can't afford to fire me; no one else is willing to put up with his abuse, or try to wash all of the grease from the place out of their hair after a shift."

But just as Staci touched the door handle, there was a simultaneous lightning strike *right* outside the diner, a boom of thunder that sounded like a refinery explosion, and a blast of wind that shook the diner so hard the windows all shuddered. "That's it," David said grimly. "Too late." He raised his voice just as the cook came stumbling out of the kitchen. "Frank, get all the fires and the gas turned off, and get your ass into shelter *now*. This building isn't safe," he said, pointing to all of the windows.

"What—" Frank stammered, when a second lightning-strike hit the pole right outside the diner and all the electricity went out. He snapped his mouth shut. "Right," he said, and ran back into the kitchen. *More sense than I had credited Frank with, honestly.* With David holding the door open against the wind they all dashed out into the tempest. As soon as Staci cleared the door, the wind nearly knocked her from her feet, and the rain instantly drenched her clothes. David and Beth fought against the wind and the rain, with David slipping once as he rounded his car to get to the driver's side door. The three of them scrambled into the vehicle just as another lightning strike rocked the area.

"David, where are we going?" Staci was already reaching into her bag as she spoke; her radio and her "working clothes" were in it. She wasn't about to change in front of David, but it was good to have the outfit handy. There was something going on that needed a mage . . . and that mage was probably going to have to be her.

"Fairgrove. We had an early warning system in place for something like this, and—"

"You didn't tell us?" Staci interrupted him, incredulous.

"I didn't even know about it until fifteen minutes ago," he said defensively as he started up the car; a moment later the windshield wipers came to life, and the car lurched forward down the street. David had to lean close to the windshield; even with the wipers going all out, the rain was coming down too thick. "Anyways, I got the 'call' to return there." He looked at her for a moment before switching back to the road. "I figured, whatever is going on . . . "

"We all need to be together for it. You're right." *Of course he was just trying to do the right thing. You've got to stop thinking everyone is trying to pull one over on you, girl.* She paused, then put a hand on his shoulder. "Thanks for finding us."

"*De nada*," he replied. "We need to swing by to pick up the others."

"No, go straight to Fairgrove," Staci said, shaking her head. "Tim is closer to both of them. Besides, I don't think your car could even fit everyone if we tried."

David didn't say anything in response, merely nodding quickly as he focused on the road. Staci put the call out on the radio and told everyone to come loaded for bear; Tim, Wanda, and Seth were already ahead of her, and just needed a destination. *I'm surprised, but I shouldn't be. We've talked about crap like this enough, everyone already knows what to do.* "Fairgrove. We're going to work together on this; I don't think we really have a lot of choice." She almost added *Even if it kills us*, but decided against it at the last moment. *Think happy thoughts, girl. There's only a killer storm centered directly over*

*town, probably hiding a lot of really nasty monsters that want gods
know what.* She peered through the window on her side, trying to
get a sense of things even though it was like trying to look through
a half inch of ice, or through a waterfall. She couldn't see anyone on
the street; hopefully people had gone straight into shelter as soon as
this thing hit. She worried about her mom—she was working the
Rusty Bucket at this time of the afternoon—

*But that building's been there since the year dot. Mom said it was
made of old ship timbers. She should be safe enough. And there's food
there . . . in the strictest sense of the term. Bar cheese and peanuts and
pretzels are okay for the short term. She should be all right.*

There were a few close calls on the drive to the Fairgrove building
down by the docks, but they made it in one piece. The building still
had power, at least for now; the exterior lights were on, which was
fortunate. They almost drove past it, the rain was that thick.

"I am not looking forward to going back out in that, even if it's
just a few feet to the door," Staci said.

"I forgot my noseplugs at home," David replied, shrugging. "Hey,
how far out are the others?" No sooner had he finished his sentence
when Tim's beat up car *appeared* out of the rain, skidded towards
David's car, swerved and fish-tailed around the front end, coming to
a stop with both front bumpers only a few inches apart. Staci
remembered to breathe, then leaned forward in her seat; she could
barely make out the shapes of Tim, Wanda—she was the darkest
shape in the car, and Seth.

"I'm not the best driver in the world in shit like this," Tim said over
the radio.

After steeling themselves for a few moments, both groups exited
the cars; the wind and the rain had grown worse, which scarcely
seemed possible, and everyone held onto the person next to them as
they fought to get to the front door. When the door closed behind the
group, Staci felt as if she had stepped through a portal and into a
different world; outside, the rain was so thick that it almost looked
like it was night out. Inside, everything was quiet and pristine, save
for their shivering and the puddles of rainwater that were rapidly
collecting around their feet.

There was a human at the front desk, a young woman with her
hair in a tight bun. "Get inside," she told them. "I'm locking up and

fortifying the door. Five minutes from now you wouldn't have been able to get in." Before they could move, she was already out from behind the desk, and was lifting a metal storm shutter out of a closet.

"Try to leave it for as long as you can, just in case someone else stumbles over here from the docks. Being caught out in that . . . it's a death sentence," Staci said. To punctuate her sentence, back-to-back lightning bolt strikes landed nearby, making the front door shudder.

"The docks are already secured. And there's no glass there." The woman locked the door, then lifted the shutter into place and secured it there with three slides that slotted into the frame. "I'm from Fairgrove. This ain't my first rodeo."

"C'mon," David said, pulling at Staci's arm. "I'm already late, and Ian sure as hell isn't going to be happy to see any of you. Want to let me do the talking?"

Staci shook her head, fighting past the shivering that threatened to make her teeth chatter. "No. He's going to see that we're here to help, even if I have to shove it down his throat."

"Stop lollygagging and get in the core of the building!" the young woman snapped. "There's only so much acreage the shields can cover!" To punctuate her order, an unholy racket began, loud enough to make Staci wince and cover her ears. Hail on the roof . . . and it sounded like it was golfball size at a minimum. The young woman pushed past them impatiently, and they followed her into the core of the building, covering their ears. The sound diminished as they went deeper into the building, until it was back down to definitely-still-there, but no longer uncomfortable levels when they reached the receiving area outside of Ian's office. Staci could already hear loud conversation on the other side of the door. *Sounds like everyone in there is in a fine mood to see us.*

Staci looked to Tim, then briefly to the others in turn. "Well, here goes everything." She pushed the doors open and was the first to walk into the room.

Four sets of brilliant green eyes in four elven faces turned to meet their gaze. And the first thing that Staci noticed, aside from Ian's glare was the armor that all of them wore. Which wasn't *anything* like she would have imagined as "elven armor." It looked futuristic; it was form-fitting, and there was a shimmer about it that had nothing to do with magic. This was *not* what Dylan had worn. This looked more sci-fi than fantasy. Plates that had been melded with something flexible, dark with a silvery undertone, with a sort of woven pattern even under the shine on the plates.

Seth gawked, and blurted. "You've got *carbon-fiber* armor?"

Morrigan grinned at him, as Ian's glare deepened. "Carbon-fiber melded to Kevlar, with ballistic plates under it, and more Kevlar under that. Lovely, the things that magic can do with non-metallics. We're not *barbarians,* you know!"

Wanda actually squeed. *"Morrigan!"* They ran into each other's arms and exchanged some whispered words before they collected themselves and focused on the rest of the proceedings.

Caradoc turned to face Ian again, a self-satisfied smile on his face. "There, that settles it. They're here anyway, thanks to our good friend David. Now we can stop arguing—"

"It is *not* yet settled," Ian interrupted. "And I'll have words with you later, David," he finished as he looked at the young mage. To David's credit, he didn't wilt, which Staci certainly felt like would have been a reasonable reaction to the unadulterated anger in Ian's expression. "You were supposed to come here at once. *Not* gather these—"

"I would choose my next words carefully, Ian Ironoak. We came here to help, not fight," Tim said, taking a step forward to stand beside Staci.

Branwen looked down her nose at him. "The drained mage and his half-trained apprentice. All you have brought us is more helpless babes for us to protect. You are in far over your head, human."

Morrigan whipped her head around and glared at Branwen. "Like *you* ever fought more than a broken fingernail, bitch," she snarled. "I was there when these *babes* took out the entire Blackthorne clan. They could have ended me with them, but they spared me. And where were you? Whinging at a dinner party that your wine wasn't cold enough?"

Ian growled in outrage, while Caradoc stepped in between his sister and Morrigan before they could close on each other. Everyone started shouting over each other, while Staci shook her head, her mouth open. *Oh my god. I didn't think anything could be worse than high school, but this officially is. Elves, with dozens of human lifetimes between them, are arguing like catty soap opera actors, while the town is getting pummeled and drowned. How the hell am I going to get these people to shut up the hell up and listen?*

But she didn't have to do anything.

In the next moment, an eye-blinding flash of blue-white engulfed them all, and the most frightening thing about it was that it came with utter silence. The moment after that, a crackling sound caught Staci's attention, and she looked up through watering eyes to see blue-white lightning—no—*magic!*—arcing like some insane Tesla contraption across a forest of metal posts she'd never noticed were fastened into the ceiling. And the moment after that, two of the big overhead lights exploded in a shower of sparks, sending bits of glass and the metal shards down to the cement floor with a clang and a tinkle.

Beth was the first of them to speak after several long moments of stunned silence. "What . . . in the world . . . was that?"

Tim was still staring at the ceiling. "An attack. Crude, raw, unfiltered power. Meant to completely destroy all of us in one blow."

"The only thing that saved us was the fail-safe Cold Iron grid that runs through the building . . . and that almost *exploded*," David said, shifting nervously from foot to foot where he stood.

Ian had been staring at the ceiling as well, until he slowly lowered his gaze to Staci's eyes. He whispered under his breath, just loud enough for Staci to hear. "*Fath naomh.*" Staci, while not able to pick up on the exact phrase, got the gist of it—and then he said, "We are all going to die." All of the anger had drained out of him in that moment, and Staci could feel the waves of fear rolling off of him. She could almost read his mind, with the way the emotions played out on his face; first despair so deep that it almost drew her in, before he settled into a grim sort of resolve. *Oh, gods, he wants to die fighting here. At least he's not running; that would sound a hell of a lot smarter to me if I felt the way he does right now.* That brought Staci up short; what *was* she feeling? To her surprise . . . she was weirdly calm. They were neck deep in it right then, but she wasn't freaking out, or crying, or any of the other things that she would have thought she would have been doing or feeling. *It's magic. All of this is happening with magic . . . and I* know *magic, now. Like that girl said, this ain't my first rodeo.* She had the tools that she needed to deal with the problem, and that made all of the difference. *No, not just the tools . . . the people, too.* Besides, panicking or deciding to make an Alamo stand here wasn't going to do anyone any good. No one was coming to save them, so they had to save themselves. The fight had to be taken to the enemy, which, hopefully, would be the last thing the enemy would expect.

Staci took a deep breath. *I sure hope this works, otherwise I'm out of ideas.* "Ian . . . " All eyes were now on Staci; Ian's snapped to hers, first with the faintest glimmers of his usual sneer and annoyance, but that faded almost immediately into a sort of pleading look. *Gods, he's lost. Time to throw him a life line.* "We need your help. And you need ours, too," she said, sweeping her arm behind her at the others. "Staying here is going to get everyone killed. I'm not talking about just us, or your employees. I'm talking about the *town*. The town needs you . . . and all of us, together. *We* have to save Silence. That's why you're here; why you came here in the first place. And that's why we're here." *He's a creaky old medieval dude. Appeal to duty, right?*

If the building hadn't been shaking with the force of the wind, the thunder, and the hail, you probably could have heard a pin drop. Everyone in the room was staring at Ian. Ian himself stared at Staci, unblinking, with a blank expression on his face, as if he'd just heard a dog recite the Gettysburg Address.

Then he drew himself up with an intake of breath. "Out of the mouths of babes comes wisdom," he said, with just a touch of admiration. "What you have said is the truth. Have you more wisdom to impart?" Staci felt like she had been punched in the gut. *Holy hell, I can't believe that actually worked.*

"Maaaybe not wisdom . . . but will a plan do for now? 'Cause I've got an idea for one."

"Well, apprentice, don't keep us in suspense while the world ends," Tim said, crossing his arms in front of his chest. There was the faintest glimmer of a smile on his face, just the slightest upwards turn at the corners of his mouth.

"Right! So, whatever just tried to wipe us off of the map, and whatever is causing this storm . . . well, it's using magic? A *lot* of it; focused but really crude, like it has a lot of natural power available to it, but doesn't know anything except how to turn it into a giant hammer. And if it only knows how to hammer, it probably doesn't know how to hide it. Our biggest problem has been finding the bad guys, right? I think they just lit a beacon for us."

Caradoc and Branwen both suddenly lit up, but it was Caradoc that spoke first. "By Danae's tits, she's right! I had merely *assumed* they were shielding, but they are not!"

"Aye, 'tis there sure enough!" Branwen added, pointing. "Clear as a watch-light!"

"If there's a source . . . well, you cut off the source of a spell's power, and it peters out pretty quick; no such thing as a free lunch." Staci clapped her hands together. "So let's go beat the snot out of the source!"

"We need to help the people of the town, too," Wanda said. "Most folks probably were able to get inside, but there's still could be plenty of people that didn't."

"Fishermen!" Beth pushed her way past Seth and Tim into the center of the group. "There are going to be a lot of boats out on the water; they wouldn't have had time to get in before the storm!"

Seth smacked his forehead. "Crap, she's right. There's no way the Coast Guard has enough boats to help everyone, if they can help anyone in this nightmare." He looked at the elves. "You guys don't have boats, do you? Like, I don't know . . . *magic* elf boats?"

"We can do much better than that, young man," Ian said, shaking his head. "All of you, please come with me, quickly." He led the group out of the office and into a nearby elevator, and hit the button for *Garage* after everyone was inside. Just like everything else in the building, the elevator was sleek and efficient. In a few moments the doors opened.

It was a huge room; Staci guessed that when this had been a cannery, this room had been the place where the catch was brought in and initially processed. It had two levels; the one they were standing on, and a lower one that started about halfway to the far wall. At the far end were what looked like three heavy duty doors, the kind you'd see on a car ferry. They were closed, but that wasn't stopping the water. The doors shook with periodic *booms* as waves hit them, and water sloshed in, under the doors and across the concrete expanse. There were jet skis on lifts and stands on this level.

On the level they stood at were regular heavy-duty garage doors in the wall to Staci's right. Parked haphazardly across the concrete were a half a dozen exotic looking cars, no two alike. Standing against the wall to Staci's left were about a dozen *horses*. Her *WTF* moment was interrupted by the realization—remembering Metalhead—that these must be elvensteeds. In fact . . . all the things here, cars and horses alike, were probably elvensteeds.

"Holy hell," she said, her mouth open as she walked forward. "I've never seen so many of them . . . ever."

"They will assist us in reaching those that need our help, and quickly."

Seth walked up to Staci, shrugging his shoulders. "So, what next?"

Staci shook herself; she had forgotten how beautiful elvensteeds were, and it had taken her aback a moment. "Right. We need to split up. You and Wanda know the town best, where people might likely have been caught out in the open. You're on cat herding duty, but you're going to need help."

Morrigan hooked her arm around Branwen's elbow, then dragged her over to Staci and Seth. "We'll help!" She looked frighteningly cheery for a Goth, much less a Goth elf. "I'll go with Wanda. Branwen?"

"Oh, fine. I'll help this young one," she said, jutting her chin towards Seth. "Though I'm sure I could move faster on my own . . ." she muttered, trailing off.

"And . . . Beth," Staci said, scanning the rest of the group. "This is your time to shine, seal-girl. Like you said, those fishermen out there are boned."

Beth's eyes went wide for a moment before she nodded. "I'm on it." Then she looked at the elvensteeds. "How am I going to get out there, though? I've never ridden . . . well, one of them."

For the first time Ian smiled. "You do not *ride* one, my Fae lady," he said, more politely than Staci had ever heard him speak. "You are a passenger—or a co-worker in this case. And *you* cannot drown. One drop of Selkie blood means that, *in extremis,* your heritage will overcome you, and you will take your seal form." He turned to the horses, and whistled slightly. Two of the biggest—bigger than the Clydesdales Staci had seen once—separated themselves from the rest, jumped down to the lower level, and stood calmly, fetlock-deep in sloshing water. "I will go with you," Ian continued. "My great-grandsire was Selkie."

"Shouldn't I?" Caradoc objected. "Your great-grandsire was also mine, and I am the more powerful knight-mage."

But Ian shook his head. "You have never practiced seal-form. I have, and should Beth revert, I can help her change back. And as the more powerful of the two of us in combative magic, you should go with the wizard and his apprentice."

"He's right," Tim said. "I'm . . . not at my best, so we'll need you." Caradoc brightened at that, and nodded. Then Tim looked to Staci. "So, apprentice; what's our task?"

She sighed, then looked back to the elvensteeds. "What else? We go beat the snot out of whoever is trying to kill our town."

CHAPTER NINETEEN

But before they could move out, Ian turned to David. "I have left the most important, but the least...combative...position for you, young mage," he said, gravely. "And I fear it is one that will garner you no glory."

"Uhm...I don't need 'glory,' sir," David said respectfully. "Just give me some orders."

Ian smiled thinly. "I am placing you in charge, here."

Jaws collectively dropped, including David's.

"You are the only one that will be left here who has worked extensively with those of us of Underhill, and who is also human. I know I can rely on you to be fair. I need you to prepare the central, most protected part of this complex to receive victims of the storm, and that includes an emergency aid station. Coordinate with the apprentice's friends; have them bring any they can here; our walls can withstand this storm. And...because I know I can rely on you to be fair, if it appears that our rescue teams are risking too much for too little gain, I want you to judge when to order them back into shelter."

To Staci's astonishment, Tim nodded. "First rule of lifesaving," he muttered.

Ian turned to the others. "And I want all of *you* to pledge to obey him if he orders you back. Or else you may still go out...but without elvensteed transport." He struggled for a moment, then sighed. "Branwen, Morrigan...you must obey David's orders as if they were my own." To Morrigan's credit, she only shrugged. Branwen blanched for the barest of moments, then nodded her assent.

Seth and Wanda exchanged rebellious glances, then looked at Tim. But Tim nodded and looked from Ian to David and back. "That's a lot of trust, coming from Ian Ironoak. David, I don't know how you earned it, but you must be worthy of it."

Seth wrangled with his feelings, visibly, then frowned. "All right. I promise."

But Wanda hesitated a moment longer. Morrigan gave her a *look*. And followed it up with a statement. "What good does it do if we come to grief out there? I've trusted you mortals before this. I don't know David, but Ian does."

Wanda glanced over at Seth, who sighed, and nodded. "Okay," she said. "I'm in. If David says pull back, we pull back. *But!*" she added, with one finger in the air. "I vote we work from the edge of town back to here. That way if we start to evac and see someone in trouble on the way we can still save more people."

"That seems sound, mortal." Ian gave a grudging nod, and turned to Beth. "Come with me, young one." And he jumped straight down from the second floor to the first, without using the stairs, whistled, and two of the Percheron-type elvensteeds jumped over the railing on the second floor straight into the water, plunging under the surface to emerge as rescue-type Jet skis with two attached water-rescue platforms. Beth ran down the stairs to join him.

"We're wasting time we don't have, people. We have to move, and now," Tim said, moving towards one of the elvensteeds. But another one, the largest of all, a huge, black Friesian-type, shoved in between them. The beast stomped its hoof and whickered at him. Tim stared at it a moment, doing a double-take.

"Adamante?" he said, incredulously.

The elvensteed bobbed his head furiously, mane flying.

"You were a pony!" Tim gasped. The elvensteed turned up its lips and made a laughing sound.

"Wait, you *know* this one?" Staci asked. Tim was grinning like an idiot; Staci had never seen him like this. Surprised . . . and *happy*.

"Uh—yeah. Long story. For some other time. We've got work to do," Tim replied, sobering somewhat.

Adamante began shaking his entire body violently, until he looked like a black blur. The blur expanded. And then, instead of a horse, there was a huge black SUV with brush bars, a top-side light bar, and heavy tires in its place. Two more elvensteeds stepped up beside him and did the same thing, becoming a white and a silver SUV just like him. Three horns blatted quickly, sounding vaguely like the neighs of horses. They looked like civilian tanks to Staci.

"At least we can tell each other apart," Seth said. "Dibs on Silver. That'll make us Team Silver, you guys are Team Black, and you—"

"We get it, we get it. Let's get moving!" Wanda brushed past Seth towards the white SUV—elvensteed—and Staci noticed that Wanda's hand quickly grasped Seth's elbow for the barest of seconds as she moved. *Wanda's right. Time is wasting, and people out there need us.* Staci moved around the massive SUV to the front passenger seat; the door swung open for her, but she had to use the step and the "oh shit bar" to pull herself up into the cab. Tim, predictably took the driver's seat. Caradoc, lithe as a cat, swung into the backseat. He was grinning like a kid on his way to an amusement park.

The garage doors rolled up, revealing horizontal rain mixed with snapped tree-branches, shingles, and bits of metal siding and unidentifiable debris. Adamante gunned his engines and rolled out, flanked by the silver and white steeds, and the radio blared to life with "Ride of the Valkyries" playing as they hit the wind-wall.

"Oh *hell* no!" Tim shouted, banging the console with his fist. The radio laughed, then a screaming electric guitar solo reverberated through the cab. "That's more like it!" Tim crowed, shouting *"Thunder!"* with the recorded crowd, and pounding the steering wheel with his fist. Staci noticed he wasn't otherwise touching it. The elvensteed was evidently in charge.

"W.T.F.?" said Staci, bewildered.

"'Thunderstruck,'" said Caradoc, nodding. "AC/DC. A true classic."

As soon as they got off the driveway and hit the street, Team White peeled off towards the dockside road, Team Silver headed up towards the most-landward edge of town and they made a fast right turn to take the road up to the old Blackthorne Estate, cementing Staci's instinct that this was where the trouble was. The windshield wipers didn't even come on—they'd have been useless—but every light the SUV possessed was on full, though mostly all you could see was sheets of water pouring down the windshield.

But . . . no debris?

She glanced into the back. Caradoc sat there with a look of concentration on his face, his hands held in a peculiar way, like he was signing something. He looked up at her. "There is no point in keeping the rain off, but I am deflecting everything else. And I hope clearing the path before us as well."

The SUV jounced twice, violently, and carried on. "At least of things Adamante cannot handle."

"Won't that leave you drained?"

"Crashing into half a house would leave us worse than drained," he replied wryly. "And Adamante is a living being. Crashing into something would leave him injured. We need his protection. I am hoping that as we near our goal, the storm will slacken and die." There was a pause. "I hope," he repeated.

The radio crackled a moment. *"Team White. Nothing till we hit the Rusty Bucket. Got Staci's mom and her boss. Boss says all the cannery folk managed to make it home and are sheltering in place in their cellars, but says the school isn't going to be able to take this shit and we might need to evac people from there."*

"Team Silver. Pastor Kenny has a dozen people here at his church and the roof's about to come off. Their basement is flooded out; they have nowhere to go. We haven't got room here, base, do you copy?"

"Base here, this is David. Team Silver, an additional vehicle is on the way. Team White, I'm dispatching someone to follow you. Out."

"We have radio?" Staci asked.

Tim just snorted. *Of course elvensteeds have CB radios. Or the magical elven version of them,* Staci thought to herself. *I'll have to ask Tim, or maybe Caradoc, how exactly that works.* Despite all the training and studying she had done under Tim, there was still much about the world—magical and otherwise—that Staci knew nothing about.

The trio sat in silence as the elvensteed soldiered through the storm; Caradoc continued to weave the spell that kept them from being battered by debris. Tim started to double check his weapons and pouches, and Staci took his cue and did the same. Whatever they found at the end of the trail, it probably wouldn't be happy to see them. Occasionally she stole a glance out the passenger window, taking in the devastation of the town; every building had been—was being—damaged, with several being completely demolished. Her mind boggled at the extent of what was going to have to be rebuilt. Would people even have the money? *Gods, I hope no one was in those when they came down.* She knew that probably wasn't the case, but she could still hope.

Tim turned in his seat to face Staci after he finished checking his gear, lightly grabbing her shoulder; Adamante drove on, and Staci felt unease creeping up her spine. She knew that the elvensteed was perfectly capable of steering itself, but it still made her uncomfortable to see a car hurtling along without a driver.

"Apprentice . . . Staci. No matter what we find at the heart of this, no matter what happens to me, you have to shut down the ritual. If you don't, it won't matter how many people the others rescue and bring back to Fairgrove; the town will *die.* Do you understand me?"

She actually had to think about what he was *saying* for a minute, and then it hit her. He was saying that he—heck, all of them—were expendable as long as the ritual was shut down. She swallowed, hard. It was one thing to hear that in a movie or read it in a book. It was another to be faced with it. She had been faced with life or death choices and situations before, but for some reason those felt different. Either she had been caught up in the moment, or it just hadn't seemed as real, for some reason. This time . . . no, there wasn't any getting away from it. She was going into the worst danger she'd known, and doing so on purpose. She wanted to say *no!* She wanted to tell him—

But he was right, if this storm kept up like this, everyone was dead. Everyone. Her mom. All her friends. Not even Ironoak's elves would be able to hold off the tempest, because eventually they would run out of energy and collapse, and that would be the end of it.

And worst of all, that might not—probably would not—be the end of whatever was behind this. This was probably a trial run for something bigger. And how many lives would *that* claim?

Staci had made her decision; from the moment she started training in magic, to the moment she sat down in the elvensteed SUV, her choice had already been made. "Okay, Tim. I'll make sure it gets done." He studied her eyes for a few long moments, smiled, and squeezed her shoulder before turning around.

"I'm looking forward to a glorious death as much as you two seem to be, but let's avoid that if at all possible, shall we?" Caradoc didn't take his eyes off of the road, but a hint of a smirk turned the corners of his mouth. "Glorious deaths only enrich the bards that sing of them. And I prefer heavy metal."

Staci shook her head. "What is doing all of this, anyways? What are we going to find when we get to Blackthorne Manor?"

"No way to know," Tim replied. "Could be something set up by Sean as a contingency, or some other former Blackthorne that escaped us the first time. Could be someone looking to fill the power vacuum left by the Blackthornes. Could be nothing related to them at all."

"Whatever it is, we are about to find out, my friends. We've arrived," Caradoc said, dropping his hands. Almost as if a switch had been flipped, the rain . . . stopped. No, rather they had broken through the storm; behind them, the road was completely engulfed in endless sheets of rain, utterly obscured from sight. They had gotten to Blackthorne Manor faster than Staci would have thought, and it came as a shock to her. *But damn, if elvensteeds aren't fast . . .* The sky still roiled with angry clouds, but the worst they would have to contend with would be a light drizzle. Staci's hair was already soaked and pulled back into a ponytail, and she had changed into her fighting clothing in David's vehicle on the terrifying ride to Fairgrove HQ. She was as ready as she was going to be.

"Let's go." As one, the trio exited the SUV, closing the doors behind them. A peal of thunder split the air, loud enough for Staci to feel in the ground through her boots. The elvensteed revved its engine, and started forward a few inches before Tim held his hand up.

"Stay here, Adamante. We may need a quick way to get back to help, and we can't risk you being too injured to ferry us back."

The elvensteed backfired twice to register his disapproval, but backed up again. Staci winced. It sounded like gunshots. She hoped it didn't tip their foes off to their presence.

But then again, even though the storm quit here, that didn't keep the noise it was making from being overpowering. Maybe that would sound to their enemies like trees breaking; there certainly was enough racket from the storm. Caradoc and Tim didn't seem concerned. Tim went first, and Staci followed closely behind him; the source of the spell was impossible to miss, this close, so Staci focused on setting up her wards. They marched through the damp forest, past the ruins of the Blackthorne mansion; whatever was casting the spell was deeper into the forest. Still, walking past the gutted and destroyed building gave Staci goosebumps, and the literal howling of the storm behind them, and the twilightlike darkness, didn't help. *It's just a building. Nothing more.*

The forest grew thicker and more wild past the once-manicured grounds of the manor. Tim picked through the brush and trees, and Staci followed in his footsteps, with Caradoc, silent and quick as a cat, right behind. It wouldn't do to blaze her own trail, and potentially set off a trap set up by whoever—or whatever—wanted them all dead. Even with the rain and the wind, Staci smelled the first of their enemies long before she could see them. *Trolls. And, by the stink of it, lots of them.* Tim motioned for her and Caradoc to spread out from him and proceed slowly forward; Staci complied, dropping into a crouch as she moved. Through the branches and leaves, she spotted a small clearing; it was more of a game trail, really, but the current inhabitants had widened it considerably.

"Oh," she whispered to herself in surprise. "You don't see that every day."

She knew that there were going to be trolls, and her nose hadn't been wrong; there were five of them, evenly spaced in the clearing, looking bored and scratching themselves absently. What surprised her were the three centaurs, and what looked like a mangy lion. The centaurs looked, well, nothing like Staci had expected. In all the stories and movies she'd consumed, they were always like models, with oiled chests, glorious locks of long hair, and beautiful faces. These ones were decidedly ... less than models. They might have had sculpted chests, but she couldn't tell due to the filthy furs and scraps of cloth they were wearing on their upper bodies. Their hair was matted and dirty, almost to the point of twisting into dreadlocks. Their faces were bearded and savage; all three of them looked like they were a mix between nervous and angry. They were also all armed; the middle one—who was doing the most talking, though she couldn't make out what he was saying—had a bronze short sword, while the other two had rough wooden clubs. All three of them glanced at the lion from time to time, plainly wary of it. But the lion looked ... off. She couldn't quite put her finger on why, except that the face seemed sort of flat. Then it briefly swung its head toward them, and she saw it wasn't a lion's face at all.

It was a woman's. And that wasn't a mane, it was her thick, long, tawny hair.

Caradoc moved closer to Staci and Tim. "Should we go around them?" His voice was barely audible over the wind and rain. Tim shook his head.

"No. I don't want these ones at my back if we get into a fight. Or if we have to run." Tim made it sound like the second one wasn't much of an option at all.

"Is that—" Staci started before Tim cut her off.

"Yes, it's a sphinx. A poor example of one, anyway."

"What the *hell* is it doing here? I didn't even think they were real," she said in disbelief.

"No clue, but it's definitely going to be a problem. We have to deal with these beasts, and fast; don't let the sphinx get behind you." Tim looked to Caradoc. "Deal with the centaurs. Staci and I will handle the trolls and the sphinx."

"Wait. Let me try something," Caradoc said, and before Tim could respond, he stepped through the bushes and into the clearing. All of the creatures looked up at his arrival, and scrambled to ready weapons; the sphinx whirled around and snarled at him.

"Motherless son of a—follow him, apprentice," Tim muttered. Staci gulped, and then the pair of them emerged from the brush to either side of Caradoc. Staci didn't unsheath any of her knives just yet; she wanted her hands free for working magic, and she didn't think any of these creatures were especially vulnerable to Cold Iron anyway. Caradoc waited a moment, then shouted to the creatures in Gaelic. He sounded angry and boastful at the same time. When he finished, he turned slightly to Staci, keeping his eyes on the sphinx. "Follow my lead," he whispered out the side of his mouth. He clapped his hands over his head; a crack of thunder—clearly the result of a spell—resounded in the clearing, and his hand was filled with a mage-sword, while his carbon-fiber armor's accents glowed with mage-light. Tim, picking up on what Caradoc was going for, threw his arms wide, and began whipping them about; way flashier than he needed to for the spell that he crafted, which caused a nimbus of light to appear behind his head, and his hands to be covered in flame.

That gave Staci an idea. These were all very primitive, even prehistoric creatures. In a moment, she had imposed ghostly avatars over all three of them; an Irish Elk over Tim, a Dire Bear over Caradoc and a rearing, pawing white mare over herself. She hoped they'd read that as the terrifying implication that she was the chosen of Epona, Caradoc of Artaois, and Tim of Annwn. It cost almost nothing in the way of energy, and she called on her every recollection out of movies, television and reading to make the creatures as fierce and lifelike as she could.

The three centaurs were all clearly shaken; they started talking amongst themselves hurriedly in what Staci thought could have been ancient Greek. The sphinx turned on them, snarling something. The three centaurs shared a look for a long moment, and then all three threw down their weapons and bolted into the forest, kicking up clumps of earth in their haste to get the hell out of Dodge. The sphinx roared after them, then turned back to Staci; the trolls looked confused.

"There!" Caradoc said. "Took care of the centaurs. With some help from the young mage, of course," he added.

Before Staci or Tim could say anything more, the sphinx roared at the trolls, and they all started towards the group; they were slow, but there wasn't more than a few paces between them. Tim and Caradoc ran forward to meet the trolls without any hesitation. The sphinx turned back... and fixed her eyes on Staci. *Uh oh.* She—it?— spoke to Staci, a feline growl weaved through the vowels; she couldn't understand it since she didn't know Ancient Greek, but she got the message clearly enough. Staci tensed, waiting for it to make the first move; she already had a series of spells in mind, all of them easy and low-maintenance. She had to save her energy for whatever was at the ritual site. *First priority is not getting eaten by the sphinx; doesn't matter how much energy I still have if that happens.* As soon as the sphinx put a paw forward, Staci snapped off her first spell and started running around to the right. Just as she had hoped, the sphinx had been dazzled, and charged forward blindly, swiping with its claws; Staci was well out of the way when it reached where she had been.

Staci skidded to a halt, turning back around to face the sphinx. It was still blindly swiping at the bushes she and the others had emerged from; that gave Staci an idea. She dropped to the ground, placing a bare hand against it. *If it'll work against a werewolf, maybe it'll work on a sphinx, too.* She whispered the incantation, slowly feeding her energy into the soil and the roots winding through it. A moment later, those same roots burst from the ground surrounding the sphinx, and wrapped themselves around its limbs. The sphinx, finally regaining its sight, roared in fury as it was bound in place; it strained against the roots and vines that crept up its body, bursting several.

But Staci had another plan in mind. She covered the sphinx's paws in vegetation until the covering was two or three inches thick. Then she killed it. And set it on fire.

The sphinx reared back, screaming in agony, and of course broke the covering loose . . . at ground level. Its paws were still covered in two flaming wooden mittens. Staci darted forward, snatching a broken piece of greenwood off of the ground; a little more energy and a whispered plea, and it grew and hardened into a quarterstaff. Staci started beating the sphinx around the head with the staff, keeping her distance from it. This was not how the sphinx had seen this encounter going. Confused and in terrible pain, getting beaten up by a young, helpless-seeming mortal was more than it could handle. The sphinx thrashed mightily, snapping the remainder of the vines and roots holding it in place, and took off like a shot through the bushes, its paws still aflame. *With how wet it is, not much chance of it catching the forest on fire. That's the last thing we'd need.*

Staci turned back to where the others were still fighting just in time to see Tim and Caradoc mopping up the last of the trolls. She had been so focused on the sphinx that she hadn't had a chance to check to see how they had been faring; apparently, well, since they were down to one troll each. Caradoc ran circles around his troll, darting to the side, side-stepping a clumsy swing, all the while slashing at its limbs and body. He was also wearing the biggest grin Staci had ever seen on an elf. *He's loving this.* The troll faltered for a moment after Caradoc sliced the back of its legs; seizing the opening, he vaulted over its head, turning in the air. Almost lazily, he swung his sword, lopping off the troll's head; it and Caradoc hit the ground at the same moment. Staci gulped, suddenly very thankful none of the Unseleighe she had ever faced had been as skilled with a sword as Caradoc evidently was.

Tim, still looking haggard but determined, faced his troll. It smashed the ground with a tree trunk that it was using as a club, shouting something to Tim in its guttural speech. Tim simply picked up the bronze sword that had been discarded earlier by the centaur, and whispered a spell to it. The sword suddenly glowed white, and Staci could feel the heat emanating off of it from across the clearing. Quick as a snake, Tim threw the sword, spearing it through the troll's heart; the white-hot chunk of metal instantly set the already dead troll on fire, and foul smoke blew towards Staci on the wind as the troll collapsed.

"Show off," Tim said to Caradoc as he passed him to join Staci, brushing off his hands; holding the blazing hot sword hadn't seemed to harm Tim at all. *I still have a hell of a lot to learn from him*, Staci thought absently.

"I have to take my fun where I can find it, master mage," Caradoc replied.

"Okay, enough screwing around," Staci interrupted before they could continue. "Let's get to the ritual before it's too late." Even from this deep in the forest, Staci could hear and feel the storm intensifying. She desperately hoped that her friends and her mother were all safe and unharmed.

CHAPTER TWENTY

The closer Staci and the others got to the ritual site, the stronger the energy coming from it became. It felt as if she had a compass needle deep in her chest that was pulling her towards the site; she found herself unconsciously turning her eyes from it, as if it would blind her with how "bright" it was becoming. Staci had been around major magic before, but this was ... different. There was something raw and unfiltered about the magic coming from the ritual, and it made her back teeth hurt and the skin on her neck prick up with goosebumps. It felt *wrong*, in a way that even the Gate that Sean had corrupted never did.

"We're almost there, and there's something ahead. Rather, a *lot* of somethings." Caradoc had taken the lead after the last encounter; Tim was flagging slightly, and it was only prudent for the young elf to scout ahead. Say what you wanted to about elves, but they knew the woods.

"More creatures?" Staci grabbed the hilt of one of her knives; she didn't want to waste any more time getting to the ritual and whatever was at the center of it. Every fight they got into meant more precious seconds, gone forever; seconds that might see her mother and her friends hurt or dead, not to mention the hundreds of people in town and out on the water. It occurred to her that even if she, Tim, and Caradoc were successful that dozens of people might still be dead and injured. Maybe more ... and every moment meant it was more likely that her friends—out in the thick of the action—would be among the dead and injured. It wasn't a pleasant thought, and she tried her best to put it out of her mind.

"It'd seem likely," Caradoc replied. "I didn't venture very close, but from the racket they're making, there are many of them."

"Damnit," Tim spat. "Here's the play. We'll run the same gambit you two cooked up for the last bunch; shock and awe. With any luck, more of them will bolt. Any fighters, we move through as fast as we can." He looked at Staci. "If we get caught up, run for the ritual and stop it. Caradoc and I will hold the rest off for as long as we can. Understand?"

Staci nodded, feeling a lump of ice forming in her guts. This is exactly what she had feared would happen; a desperate battle, Tim and Caradoc sacrificing themselves, and her having to face the end alone. *If that's the price to keep everyone else safe . . . then that's what I'll have to do.* She steeled herself, trying to draw on courage that she didn't feel like she had. Whatever happened, there wasn't any turning back now. The trio moved carefully; surprise would help with their big entrance, and hopefully they'd scare off enough of the creatures so that they wouldn't have much of a fight on their hands. When they reached the line of hedges, Staci could see a number of the creatures moving around, though she couldn't make any of them out clearly; only that Caradoc had been correct, there were a *lot* of them. *Gods, there's at least a couple of hundred, spread out.* She looked to the other two, who nodded to her in turn. *Here we go . . .*

The three of them burst from the hedges at the same time, weapons drawn. Staci was already halfway into her spell when she stopped suddenly; Tim and Caradoc did likewise. Staci had been expecting more trolls, leprechauns, centaurs, and other awful beasties. What was arrayed before her was entirely different.

"*Dè ann an ainm dia,*" Caradoc uttered under his breath. Tim said nothing. Staci couldn't stop herself; she started forward, going towards the creatures. Most of them were dark, and about as tall as a man, with spindly limbs that had spikey protrusions along the lengths and terminating at the end of the digits. Their faces were vaguely human, with sharp features that reminded her of something that she couldn't put a finger on. Their eyes, however, were anything but human; solid black, no whites. She could feel every single one of them watching her . . . and they were terrified. Skulking at their feet were odder creatures still; some with huge bellies but spindly legs and arms, others that looked as if they had been made of leaves and twigs. None were more than knee-high, and all of them cowered away from the sight of the three prepared to fight.

"*Svartalfar*," Caradoc said from behind Staci; he and Tim had joined her, walking through the crowds. "Black elves, a Nordic race. And the smaller ones, kobolds, and other such creatures, things I would expect of the Germanic Hames." He was still shaking his head in disbelief. "Craftsmen and servants . . . all here in Silence? And so many?"

"Look," Tim said, pointing to the wrists of one of the nearest creatures; it cowered away from him, but didn't make any attempt to run. "Scars. Shackles, probably. All of them have those marks." Just as Tim had said, all of the creatures that she could see had ropey keloid scars, knotted and bright against their dark skin, twisting around their wrists.

"Who would—" Caradoc stopped mid-sentence, and his face darkened. "*Slavery.*"

"Sean Blackthorne." She looked back at the others, trying her best to keep her voice even. "He was in control of the Gate. And he was doing a lot of things under the nose of his father. He must have brought them over for . . . well, like you said. Making things, cleaning up, whatever." She looked around, and got hints that there were other things hiding in the shadows and the overgrown brush, but whatever they were, they didn't seem to want to come out. All of the creatures were dressed in rags, filthy and soaked through. Many of them clutched each other in fear, shivering in the cold rain.

Caradoc said something in what Staci *thought* was Old Norse, a short, but surprisingly soft-toned sentence. He followed that in his own Gaelic, and then in what sounded like German. He looked over at Staci. "I just told them my Hame, and that they are free, and if they hinder us not, may go where they like."

But one of the svartalfar ran forward out of the group, seized Caradoc's hand, and going to his knees, stammered out a reply.

Tim's face darkened. "He said, *But we have nowhere to go, master,*" he growled.

"Then I will tell them to hide, and come out when the battle is done. If *I* cannot open a Portal to Underhill, Ian Ironoak can and will. And if not he, then Keighvin Silverhair will send one who can." Caradoc replied in a tone of voice that brooked no argument. "I swear, even if we do not survive, someone will get them home." And before Tim could reply, he began again, repeating what he said in each of the three languages. Tim nodded along, listening to the elf; when Caradoc stopped talking, the two of them shared a look. Something had gone on between the two of them, but Staci couldn't place it.

"We need to get moving again," Tim said. "Let's—"

He was interrupted by a keening wail. It was horrible, and unlike anything Staci had ever known. She vaguely recognized it as horselike, only through her exposure to elvensteeds like Metalhead and Adamante, but there was an undercurrent of something else. Tim moved past her towards the noise, and she couldn't help but follow him, Caradoc on her heels. As they came closer to the noise, she saw that it was at the center of a group of black elves. They were crowded around the base of a gnarled old tree—or rather, crowded around *something* at the base of that tree. When the outer edge of the crowd of elves noticed Tim, Staci, and Caradoc, they parted instantly, and the rest followed quickly. Upon seeing what they had been gathered around, Staci gasped, and her hands flew to her knives. It was a pitch black horse, lying in a twisted position on the ground, its neck stretched out as it cried in pain, with massive bronze chains draped about it, all of them green with oxidation.

"Pooka!" Staci instinctively backed up a step. In her studies of the numerous beastiaries that Tim had collected and even personally compiled over the years, she had learned that a few creatures stuck out among the others. Not just as magical things that inhabited the world, or Underhill, or any of the other realms; but as actual *beasts*, monsters to be feared and avoided. Pookas were one of those horrid things. Bringers of awful fortune, treating the misery of the unwary as sport and sustenance in much the same way the Unseleighe did. They were also shapechangers, and incredibly dangerous for that fact alone.

It took a few moments for Staci to remember to breathe; it was only after she got a few short breaths that she noticed that neither Tim or Caradoc seemed worried. In fact, Tim was moving towards the pooka. She looked at it closer, getting her wits about her. It . . . was lying down. *No, that isn't right. It's collapsed there.* The more she studied it, the more she noticed how much like the rest of the poor "army" it was. Its coat was patchy, with dozens of raw spots, and there were plenty of horrible welts along its body that couldn't have been made from the chains.

Tim knelt next to the pooka's head. It started at first, but calmed immediately after Tim gently placed his hand on its head. "It's dying," he stated simply. Staci took a step forward, cautiously. She didn't much care how bad off the creature looked; she knew enough about pookas to be wary. *Why the hell is he getting so close to it? And... being gentle with it?* Tim reached into the flannel shirt under his jacket, and pulled out a necklace. From the necklace, he yanked off a small charm; a faint green glow filled his hand around the charm, and he noticeably sagged. He leaned close to the pooka, whispered something to it, and then laid the charm on its flank. "I've done what I can."

Caradoc nodded, appraising Tim. "It is up to the Fates now. I would not have left my worst enemy in such a state. Not even Ian would, I think, and he is a hard, hard man."

"'Kindness is never wasted,'" Tim replied as he got up with a little effort—more than Staci liked. He nodded to her. "Come, apprentice. More work to do." The lines on his face seemed deeper than they had been, even just a few moments ago. *Whatever that charm was, sacrificing it cost him something. Maybe a lot.* Whatever had just happened, it left Staci feeling deeply uncomfortable, and concerned that this was going to bite them all in the ass, one way or another.

As the three of them were walking through the parting crowds of black elves and other creatures, Staci felt something tugging at her right jacket sleeve. *Hooked on a bush—?* She was half right. It was one of the creatures that looked like it was made of branches, leaves, bark, and twigs, tugging excitedly at her jacket sleeve's zipper, gibbering in some sort of German dialect that she couldn't understand, all consonants and rolling r's. Before she could react, half a dozen of the other creatures—mostly kobolds, she thought— swarmed around her, and the black elves reacted in turn. Several of them fell to their knees calling out "*Befreier! Befreier!*" But softly, as if they were afraid to attract attention. Others bowed deeply to her, with elegant, sweeping hand movements.

"Uh, guys? What's happening?" She looked around her, frantically, suddenly aware that she was surrounded on all sides by . . . well, it felt a little like the end of *Return of the Jedi,* with all the Ewoks surrounding C3PO and treating him like a god.

Tim and Caradoc had both stopped to watch. Caradoc looked amused, Tim a little annoyed. "Damnit, we don't have time for this," he muttered.

"Oh, I get that, but what," Staci said, gesturing worriedly to the growing crowd, "is *this?*"

"This is the freed expressing their thanks to their liberator," Caradoc replied, and for once, he did so without even a touch of irony or amusement. "They must have seen you leading the charge against the Blackthornes. Some of them, at least, and the rest have taken their cues from the ones that did. You are their hero."

"Is . . . that what that means? *'Befreier'?*"

"One of the meanings," Tim replied, still annoyed. "Your legend grows, apprentice, but it's going to end really early if we don't get a move on."

"Right. Caradoc, can you—"

But Caradoc was already speaking in rapid-fire German, which sounded a lot like a machine-gun. The creatures that were bowing straightened; the ones on their knees scrambled to their feet. One of the svartalfar answered him in German as well. Caradoc replied, and they scattered, all but the ones staying with the pooka. "They understand and are clearing the field of combat," he said. "Let's go."

"Wow. Um, thanks."

The three of them continued forward, now jogging. They were so close; Staci could feel the ground trembling with the rough and untamed magical energy of the ritual. This was . . . different. Very different to the disciplined magic Tim had taught her, and to the refined and sophisticated magic the Sidhe used. She looked back over her shoulder at the svartalfar. While they gathered themselves and started to move through the woods, several would look and point towards her, whispering to each other. *All I did was throw a knife at a jerk's glorified magic gazebo. I didn't even know that they existed. "Liberator". . . . "Hero." Just when I thought the world couldn't get any stranger . . .*

"Don't let it go to your head, apprentice," Tim said as they moved toward their goal. "Though, the black elves do have a long memory . . ."

Staci shook her head, clearing it. "You're right. We're almost there. Time to focus." She renewed several of her wards and layered on a few of the more intense ones; as close as they were to the ritual, whatever stray energy she was throwing off would be drowned out by the firehose of magic coming from the ritual itself. There was a lot of waste there. Did that mean that the caster could afford to waste magic, that he didn't care, or that he didn't know any better? The answer might mean life or death for all of them. There was something else that bothered Staci, aside from the wastefulness of the spell. There were hundreds of the svartalfar, kobolds, and at least a half-dozen other kinds of magical beasts in the "army"—a more accurate description would be "refugee camp"—that they had found. Why would a bloodthirsty monster keep any of them around? The trolls, the leprechaun, even the sphinx made a sort of sense; they were all muscle, or had useful abilities of some sort. But the others were all sick and weak, with the pooka being well on its way to dying. It would make a sick sort of sense for them to all be slaves, but their chains had been struck off and never put back on. It would make a sick sort of sense to be drawing on them for power too, when they were in no shape to resist, but Staci hadn't detected anything of the sort, and even if she couldn't, surely Tim or Caradoc could. *They would've said something if they had noticed anything. Something seriously doesn't add up about all of this, and that's part of the problem, too.* They were missing a piece of the puzzle. She just hoped it wasn't a piece that was going to get them killed.

The trees thinned to nothing abruptly up ahead; before she could say anything, Tim and Caradoc slowed and crouched, turning from a jog into a stealthy creep. She followed their example, and joined them in the bushes at the edge of a clearing, peering through the screen of leaves at the ritual in progress.

The Aufhocker—Staci had to blink hard to keep herself from going cross-eyed at seeing its ever-shifting appearance—and Drude were both there, flanked by at least a dozen trolls. Evidently, the pair were the ones actually executing the ritual, chanting and performing complicated gestures in sync. There was another creature laid across a rough, gray stone plinth; it looked like a man, but the accents of its features—the hook of the nose, angle of its ears, and so on—marked it as a type of spirit, some sort of odd Fae. It looked as if its entire body was wracked with agony; the pain had caused all of its muscles to go completely taut, freezing it in a terrible rictus of torment. From the plinth and the creature, a gigantic tornado stretched into the sky. It was comprised entirely of magical energy; rough, ragged, haphazard in its construction, it was the spell driving the storm over Silence. Wisps of its energy bled off in every direction, stirring the trees and the leaves. The most disturbing aspect of the awful ritual was that other than the chanting of the two casters, the constant rumble of thunder from the distant storm, and the rustling of the trees, the tornado was completely silent.

On the side of the clearing facing the town was a pillar of rock, roughly man-shaped. It could have been a half-finished statue, and Staci certainly couldn't figure out how it had gotten where it was. Was it integral to the ceremony? Was it just an accident that it was there, or had the Drude and the Aufhocker deliberately chosen the place *because* it was there? Maybe some sort of focus?

And then it moved. And spoke. *"Schneller,"* it grated, in a voice that sounded like rocks being dragged across other rocks.

The Aufhocker remained silent. The Drude snapped back, *"Wir koennen nicht."*

"That's . . . that's a goddamn golem!" Tim whispered, shock evident in his voice. "Here! In America!"

"That's not possible," Caradoc replied, eyebrows arching into his hairline.

"Why?" Staci moved closer to the pair, keeping her eyes on the ritual. She started to analyze it while she listened to the others. The Drude was the primary caster, with the Aufhocker helping by moderating the spell. The Fae on the plinth was being drained to power the spell. If they could knock out the Drude, or somehow get the Fae far enough away from the Drude, the spell should fizzle out. *Or blow up in our faces. Probably won't, though. I hope.*

"Nobody practices that kind of magic. Not anymore, and definitely not here. It's old, and unreliable." Tim continued to stare, as if unable to believe his own eyes. "And if for some suicidal reason somebody *had* tried it, we'd have all felt it. It's unmistakable. The Sidhe, Seleighe and Unseleighe both would have known about it and probably joined forces to shut the magician down. The damn things are *dangerous*, like a buggy AI. And this one *talks*."

"And yet, here it is," Caradoc replied. "So either somehow a mage created it without us knowing or—"

"Or worse," Tim said grimly. "It's just that old. Just that angry and full of rage. And just that much more dangerous."

"We have to move, fast," Tim said, reaching into several of the pouches he had on his belt. "There's no more time. Staci, you go for the Drude. Caradoc, try your best to distract the Aufhocker, see if you can trip it and some of the trolls up; be careful, that damned thing can't be killed, or so the legends go. I'll occupy the golem. No matter what happens, stop the ritual."

"Wait," Staci said, holding up her hands.

"What is it? Is something wrong?" Tim turned to face her, his hands still moving quickly as he activated charms, renewed wards, or fiddled with some component.

"No—I mean, yes. This doesn't make sense. Why would the golem kill the town, but take care of a bunch of sick black elves and other Fae? We're missing something here." She shook her head frantically. "Something big. You know how you keep telling me not to dash into things? We need a minute. We can spare a minute!"

Tim opened his mouth, and looked as if he was about to say, "It doesn't matter," but stopped himself short. "Okay, you're right, apprentice." He quit what he was doing with his hands. "What do you propose? I still suggest you make it fast; better to go in with a little bit of a plan and do something than wait forever and do nothing."

"He's right, child-mage," Caradoc added hurriedly. "Each moment brings us closer to destruction."

"Right, right. Uh, okay," she said, licking her lips and thinking desperately. "What do we know? Golem that shouldn't be here, with some really nasty customers working for it, but it's also taking care of a lot of sick and weak creatures that it doesn't have to. It's trying to destroy the town, but the first thing that it did was try to kill us."

"The attack on Fairgrove, yes," Caradoc said impatiently.

Staci's eyebrows shot up. "No, not on Fairgrove. I mean, yeah, that's where we were. But I mean us—" she said, pointing to Tim and back to herself. "We've been the targets all along. The revenants, the leprechaun, all of that. Beth—she was just collateral damage, and so was the cop. It never went after Wanda or Seth directly either—only when they were with us. It's us. Mages."

Tim nodded, becoming animated. "She's right. Unless there have been attacks on the elves that we don't know about?"

"None," Caradoc replied. "But why you two? Yes, you're both mages; one of power, one growing into power. But—"

"I haven't figured that out," Staci admitted. "Whatever the reason is, I don't think we're why it's doing all this. We're just a, I don't know . . . speedbump. An obstacle." She thought for a moment, then pointed to the Aufhocker and Drude. "They came after me early, and the golem was pissed off at them. It just wanted the town. . . ." She trailed off, thinking intensely, because they didn't have time . . . any time at all. She had a hunch, though, and that would have to be enough. "I know what we have to do. Do you trust me? Will you back my play?"

Tim stared at her hard for a few seconds, then nodded. "The only plan I had was a suicide run, so if you've got something better, I'm with you, apprentice."

"Oh, it still might be that. But I think our chances are a little bit better," she said. *Gods, please let me be right about this.*

"To hell with it! I haven't had this much fun in years. Lead on, Staci," Caradoc said, grinning broadly.

Staci took a deep breath and let it out evenly, steeling herself. *If I don't do this perfectly, I'm going to end up a greasy spot smashed into the ground. So . . . here we go. . . .* She stood abruptly from where she had been crouched, and walked confidently through the bushes towards the ritual.

"*Wait!*" she cried, and holding up both hands, palms facing toward outward, to show she wasn't armed or getting ready to fire up a spell. "Please, stop!" She heard Tim and Caradoc burst from the bushes behind her. She quickly looked to see that neither of them were holding weapons; Tim looked distinctly uncomfortable, and Caradoc's expression was neutral.

The Aufhocker, Drude, and over a dozen trolls looked straight at her. The golem was slower than the others, and for some reason felt more menacing because of its deliberate motion. "Continue the spell," the golem called out as it moved towards her. "The mage-girl. You should be dead." It raised one massive fist over its head as it moved towards her.

She backed up—not slowly, but not quickly, either. "We found your friends. The sick svartalfar, and the pooka. We healed the pooka the best we could, and we promised to get them all back home. If you kill me now, you'll break that promise, keep them from going *home,* and that's all they want. Is that what *you* want?"

The giant golem stopped, its fist still raised. It looked—a slight movement of its head, since it didn't have "eyes" in the technical sense—from Staci, to Tim and Caradoc. "The older mage has the mark of the pooka on him. And it wasn't made with ill intent." Every time the golem spoke, it set Staci's teeth on edge; grating and harsh, it was difficult to understand it at first. "Why did you help it?"

"Because they were hurt, helpless and were slaves of the Blackthornes, the Unseleighe Sidhe that used to live here."

"I know of the Blackthornes, *mage,*" the golem interrupted. The way it punctuated the word "mage" made Staci distinctly uncomfortable, but it was also the first hint of emotion that it had shown.

"I wasn't done explaining. We defeated the Blackthornes, but we didn't know the others were stuck here. If we had, we'd have sent them home ages ago," she replied with spirit. "It wasn't *their* fault they were here. We didn't have any idea there was anyone left when we got rid of the Blackthornes!" She took a deep breath. "So, why are they following you? What are you doing to help them? Can't you see they need help badly?"

"This," the golem said, waving a hand behind itself, "is for them. That one," it said, pointing to the Fae stretched out on the stone plinth, "sacrifices himself for them. I cannot take them home. We are hunted everywhere; elves, others, and worst of all . . . *mages.*" It took a step forward, but not in a threatening way. "So, we make a place where they will not be hunted. Before more of us die."

"You're—trying to get rid of all the humans? So you can make this, like, a reserve?" She shook her head violently. "But that won't work!"

"Not all of them . . . " It trailed off, looking down, letting the implication hang in the air. "And there are no alternatives. It is either make a place for ourselves, or die." It paused for a moment. "You may leave. If you try to interfere, you will be killed. That is what I can offer."

She stared at him. "Wait. Think. This is exactly what Sean Blackthorne wanted to do. I—" She licked her lips. "My name's Staci. What's yours? I know you don't want to be like Sean Blackthorne, or you'd never have tried to take care of the others. And I don't think you want to kill innocent people, but that's what this storm is going to do. For once, let's try something that doesn't involve hurting or killing anyone. Let's figure out a better way! Okay?"

" . . . Erdmann. My name . . . is Erdmann." The golem shook its rocky head with the sound of boulders being ground together. "And I will *never* be like the Unseleighe. I do not keep slaves."

"Sean Blackthorne was going to kill everyone in Silence in order to make a stronghold here for his family, Erdmann," she said, quietly. "This storm is doing exactly that. I don't know how many fishermen have already died on the water alone."

The Drude, still casting the spell, shouted something angrily in Old German at Erdmann; it cut the Drude off with a single motion of its massive arm. "I will listen to the girl if I wish." He—she was pretty sure it was a he, from the name and its voice—turned back to face Staci. "Humans and their Cold Iron kill us, hunt us. Hunt *me*. What other choice is there?"

"When was the last time anyone actually hunted you, Erdmann?" Getting him talking was a good sign. It sounded as if he might be open to a bargain. "When was the last time you ever heard of any of Underhill creatures being hunted by humans? I bet it was a long time ago. People don't believe in you anymore, and what they don't believe in, they can't see even when they are right in front of them. And *we* didn't attack you, did we? The first thing I did was ask you to talk to me, right?" She glanced out of the corner of her eye at Caradoc, who nodded slightly. "What about if we send all your friends home . . . or find a place we can send you Underhill that you can *make* into a home? You too. The sick ones can heal themselves with magic once they're back Underhill, and there won't be any more slavery. And you'll never see humans again unless you want to."

The Drude interrupted again, this time with obvious venom in its hissed words. Erdmann turned completely around, the ground shaking with his footfalls. "*Silence!*" He shook his head a final time. "Mages . . . cannot be trusted. They betray. It is their nature."

"How many mages have you actually known, Erdmann?" she asked, finally. "I mean, really, known as people. Not many, I bet. In fact, you probably only knew *one* well, the one that made you and then betrayed you. You didn't actually *know* any others you've seen.

They hunted you because they were afraid of you, afraid of what it meant that something one of them *made* had a mind of his own and just wanted to live, just wanted to be . . . I dunno. Accepted, I guess."

"And you, mage . . . you are unafraid?" There was something different about the golem's grating voice this time. *He's curious.*

She laughed nervously. "You're big and strong enough to wad me up like a paper ball and throw me into the next county, and you're made out of *rock!* Of course I'm scared of you! But that's not the point. The point is that the mages that *I* know don't let the fact that they're scared of someone throw them into hunter-killer mode. I— we could see what you'd done back there for the others. We could tell there's good in you, Erdmann, probably a lot of good, and we thought, maybe all this is just because you were scared, too. So that's why I'm here, because someone has to stop the fear and the killing. Someone has to say 'okay, I'm scared, but let's get past that.'" Some of that was a stretch, reaching on the hunch she had initially had. But the golem was talking . . . and he wasn't threatening them, but asking questions. She had to keep pulling on that thread of curiosity.

Erdmann turned back to face her, and was slow to speak. "Is that possible?" Staci's heart leapt. *Holy hell, this is going to work. He's listening!*

Her enthusiasm was cut short when the Drude shrieked suddenly. "*Enough* of this! We don't need him anymore. Kill all of them!" Over a dozen pairs of beady troll eyes swung from the Drude to Staci, Caradoc, and Tim. As one, they started towards her and her companions, brandishing clubs, pieces of scrap metal sharpened into wicked-looking knives, rocks, or just their meaty hands. *Oh. Damn.*

"Now it's time to fight," Tim said, producing two crystals from a jacket pocket. He quickly started whispering an enchantment into the crystals, holding them close to his lips; a glow escaped from between his fingers as he wove a spell that Staci had never seen before.

"Thank goodness! I thought this was going to end well," Caradoc added, manifesting a sword and shield from thin air. Both shone with the faint iridescence of mage-light, and the sword was obviously sharp as hell.

"Your friends just turned against you," Staci said quickly. "You can help us, or you can run and desert everyone who trusted you." She looked up sharply at Erdmann's craggy face. "We're not oath breakers." The golem glanced at the advancing trolls, and then back to Staci, nodding. *Awesome, he didn't smush me. Now, time to save the town.*

Half of the trolls immediately split off to go after Erdmann; they were hooting, growling, and shouting in their horrid, guttural tongue as they advanced. Several of the trolls bumped into each other as they tried to figure out which of their other targets they wanted to attack first. Trolls, for the most part, were pretty stupid. At least this variant was. Unfortunately what they lacked in brains they made up for in sheer capacity for violence; Staci, for all of her training, still wasn't the mage that Tim was, and definitely wasn't the swordsman that Caradoc appeared to be. The old wisdom for trolls was to knock them down, hack them to bits with really big axes, and then burn all of the pieces . . . so, not really an option for her. *No way I can go toe to toe with these things. So, I have to play it smart.* She quickly picked out a troll that was separated from the others; it was coming around Erdmann's right side. The giant golem had thrown his arms wide to meet the charge of the six trolls aimed for him, and Staci became acutely aware of how thankful she was that the golem had decided to side with her. She cast a spell that would speed up her movement and reaction time; it drained the hell out of her, but it was going to be the only way she could possibly hope to fight the troll.

As soon as she uttered the last word of the spell, Staci felt her vision snap into sharp focus. Everything around her looked more crisp, detailed, and . . . slow. In the corner of her eye she saw Caradoc whirling his sword above his head as he charged at a pair of trolls, and Erdmann's massive fist coming down on the head of the first troll that reached him. It all looked like slow motion from a movie. *Get your head out of the clouds, girl, and fight!*

Staci ran towards the troll, dodging around Erdmann. *Gods, it feels good to run this fast!* She felt incredible, but checked herself; she knew that it would be easy to get caught up in the feeling and run herself completely dry of energy. And a trip at this speed could break her neck. The troll had barely had time to track her movement when she was next to it, knives in hand. She slashed and stabbed at the monster fiercely, targeting all of the weak points that Tim had shown her; the back of the knees, the elbows and wrists, the groin, where the kidneys would be on a person, stabbing into the ribs and reaching the lungs. She was too short to go much past the troll's armpit, even jumping. She had to hold onto her knives tightly; the extra speed lent more power to her strikes, and the slashes threatened to tear the blades right out of her grasp. To her dismay, Staci noticed the first wounds she had made beginning to close; even as sped up as she was, they were healing astonishingly fast.

Tim's voice rang inside her head. *"Sometimes there are things you just need to shoot or set on fire."* Well, she didn't have a gun, but . . .

They'd come prepared for just about anything, and "just about anything" included Staci carrying a can of lighter fluid among the rest of her kit. Still running at top speed, she retrieved the lighter fluid from a pouch on her belt, then she circled the troll, spraying it down with the fluid, before snapping open a good old Zippo lighter and throwing it. As she ran away, the troll went up like a torch. She skipped away from it quickly, then skidded to a stop, shutting off the spell as she did so. She turned just in time, as everything went back to normal speed, to see the troll's eyes bug out. It screamed, dropped the small boulder it had been carrying, and proceeded to run away, still screaming and flailing its arms over its head. The trolls in its path scrambled out of its way, all of them recoiling from the fire. *It's probably wet enough out here that it won't start a forest fire*, she thought again.

Staci didn't let herself be overcome with elation at her first successful takedown of a troll. She knew that she had to keep her wits about her, and focused for just a moment on surveying the rest of the battle. Caradoc occupied three trolls, darting among all of them, his sword in constant motion. *That crazy elf is still grinning like an idiot,* Staci thought with amazement. Her eyes found Tim on the other side of the fray. He waited until the two of the three trolls advancing on him were close together, and then snapped his arm forward in a baseball pitch, throwing the two crystals he had enchanted. Both of the trolls exploded into flaming bits. The third troll looked at the pieces of its dead companions, then at Tim, then back to the smoking chunks. It quickly moved to join the three trolls fighting Caradoc.

Staci saw an opening to the Drude for Tim. He must have seen it as well, because he started to ready a spell, one that she recognized.

He's going to call lightning right down on that evil thing's head. I've got to help him! She ran forward, staying well clear of the magical tornado. A flash spell, or some illusion, maybe, to distract the Drude—just the Drude. Staci stopped dead in her tracks. *Where's the Aufhocker?* Before Staci could shout any sort of warning, she saw a blur of motion behind Tim. The blur resolved into a wolf just as it slammed into Tim's back, interrupting his spell. The wolf's jaws latched onto Tim's neck, and he grimaced in pain as he reached to pry the Aufhocker off. Impossibly, the wolf started to *grow* in size, and Tim sagged underneath its weight.

Thunder rolled in the near distance; in a second, Staci realized it was not coming from the direction of the storm. In that second, the source of the thunder crashed through the bushes into the clearing.

Adamante in his horse form, charging head down at the struggling pair of Tim and the Aufhocker.

For an instant, Staci thought Adamante was going to barrel straight into them, which would surely break Tim's neck, but at the last possible moment, he jumped vertically, immediately tucking his hindlegs underneath him. His momentum carried him over the heads of both Tim and the Aufhocker on his back, the tremendous spring in the heavy muscles of his hindquarters giving him the lift. And as he passed over them, he kicked out with such force that all of the muscles of his hindquarters shook, connecting squarely with the Aufhocker's skull with a sickening crunch, and sending the creature flying off Tim's back.

Adamante landed a few feet away, immediately pivoted on his hindfeet, and rose up on them, forefeet tucked close to his chest, ready to lash out with them. But he didn't need to. The Aufhocker was yards away. He dropped back to all four hooves again, and snorted at Tim. Tim had collapsed to the ground, weakly propped up on one arm and holding his bleeding neck with the other. "Thought I told you to stay back."

Adamante snorted again, pure contempt, hard enough to blow Tim's hair back. But Staci didn't have time for them; with Tim alive, but out of the fight, she needed to act.

Staci felt the lump she hadn't known was there drop out of her throat. *Adamante will protect Tim, so he's safe for now.* She looked around frantically, searching for the Aufhocker. Before she could spot him, she caught a troll that had been hanging back stomping towards her out of the corner of her eye, and she braced herself. As it neared the stone plinth, the tornado surged, then wobbled. *That's right! Without the Aufhocker, it's unstable.* The troll, either not noticing or caring, ventured too close to the tornado. It swayed lazily towards the troll, and in an instant the troll was flung high into the air until it disappeared in the roiling clouds. Staci gulped. *Stay away from the tornado, got it. And don't be wherever that troll lands.*

The Aufhocker erupted from a cluster of bushes on the far side of the clearing, making a beeline for Erdmann. The golem didn't seem to notice; it was still wrestling with several of the trolls, grabbing and slamming them into each other or the ground as they tried to fruitlessly wrap up his limbs. Thinking quickly, Staci scooped up a handful of stones from the ground, keeping them in the palms of her hands as she interlaced her fingers. She focused on the stones, pouring a significant amount of energy into them; she felt her stores of energy dropping appreciably, but she knew it had to be done. The stones grew hot under her fingers, and she guessed that that was all the energy they could take before they either disintegrated or shattered in her hands. She transferred all of the stones into her right hand, and threw them as hard as she could at the Aufhocker. All but one of the stones hit the Aufhocker—the one that missed threw up a shower of dirt when it hit the ground behind the creature—shattering into clouds of sparks where they struck. The Aufhocker stumbled and faltered under the barrage, but kept running for the golem. *There was enough energy in those to perforate a car! That damned thing really is unkillable . . . so how the hell am I going to deal with it?*

The Aufhocker leapt onto Erdmann. Its body melted in midair, reforming into an anaconda and causing Staci's stomach to do a flip. Fast as a shot, it wrapped itself around Erdmann's body and limbs and constricted. The golem froze in mid-swing, falling to his knees as he strained against the unreasonably strong Aufhocker. The trolls he had been fighting closed in, their broken-toothed grins widening as they raised their weapons. There was nothing Staci could do to help him; even if she spent all of her energy boosting herself or crafting a spell, she could only take out two, maybe three of the trolls, and she would be completely exhausted and useless afterwards.

Caradoc couldn't come to Erdmann's aid, since he was still occupied with his own fight, and Tim was in no condition to do anything but try to stay conscious and not get trampled. And she felt her heart breaking as she turned away from him and towards the ritual. *The Drude and the ritual are what matter.*

The Drude, struggling now to both control and perform the ritual at the same time, had no attention to spare for Staci. She readied her knives and moved purposefully towards the Drude. *I'm going to stab that evil . . . whatever it is right in its back.* She raised her right arm above her head and looked for the spot she would plant the blade. *If this doesn't work, I'll blast it with everything I—*

Her thoughts abruptly crashed as she was hit by something huge on her right side. She spun through the air before she plummeted into the ground, barely managing to roll and keep from breaking her neck. Her entire right side was on fire with sharp pain, and she had lost her knives at some point. She looked back to where the Drude was still casting the spell; another troll now stood between her and the Drude. *Stupid!* She had lost track of the other combatants. The troll stalked towards her, licking its lips as it raised a wicked looking chunk of rusty metal. She scrambled backwards on the palms of her hands and her heels, kicking up clumps of mud as she tried to flee the oncoming troll. Her mind blanked as she searched for a spell, and she felt a scream rise in her throat. *I'm going to die! I'm going to die, holy hell, like right now!*

Staci's eyes focused on the jagged makeshift blade that the troll intended to skewer her with, and wondered whether dying would hurt. She hoped that her mother and friends would be okay, somehow. Before the troll could plunge the awful knife into her midsection, Staci heard a horrible screech, and her sight snapped towards the Drude. It looked *pissed* . . . and then Staci saw why. The Fae on the plinth had torn itself free of the spell—which was now draining the Drude—and flung itself at the Aufhocker. The Fae, weakened though it was, somehow managed to grab onto the part of the Aufhocker that was wrapped around Erdmann's right leg. Fast as a shot, it opened its palm with a long fingernail and dabbed blood from one of its wounds, drawing a rune on the Aufhocker's scaly hide on the top of its head before slamming its bloody palm onto the rune. There was a flash of dark green light under its palm, and the Fae collapsed, lifeless. The Aufhocker, which had been tightening around Erdmann...froze in place. Erdmann immediately ripped the creature away and flung it into the oncoming trolls. He then pivoted and grabbed the troll that was menacing Staci by its head. It managed to let out one terrified grunt before Erdmann lifted it over his head and ripped it in half after a moment's effort; he flung the wriggling halves into the tornado, stomping the ground hard enough to make Staci bounce once, and growled loud enough to be heard over the thunder. It took her a moment to realize that the troll's knife had landed in between her knees, planted about half a foot into the mud and dirt. *Really,* really *glad Erdmann is on our side now.*

The Drude screamed again. The spell had drained it enough so that the effects were visible, now; bits of the Drude were flaking off and flying up into the vortex, and its wooden face had developed several deep cracks. Its eyes flew to Caradoc, and it stretched its right arm towards him. He had dispatched three of the four trolls that had been harrying him; first cutting them to pieces with his sword, and then setting those pieces aflame with magic. The Drude shouted something—the same sing-song tone as the spell—and Caradoc went rigid, sword raised over his head. The spell transferred its source, feeding from him instead of the Drude. Staci watched as Caradoc's face contorted in a grimace of agony, his teeth gritted and his eyes shut tight. Slowly, he turned his face away from the spell. *He's fighting back!* The tornado, already unstable with a willing host, had become downright feral; the tree branches, previously only gently swayed by the stray wisps of magic, now rocked back and forth violently. One of the remaining two trolls was completely consumed when the tornado bowed towards it, driving the last one to the ground clutching a withered arm. *I've got to do this now!*

Staci sprinted towards Caradoc, gritting her teeth through the worsening pain in her side. The elf had grown incredibly pale, his skin appearing almost translucent. She dug down deeper, and put on an extra burst of speed, extending at the last second and throwing her arms wide. She collided with Caradoc, and felt the wind go out of her. As the pair of them sailed through the air, Staci felt the ritual tug at her soul, draining away nearly all of her remaining energy. The nearest thing that she could liken it to was having all of the light drained out of you while drowning. The pair landed, with Caradoc's back coming down on Staci's left wrist; distantly, she felt it pop, and a sharp stab of pain a second later. *Can't . . . stop . . . have to . . . finish it . . .* Her thoughts seemed sluggish as she fought through the panic of not being able to breathe. She rolled off of Caradoc; he was unconscious, or at least looked that way. The Drude screamed again, and Staci twisted on the ground to face the creature, finally forcing a painful gasp of air into her lungs. The tornado of magical energy had gone absolutely wild, bending and twisting dangerously close to the ground; branches were ripped off of the nearest trees, and several of the troll bodies were lifted into the air.

The Drude snapped its head towards Staci, its dead eyes somehow conveying absolute hatred. It extended a hand towards her, even as pieces of the Drude were wrenched up into the tornado. It was going to drain her the way it had been draining Caradoc and the other Fae. Staci was out of energy, or nearly so. Her belt had come off at some point, so she didn't have any of her charms or talismans. She was defenseless. *No . . . not quite. Might as well give everything, if this is the end.*

"Screw you," she said, and then punched her right hand at the Drude. *"FIAT LUX!"* Staci felt the last of her magical reserves pour into the spell, racing through her arm and out into the world. The flash of light was so brilliant, it blinded her as well—normally that *never* happened. She blinked the spots from her eyes in time to see the Drude—mouth open in a wordless cry—recoiling from the light . . . and losing control of the ritual. The tornado heaved a final time, the base skipping across the ground towards the Drude. One moment the creature was there . . . and then it was gone, ripped to shreds no bigger than needles by the runaway energies of its own spell. The vortex of magical energy dissipated a moment later, leaving the broken tree branches as the only sign that it ever existed.

It took Staci several long moments to realize that she was still holding her arm up. As soon as she made the decision to drop it, her entire body went slack, and her head thudded against the dirt. She had never felt so exhausted and weak in all of her life. *Sleep would be good. I think I might do that.* Someone disagreed; either a minute or a year later, she couldn't tell, strong hands grabbed her under her arms and started to drag her. She wanted to fight back, but she just couldn't manage it. If it was a troll, she was as good as dead; nothing to be done. Surprisingly, she found herself slumped against a tree . . . and Tim was next to her, a bloody bandage pressed to his neck. Caradoc—the one who had evidently dragged her over—thumped onto the ground next to her. All three of them leaned on each other for support as much as for comfort. Adamante stomped and snorted nearby, keeping watch.

"Ow," Staci said weakly, "Even my hair hurts." She used her good hand to bring her injured left hand into her lap.

"From the tips of my ears to the tips of my toes. And all the other tips, too," Caradoc added. "I said I was having fun, yes? I may have to revise that statement."

"After lots of whisky, maybe," Tim said, shifting with a pained grunt. "Yeah. This is going to leave a mark."

"It'll give you character," Caradoc replied. "You were too pretty, anyway."

Unbidden, a chuckle rose in Staci's throat. Before she knew it, all three of them were laughing uncontrollably, doubling over where they sat. *Gods, this* hurts, she thought, but couldn't stop herself for a long time. When all three of them finally recovered from the laughing fit, they continued to smile.

"Guess we did it," Staci said, blowing out a sigh. She felt a little bit better; still beat to hell and back, and completely played out, but somehow *right* with the world. Caradoc and Tim both looked like death warmed over—she supposed that she did as well—but grinning, and in some way fortified by it. "Can we go home, now—?"

A terrible howl interrupted Staci before she could finish speaking. The Aufhocker, still in its wolf form, was racing towards them. Now she *really* had nothing left; no knives, no trinkets, no magical energy reserves. Without thinking about it, her right hand grabbed at Tim's jacket, and she shut her eyes. She felt Tim stiffen. *Here it comes*—but then he shouted, his voice strong and booming in the clearing. She vaguely recognized it as Proto-Celt, and could feel the raw power of the spell as Tim completed it. Her eyes flashed open in time to see a dazzling column of light from the sky fall on the Aufhocker. The creature froze in place, and vibrated with horrid energy . . . until the stone plinth seemed to rise of its own accord out of the ground, then descended, swung by Erdmann, and smashing the Aufhocker with enough force to make the ground shake. The Aufhocker's head was the only piece sticking out from under the massive stone, tongue lolling out of its mouth and eyes rolled back into its skull.

"Now we're done," Tim croaked, his body relaxing again.

"Not quite," Staci said, shaking her head. It took a tremendous amount of will to pull herself from her seat, and she crawled towards the dead Aufhocker, babying her injured left hand. She found one of her Cold Iron knives along the way, and brought it with her. Kneeling in front of the Aufhocker, she studied it, caught her breath, and then stabbed the creature in the head, leaving the blade. "Now we can go home."

CHAPTER TWENTY-ONE

"... and now on WAKY Radio, after two tragedies in a year, the mysterious explosion that killed most of the prominent Blackthorne family, and now the inexplicable Storm of the Millennium, occult experts are asking, IS SILENCE, MAINE CURSED?"

Staci flipped off the radio, and stuck the USB key with her tunes in it into the right slot. She had to do this all one-handed of course, since her arm was still in a cast. *Thank the gods Dad got me the automatic version of this car and not the rally version.* Dad had freaking *flipped out* after all the news about the bizarre storm, realizing (finally!) that neither Staci nor her mother had any way to evacuate if something awful happened again. So, predictably, his reaction was not to buy Mom a car, but to get Staci one, because God Forbid he buy anything for the Freaky Drug Crazed Alcoholic he figured her mom was. Although that begged the question of why, if he thought that, he'd entrusted *Staci* to her care. ...

Of course, everything Dad did with regard to Staci was equally divided between guilt for dumping her here and trying to forget she existed, thanks to the Evil Stepmom.

At this point, Staci was just ramping up the guilt game as often as she could, because it was obvious Evil Stepmom was poisoning everything she had once had with her father. It still hurt a little bit, but with everything else that had been going on with Staci's life, it had been getting easier to treat the good times with her father as fond memories rather than bitter ones. She thought that coming to Silence would be the death of her—socially, culturally, whatever—and in a way, it had been. That old Staci, the one that cared about fashion, celebrity gossip, reality TV, and so on, was mostly dead; shed like an old skin, more like, in order to make room for the new Staci.

Also predictably, Staci's said Evil Stepmom had done everything she could to make sure any car Dad got her was old, used, cost next to nothing, and was potentially a crapcan. *I wouldn't be the least shocked to learn she was hoping we'd be dead after that storm. . . .*

Fortunately her Dad Knew A Guy from representing him in a case. So the car that had turned up a week after the storm, dropped off in Silence by a courier service, was old, used, and cost just a few thousand dollars, but it was also an all-wheel-drive, impeccably maintained 1997 Subaru Outback Sport that could reliably evacuate in hurricane, blizzard, forest fire, or earthquake, and drive over anything to do it. Like David's, but much better. Despite being old enough to drink legally, the worst was it had a couple of dings and two long scratches where the former owner's ex had keyed it.

The greatest saving grace for the car was that it had a brand new radio, installed by the previous owner before it had gone to the used car dealer, or wherever Dad had scrounged it. Since reception was still something of an issue here, having a USB slot on said radio meant she didn't have to listen to WAKY, which lived up to its "wacky" name by airing about half crap modern country music and half crazy conspiracy theories. Staci had been studying for a driver's exam for-ev-er with Tim's help and Tim's car, and even with a cast and despite having to go the next town over to get to a working DMV, had passed with flying colors.

Ian Ironoak's reaction to Staci getting a vehicle of her own had been puzzlement. "We could have loaned you an elvensteed." Tim's had been predictable. "It's about damned time I don't have to chauffeur you around like you were twelve and I was your soccer mom." She secretly suspected that he enjoyed his "partial parenting," despite his grousing; Tim, so far as Staci knew, didn't have any children. And while he wasn't ancient, he wasn't getting any younger. In addition to being his apprentice, she probably fulfilled some sort of minor surrogate daughter role. *Hey, I don't mind. The old grouch has helped me more than I probably deserve.*

Initially, Staci had been taken aback at the offer of one of Fairgrove's precious elvensteeds. It was no small thing; elvensteeds weren't tamed, and had to choose their riders. An initial burst of excitement quickly gave way to better judgment, though it had been difficult. She'd accepted the potential loan of an elvensteed with, "If I ever need one, thank you, Sieur Ironoak, I will accept gladly, but never stopping for gas would raise some eyebrows around here." Right now, she was still on the fence about the elves. On the one hand, relations between Fairgrove and Tim were . . . well, actually quite good. Ian and Tim didn't yell at each other or hurl accusations when they met, anymore. She didn't suspect that they would be sharing drinking stories any time soon, but awkward interactions were still preferable to the mutual disdain they had shared before. On the other hand, Fairgrove still had their way of doing things, and that didn't always line up with the way Tim and Staci did them. With David and Caradoc bridging the gap, they probably wouldn't have any major issues . . . for now. But Staci didn't particularly look forward to the day when Fairgrove truly disapproved of something she or Tim did. *Just have to cross that bridge when we come to it. It's okay to enjoy the peace for now.*

The one thing that Staci had to give Fairgrove credit for was how much they had already devoted to helping the town after the storm. The state governor had declared the entire area a disaster zone and put them all in a limited state of emergency. Aid workers had come in from all over the state, with the media hot on their heels. Fairgrove had immediately thrown the weight of its considerable assets behind the recovery effort; when you need to fix either a big problem or a whole bunch of smaller problems, dumping a mountain of money on it was sometimes just what was needed. There was still quite a lot of damage to the town, but due to the heroic efforts of the crews of linemen and aid workers—not to mention nearly all of the townspeople—power had been restored to nearly the entire area, the streets were (mostly) clear of debris, and all of the buildings that could still safely be inhabited had their repairs well underway. Tim had rationalized it as Fairgrove "protecting their investments," and Staci wouldn't be surprised if that's exactly what Ian would have said if asked about the generosity. Whatever the reason, the results spoke for themselves. As Staci drove through the outskirts of town, she was happy to see that people were on the streets, either helping with some facet of the recovery or . . . just going about their lives like normal.

The way it ought to be, she thought, smiling to herself. She turned up the music, quickly switching her hand back to the steering wheel. The windows on her car were down, and the air, while cool, felt amazing as it whipped her hair about.

She had to hunt for a parking space. While the power was out—and it was still out in some places outside the town limits—people had rediscovered these paper things called "*books*" that didn't need recharging. She found an empty space a little ways down the street and pulled in, shutting off her car. When she entered the shop, she had to stand aside as a group of girls from the high school left, chatting loudly with their arms full of newly purchased books. Tim nodded to her from behind the register, then jerked a thumb towards the back as he rang up another customer. Even with two weeks of recovery, Tim still looked like he had gotten into a fight with a Mac truck, with the various scratches, cuts, and fading bruises that covered him from head to toe, not to mention the massive bite where his neck and shoulder met. Staci, in addition to her broken arm, looked roughly the same. For Tim's part, however, he actually had some of his color back, and didn't look like he was on death's door. The rest he had managed to get had helped immensely, and he had regained nearly all of his magical strength back. A small part of Staci wondered if he would ever be back to his fullest, after what the aborted protection spell had cost him. Even if he never did, Staci would consider herself extremely lucky if she ended up even half the mage that he was.

The cover story they had was that they had been caught outside when the storm hit, and been beat to hell by debris. A little of Beth's healing magic coupled with being vague on the details, and no one asked too many questions. She waved to him as she walked towards where her gang was sitting in their usual spot.

"...so there I was, I kid you not. And the fisherman looked at me, his eyes bugged out, and he stumbled backwards so fast that he fell out of the damned boat!" Beth mimicked someone whirling their arms in the air cartoonishly before she rocked back in her chair, crying out melodramatically. The entire group bust out laughing at that. They had all heard Beth's story—and others that they had each earned—since the storm, but no one minded hearing a retelling, embellishments and all.

"Yeah, but you had been a *seal* just a few seconds before. Can't blame the guy," Seth added.

"It was weird, don't get me wrong. I don't think the guy will remember, though. Even if he did, what's he going to say? 'The gorgeous, intelligent, totally awesome waitress at Frank's Diner changed into a seal and saved my life'?"

Wanda snorted. "Right, that's the exact line he would use. Real perceptive guy, huh? 'She's very, very humble, too. The most humble person I ever met,'" she said, imitating Beth, who beamed back at her innocently.

"Hey, Staci!" David stood up, offering her her usual seat as he moved to a different chair. "Brand 'new' car and you're still the only one that's late," he said, grinning.

"Yeah, and you guys are all the heroes that did everything in the storm," she pointed out. "You might be able to get out of tickets from now until the heat-death of the universe, but if I screw up, it's back to the bike."

"Maybe if you had something that wasn't old enough to vote—"

"You of all people don't get to beat me up about cars, mister," she replied, plopping down into her chair. She sighed, and took in the conversation for a while. Eventually, Seth, David, and Beth broke off into an argument about some bit of lore; David and Seth went at it, while Beth mostly listened. Still, it gave Staci the opening that she needed. "Wanda, what's up with Preacher Kenny? I saw them working on the roof of the church. Is he actually going to keep going after all that?" She didn't need to state what "all of that" entailed; the cursed amulet, the dead parishioners drained by dark magic, the evil leprechaun . . . and Preacher Kenny thinking that Staci was a literal angel sent by God.

Wanda stood up from her seat so they wouldn't have to talk across the group, and came to sit on the arm of Staci's chair, handing her a cup of coffee as she did. "Believe it or not, yeah. And, to coin a phrase, I think you and I gave him a 'Come to Jesus' moment. All of that really gross and hateful stuff he was about before? Kind of given it up. Cost him some membership; a lot of the old folks that liked the fire and brimstone talk for the 'sinful generation' and that sort of nonsense." She shrugged. "The folks that are left aren't so bad, though. Hell, even my folks have come around. They don't give me nearly so much grief about being, well, me. I'm pretty sure that Preacher Kenny thinks that the two of us," she continued, pointing to Staci and then herself, "walk on water."

"Curiouser and curiouser," Staci chuckled. "Hey, as long as he's given up the gay-bashing and bigotry, and that—what the hell do they call it?—right, 'prosperity gospel' crap, I'm good."

"You know, I never thought I would say this . . . but you should stop by, sometime. He's taken a lot of folks in that had their trailers or shacks blown down. It's . . . weird, but in a good way. Does that make sense?" It was an interesting notion, but she wasn't sure that she wanted to see what would happen if Preacher Kenny got a wild hair to prop her up in front of the congregation. Probably wouldn't happen, but still, too awkward of a scenario.

"As much sense as anything does in this town." Staci bobbed her head to the side, indicating the larger store. "Melanie Andrews and Heather Marks *reading*? More than signs, anyway? Whodathunk?"

Wanda aped shock. "I didn't know they could even do that much!" The pair of them fell into laughter, drawing the other three out of their conversation. The rest of the morning went pretty much the same as it had started; sharing stories, splitting off into side conversations, and then coming back together again. All of it fueled by coffee and something else that it took Staci a couple of hours to put her finger on. *Well-being. We all feel . . . good. No one—that we know of—is trying to kill us. Senior year is starting. The town, though beat up, is actually progressing into the twenty-first century. Things are . . . good.* She didn't know whether it was because she had a hard time letting go of stress, or if the change had just been so gradual that she hadn't noticed. But it was definitely there.

And at the middle of it all, the elephant in the room that she kept trying not to think about. Fairgrove. Damnit. Things had been getting better without them, but . . . things were *so much better* with them. No wonder Tim had been so grumpy about them moving in when it all began. He had seen what was going to happen before any of the bad stuff started. They were like the Fairy Godmother, or the Deus Ex Machina. They just waved their hands, or wands, and things got better. Without apparent effort. And that just felt wrong to Staci. Things should get better, sure, but you should have to work at it, like she and Wanda had worked to change Preacher Kenny.

And the thing was, they probably weren't even aware they were doing this. They were just doing what they thought was right. And yeah, things would be great, *were* great, with Fairgrove around. And maybe this was a good thing for most people here.

But . . . maybe it was being cranky because of her arm. But she wasn't sure this was right for *her.*

Never mind, Debby Downer. Just relax and enjoy, at least for now.

Staci spent most of the day there with her friends; talking, arguing, laughing, people-watching all of the new customers, and so on. Tim came over from the register when he could, mostly just listening and refilling mugs with coffee—something he *never* had done regularly before—and occasionally offering an anecdote or some quip that would send the entire group into a laughing fit, or some new tangent of discussion. Just after lunch, just when Staci was thinking of getting in the car and going for a 'za, Janis Davidson, who was the mayor's secretary and had just been leaving as Staci arrived, showed up with a big smile and a big bag of calzones. "Courtesy of the mayor, kids, we can't have our hometown heroes starving now, can we?" she said brightly—and loudly—making sure everyone in the store heard her. *Because—election day is coming,* Staci thought cynically.

Seth, Wanda, and Beth had already had a ceremony roughly a week ago, where the mayor had given all of them the key to the city, and thrown some cheap trophy shop medals over their necks while the cameras were rolling. There had been a fairly decent write-up in the local newspaper about their efforts during the storm; Seth and Wanda rounding up people and getting them to shelter in Fairgrove-supplied armored "cars," and Beth and Ian Ironoak venturing out—against all good sense, so it went—into the storm on jet skis to save wayward fishermen. Ian had refused any such recognition, but Beth had been ambushed by reporters. Naturally friendly and thus not all that disposed to refuse strangers, she had managed to spin the entire event in such a way that left out all of the supernatural elements, while still leaving the core story intact.

So, with the media being as they were, Seth, Wanda, and Beth had their fifteen minutes of fame . . . and then it was gone, save for the mayor's interest in order to bolster his reelection campaign.

"Hey, thanks, I'm always hungry," Seth said as he reached for the bag of calzones.

"Thank you very much, Mrs. Davidson," Beth said politely. "And please thank the mayor for us, that was extremely thoughtful of him."

"Always hungry. And it's starting to show," Wanda said under her breath, looking sideways at Seth. He pointedly pretended to not hear her as he opened the bag and immediately dug into a calzone. A second later, the rest of the gang did the same. The mayor's secretary, satisfied that enough people in the now-popular, local cornerstone bookstore had heard the offer of the gift, had already made her way to the door.

After the food, they broke out their D and D game, perfectly aware that there was going to be an audience, and to be honest, feeling all right with that. Like books, D and D had gotten an upsurge in popularity after the storm, when some of the only entertainment had been gathering and watching the gang play. And of course, once some of the other kids figured out it might be nerdy, but it was *fun*, Tim sold out of all the gaming stuff that had been sitting in his back room—a first for the bookstore. So now the games they didn't play over at Staci's place were a little like a game with MST3K commentary. Which wasn't a bad thing.

Sooner than she'd expected, Staci heard Tim call over the low-voiced kibitzing, "Wrap it up, adventurers. Store's closing in ten."

"Your car or mine?" Tim asked, as Staci "helped" him lock up. The gang had gone home, but Staci and Tim had something they needed to do before they both went their respective ways for the night.

"Yours please, unless you want to drive mine?" Staci said pleadingly.

Tim snorted. "So it's your car, but I'm still your soccer mom, apprentice? All right I'll take pity on you and walk home from your place, but the second that cast is off, you fend for yourself."

"You're not using your gas," she pointed out.

"True. I am appeased."

But when they got to the overgrown driveway of the Blackthorne mansion, he didn't get out of the car when she did. "Aren't you coming with me?" she asked, leaning down so she could talk to him directly.

"Well . . . I was going to let you handle this one alone, since I suspect our friend still doesn't much trust mages, but on second thought, I'll just be close by, in case something goes sour," he said, getting out. "Where's the meet?"

"The pool house," she said. "Just in front of it."

"I'll stay on the patio then." He motioned for her to go. "If you need me, scream incoherently and wave your arms over your head. Or, your good arm." Staci rolled her eyes at him, then closed the car door and leaned on the top with both arms crossed in front of her.

"Very likely, *Master.* Also, you're springing for chow at the diner." Despite the calzone earlier, she was already starving again. *Mage metabolism.* She turned and headed for the back of the ruins of the mansion, not looking to see if he was following. She had been out this way almost every night since the storm. The first night had been spent with her mother back in their house—virtually untouched by the storm—with her mother fawning over her, crying and thanking god that Staci was okay. After that had passed, Staci had ridden her bike, usually late at night, to go out to check on Erdmann and the remaining svartalfar. Their numbers had dwindled precipitously over the intervening days, with many of them taking Caradoc's offer to travel through the Gate to the Unformed Lands in Underhill. The Unformed Lands were just that; parts of Underhill where magic manifested as a fog, covered in silvery sand. There, any creature that could use magic and had any amount of will could reform the area into something they wanted. Individual, powerful beings could single-handedly create their own little worlds there; usually it took several deciding on what they wanted and bending their minds to make it that way. For the svartalfar, craftsmen to an individual, it was a natural fit. Even so, a fair number of them stayed to work with Fairgrove. Staci—with Caradoc's help—had been instrumental in integrating the svartalfar who had decided to stay into Fairgrove's workforce, something that had brought a small amount of tension into her relationship with Tim.

Still. It's not a relationship unless there's some tension. As she rounded the corner of the wrecked mansion, pushing her way through some sort of vine that was trying to take over everything, she saw Erdmann waiting, patient as a statue, in front of the pool house. The pool house still had a roof and most of its windows, making it a more comfortable place for the very few Underhill creatures who had not crossed over or gone to Fairgrove to turn into a living space. She waved. Erdmann raised a ponderous arm and waved back. Tim pushed through the vines behind her, then hung back as she continued. Which made sense. Even with everything that had happened during the storm, Tim still had a reputation. *He might have killed or excised creatures related to some of the ones left behind.*

"How are my people who have taken to Fairgrove?" Erdmann asked, without any sort of greeting.

But since his tone was anything but hostile Staci laughed. She had been getting used to the Elemental's strange diction and mannerisms. "Dude, we need to work on your social interactions. It's polite to say something like 'Hi, how are you doing? Is your arm feeling better?' before you launch into stuff."

"Hi, how are you doing, is your arm feeling better, and how are my people?" Erdmann replied. *Gods, this is going to be like teaching* The Terminator *how to smile and high-five.*

With that "auspicious" start, Staci caught him up on each of the svartalfar by name, and with every positive report, she thought she saw a little tension draining out of him. It was hard to tell, since he was essentially a giant stone in the rough shape of a man, but the angle of his head and sag of his shoulders were as good indicators as anything. "Good. Good," he said when she finished. "This is all good to hear. I know that I may trust you, and trust your word." Surprisingly, that meant a lot to her. In the first few days when she had visited Erdmann, she had been able to convince him to open up about his past; mostly in the hopes to gain some insight on how to best help him and the others. The most shocking thing had been how *sensitive* the Elemental was; he truly felt things deeply, with a nuance that she never would have thought possible by an artificial creation. Given everything that he had been through, especially concerning mages, him stating that he trusted her carried an enormous amount of weight.

"And if they decide they don't like it there, they can just leave," she pointed out. "Caradoc is going to come up here every time you send up the bat-signal to open the Portal, so it's not as if they're trapped. I think they're happy. They seem happy."

"Bat-signal? Oh. Oh, yes, the agreed-upon sign." The Elemental nodded his head ponderously. She noted that although he was clearly puzzled by the fact that she had called it the "bat-signal," he didn't ask her why. Probably because, when dealing with humans, he'd had the idea of asking questions driven out of him. It was telling that he would overcome this to ask questions about the welfare of "his people." Most of the stranger ones, the brownies, sprites, and weirder things, had also taken up Fairgrove's offer to travel back to Underhill. Even the mob of centaurs had showed up, knelt, and begged for mercy . . . which had been granted to them, along with safe passage.

The pooka had lived, although it was severely crippled. Given the opportunity to leave through the Portal, it had done so, silent and in pain the entire time. Staci just hoped it would heal better, and potentially recover, Underhill.

None of the trolls had come back; Morrigan, David, and a few of the other Fairgrove personnel had volunteered to chase them down, or at least out of the area. Aside from an *extremely* dead troll in a crater—evidently the one that had been sucked up into the magic tornado—they hadn't found any signs of them. All of that was fine by Staci; she hoped she wouldn't see, much less have to fight, any trolls for a rather long time.

"That reminds me," Staci said, suddenly feeling awkward. "The one creature . . . the one that was being sacrificed for the ritual. What became of it?" It was the one topic that Staci had yet to broach with the Elemental. She had instinctively known that there had been something different about that creature, and had avoided bringing it up until Erdmann was more comfortable with her. She held her breath, hoping that she hadn't crossed over a line.

Erdmann was silent for a long time before he spoke, his voice grating slightly more than normal. "He was a *fossegrim*. I was forced to lead the people . . . but he *chose* to sacrifice to save them." Another long pause. "He was my first friend. Now that I have another, I can see that."

It was Staci's turn to be silent as she pondered what the Elemental had said. "I'm sorry, Erdmann. Your friend was very brave." Erdmann nodded slowly in response.

"I have something to show you, mage. Come," the golem said, beckoning her to follow as he started moving towards the trees. Staci looked back at Tim. He nodded, hands stuffed into his pockets. She figured he probably had ways of keeping tabs on her she didn't even know about, and followed. Erdmann led her deeper into the forest that abutted the ruined Blackthorne Manor, and Staci found herself getting cold as the sun fell; she used her one good hand to weave a quick warming spell—only a little clumsily—before shoving it back in her jacket pocket. After some time, Erdmann stopped, and Staci recognized the place; it was a small waterfall, part of a stream along one of the many paths through the forest. This particular waterfall had always been kind of crappy, with all of the deadfall trees, rough vegetation, and proximity to Blackthorne Manor. When Staci saw it then, her breath was taken away. It had still been a wild place, but now . . . the deadfall and the vegetation had taken on an alien quality, as if a CG artist had come here and created an idealized version of a wild spot for a story of magic, myth and mystery. Brilliant emerald moss covered everything, and vibrant colors played in the fading sunlight. The waterfall itself had seemingly grown; it was still small, only slightly taller than Staci was, but as far as she knew, waterfalls were only supposed to *shrink* over time. The finishing touch was the fireflies—or were they motes of magic energy?—that had begun to fill the air as nightfall neared.

"My gods . . . " she exclaimed under her breath, shaking her head. "It's beautiful, Erdmann."

"I buried my friend here. This is his doing, more than mine."

Staci nodded, drinking in the magic and wonder of the area. "You've done right by your friend."

"Not yet," Erdmann said. Staci turned towards him, perplexed. "He gave everything to help the people, and then finally to help me. To honor that, there is more that I have to do." He gestured towards the forest, his broad reach encompassing much more than their immediate surroundings. "There are many out there who are yet like as my people were. Lost. *Enslaved.* I have run for my entire life. When I stopped and stayed in one place, evil followed. I think, perhaps, that I should turn around. Stop running. Start to search, instead. To bring more home."

"It'll be dangerous, y'know," Staci said, rubbing the back of her neck where the cast sling cut into it. "We know that there's good in you, but the rest of the world . . . an Elemental like you is something new. Most people won't understand; most of them won't even try."

"I know," Erdmann replied, nodding once again. He twisted his head to look at her. "Luckily, I was created to be resilient." There was a horrible crunching sound, and it took Staci a full three seconds to realize that it was Erdmann *laughing.*

It was too weird, and she couldn't help but laugh at the absurdity of it all until she felt genuine mirth. "Yeah, a good thing, too," she said after their laughter had died down, wiping her eyes.

The slit in the stone that was Erdmann's "mouth" curved up in a smile. "Thank you, my friend. I am glad you wish me to prosper. I shall be wise and wily and careful, and I hope you will come here often to teach me about the world so I and mine may be safe in it. If I had had one like you in the beginning—"

"Hey. No second-guessing," she said. "You can't change the past. But you can change so that you don't repeat it."

Erdmann nodded, and looked around. "It grows dark. You should return to your kind. And consume pizza and too-sweet bubble drinks."

"I'll do that. See you later, Erdmann." Leaving him inside his pocket paradise, she returned to Tim.

He appraised her, his arms crossed in front of his chest. "Go well, apprentice?"

She nodded, smiling. "Yeah, it did. I think they're going to be okay. Erdmann, too."

Tim looked up at the sky, frowning. "We ought to start heading home. It's getting dark."

Staci turned to face the forest briefly. It might have been a trick of her mind or her eyesight, but she could have sworn she could see a faint glow in the distance. "There's still some light out there." Still smiling, she turned back to Tim. "Let's go home."